heart warriors

A Family Faces Congenital Heart Disease

by
Amanda Rose Adams

Behler™
PUBLICATIONS
California
USA

Behler Publications
California

Heart Warriors: A Family Faces Congenital Heart Disease
A Behler Publications Book

Copyright © 2012 by Amanda Rose Adams
Cover design by Yvonne Parks - www.pearcreative.ca.
Back cover and interior photos used with permission by Photography by Desiree

Some of the names have been changed and some conversations have been condensed in order to retain the flow of the narrative.

Library of Congress Cataloging-in-Publication Data

Adams, Amanda Rose.
  Heart warriors : a family faces congenital heart disease / Amanda Rose Adams.
    p. cm.
    ISBN 978-1-933016-80-1 (pbk.) -- ISBN 1-933016-80-9 (pbk.) -- ISBN 978-1-933016-79-5 (ebook) 1. Congenital heart disease in children. 2. Parent and infant. 3. Bereavement. 4. Adams, Amanda Rose. I. Title.
  RC687.A38 2012
  618.92'1204375--dc23
                                        2011049378

FIRST PRINTING

ISBN 13: 9781-933016-80-1
e-book ISBN 978-1-933016-79-5

Published by Behler Publications, LLC
Lake Forest, California
www.behlerpublications.com

Manufactured in the United States of America

To my sweet Liam,
who holds so many hearts in his small hands,

~

To Jim & Moira,
because the heart of our family has four equal parts,

~

In Memory of Steve Catoe,
the Funky Heart and original Heart Warrior,
The world is a far better place because you were in it.

I said, O Love
I am frightened,
but it's not you.
Love said to me,
there is nothing that is not me.
Be silent.
~Rumi

Out beyond ideas of wrongdoing and right doing,
there is a field,
I'll meet you there
~Rumi

Table of Contents

Foreword

One out of every hundred babies is born with congenital heart disease (CHD). This is the most lethal disease of children, and those who fight it every day must truly be warriors.

I am a congenital heart surgeon, and underwent sixteen years of intense surgical training to learn how to repair complex heart defects. The best moment of my working day is telling a mother and father that their baby's operation is finished, and that everything went well. You can see the profound relief in their eyes. As congenital heart surgeons, those moments sustain, complete, and define us.

The worst moments of my working life have been when I've had to place a dying child in his mother's arms, so that she could hold him during his last seconds of life. When surgeons fail, we can only pray and bear witness to a parent's grief.

I am married to a great pediatric cardiac intensive care unit nurse, we met in the CICU at Boston Children's hospital, where we both worked, and we are now the parents of three wonderful children. When our firstborn daughter was two, someone asked her what her father did. She promptly responded, "He cuts the babies and makes them cry," innocently expressing the ultimate surgical irony—we have to hurt our patients to heal them. Her answer perfectly synthesized the disconnect between physicians, who hope and believe they are "fixing" everything with a good operation, and parents, who are absolutely traumatized by having their child's "chest cracked," sometimes repeatedly.

Most congenital heart surgeons have repaired thousands of babies with complex heart defects, but haven't ever been the parent of one, and simply could not adequately describe the family's experience. A mother has a unique biologic and emotional connection to her child—she is the first heart lung machine for a baby with congenital heart disease, and clearly the best one. **HEART WARRIORS** is the story of family's lifelong fight for their child with congenital heart disease, and is a story that only a mother could tell, a mother like Amanda Rose Adams.

In **HEART WARRIORS**, Ms. Adams gives us a compelling and brutally honest portrait of parents fighting for their children with congenital heart disease. Her insightful narrative intricately details the long and often terrifying hours, exhausting days and endless years she spent in prenatal echocardiography, cardiac intensive care units, surgical waiting rooms, hospital wards, cardiology clinics, and chapels. She describes the evolution of her knowledge about heart defects and medical care, and her frustration with the lack of awareness most of us share about the relentless disease she is fighting. She provides a comrade-in-arms view of her fellow warriors—her gentle husband, her heart baby's "normal" sibling, their devoted family, and the other brave parents and children fighting in hospital beds alongside them, engaged in their own desperate battles. She gives us the arc of her son's life.

Surgeons partition the treatment of congenital heart defects into discrete events and phases: the diagnosis, procedure, postoperative care, and follow-up. We measure our performance in terms of survival statistics and complication rates. Amanda Adams experienced those discrete events with her firstborn son, and opens our eyes to every moment in between, revealing the daily human impact of those events and outcomes on a parent, child, and family—the tears of pain, cries of frustration, relentless guilt and second guessing, the lurching emotions between desperation and joy, the bottomless fear of potentially losing a baby, and ultimately, the cumulative emotional trauma endured by the family of a child with a heart defect.

For a parent, this book will forewarn you of the coming storms, prepare you for the intensity of the fight, and arm you with crucial information and hard earned knowledge. For physicians, nurses, and hospital employees, this book will deeply connect you with the consequences of our actions on patients and their families, and remind us of the profound impact a single errant suture, or simple kind word, can have on another human being and their child, when both are engaged in the fight of their lives. For those who decide to join the fight, and advocate for the millions of patients who are engaged in the struggle against congenital heart defects, **HEART WARRIORS** is a powerful call to arms.

Redmond P. Burke MD
Chief, Division of Pediatric Cardiovascular Surgery
Miami Children's Hospital

1
In the Thick of It

Denver Children's Hospital, Cardiac Intensive Care Unit (CICU), Mon. Apr. 10, 2006, 9:30 P.M.:

Liam won't sleep. He won't eat. He won't calm down. He's almost three, but his whining has morphed from the standard toddler protestations to preternatural whale-song. Liam had his fourth open-heart surgery five days ago, but despite his exhaustion, he won't sleep. His lungs are full of fluid, so I force my son to walk.

"No, Mommy, Liam no walk," he weeps.

His tears tear me apart. I want to weep, but I will not cry in front of Liam. Instead I negotiate. "Sweetie-pie, if you walk three laps around the unit, Nurse Maggie will let you pick a prize out of the treasure box."

He peers in the cardboard box Maggie is holding and spies the tell-tale blue of a Thomas the Tank Engine push and go toy. "Liam want Thomas."

"You can have Thomas when we make it all the way around, three times. Let's chase Thomas! Let's count to three!" I try to sell my son an adventure instead of a chore. But it is a chore.

Before Liam can leave his bed Maggie unhooks his saline drip from the dancing rack above his bed and moves it to a rolling pole while I pop the oxygen tube off the wall-mount behind his bed and squeeze it onto the nozzle of the portable tank. As I drop the side-rail of Liam's crib, Maggie double-checks the oxygen gauge and hooks the tank to the IV pole. Before Liam can stand, Maggie clamps the bulbs at the end of each of his three chest tubes to his diaper. The bulbs catch the fluid that drains from his lungs. They now rest at his hip like plastic grenades and quickly fill with bubbling pink fluid as my son sits on the edge of the bed.

Maggie checks to make sure all of Liam's lines, oxygen, pacemaker, IV drip, and chest tubes won't catch on the bed rails, and together we scoop him off of the bed and stand him gently on the floor. I feel like Herr Drosselmeyer propping up a dancing doll.

After we turn out of Liam's semi-private room, Maggie sets the train on the floor and pushes Thomas' funnel so the toy will zoom ahead of us. Holding both our hands, Liam struggles, step by step, to follow Thomas. We are quite the sight. Maggie drags the oxygen tank and IV pole behind us while I grasp the portable pacemaker in my right hand that is tethered to my child's heart.

As Liam staggers after Thomas, he sees babies in their cribs and wrests his hand free from mine to wave. In his sweet voice, still scratchy from the ventilator tube, he croaks "Hi, baaabies!" to every broken-hearted child we pass.

We make it two and a third laps before Liam is shaking.

I scoop him in my arms and take the shortcut through the break room with Maggie and the equipment trailing us like a bridal train. I deposit my son back in his bed and Maggie and I perform our ritual of repositioning all the lines and bulbs and bags where they belong before she strips the chest tubes and drains the fluids.

Physically spent, Liam doesn't care about his toy anymore. Despite his exhaustion, he whines and refuses sleep. He's so tired.

We are all so tired.

At least Maggie gets to go home eventually.

CICU, Tuesday, April 11, 1:00 am:
   Liam won't sleep, but I'm beyond exhaustion. One of the nurses offers me the dark silence of the bereavement and family counseling room. For twenty minutes I attempt to unwind on the tiny loveseat, but never attain sleep. The nurse comes back into the dark room to clear me out. They need the space for a family en route on the flight-

for-life helicopter. Another dying baby will be here soon with its new parents, and I retreat to my narrow reclining chair at Liam's bedside.

I'm an old parent with my walking talking son. I'm the veteran on this battlefield. Liam is supposedly recovering, but after almost a week in the intensive care unit I'm unsure we're going anywhere but in circles.

I haven't slept more than two hours for more than three days. Every time I think Liam is asleep, I lean back in the chair, and he whines, "Mommy, come here." This happens over, and over, and over again. Finally, I burst out of the CICU just after 2:00 A.M. and walk, unescorted, back to my room at the Ronald McDonald House (RMH). I'm too ashamed to wait for the security guard. I'm ashamed because I'm supposed to stay. I'm on night duty. It's my duty as Liam's mother to stay, to wait, to never leave him alone. But I'm so sleep deprived I can't function. I can't stay, and I hate myself for leaving. Even when I get back to a quiet bed, I won't sleep because I burn with guilt for leaving Liam awake and alone.

I didn't know it at the time, but as I crossed that dark street alone a notorious rapist was one block over committing a crime spree as I stomped between the hospital and the Ronald McDonald House. He stayed off my street. I'm just lucky, I guess.

CICU Tues. April 11, 2006, 8:00 P.M.:

Jim sat with Liam all day. I'm on the night shift. Liam's bed got moved to the less intensive side of the Intensive Care Unit. Progress?

Our new bedside neighbor is dying. I know this because Jim and our daughter Moira ate dinner with Charlie's family at the Ronald McDonald House. Charlie is fifteen months old. His mother asked the charge nurse to press his hands in clay tonight while she prepared her older children.

Charlie will go home for hospice care this week. His parents prefer their son's death to happen at home. They only get to choose the venue. The event is beyond all control.

I won't cry for Charlie in front of Liam. Instead I sneak off to the quiet bathroom upstairs to sob privately. I can't stand to sit next to that dying baby right now.

When I return, Liam and I walk again. Liam whines. Liam weeps. He doesn't understand that I'm trying to walk him home, willing him to heal by walking. I'm trying to convince my child to "walk it off," but it's open-heart surgery, not a cramp.

Walking it off fills the bulbs again, but it's not getting us anywhere but back to bed. Liam cringes as tonight's nurse tugs and strips the standing fluid from the tubes that are stitched into his skin.

We have a routine to distract him. "Tell it goodbye, Liam."

"Bye-bye juice."

Liam's lungs just keep producing juice, and he keeps telling it goodbye. All of that juice filling those little grenades is what keeps us here. When the nurse is done stripping the tubes, she drains the grenades, measures the juice, and takes it away, but we remain. We are standing water that will not evaporate. We are the juice.

"Liam hurts," he whines and leans back into bed. He won't play with his Bob the Builder toys. He doesn't want any stories, not even his favorites *James and the Red Balloon* or *Thomas and the Jet Engine*. He has stopped loving the things that make him Liam.

He still will not sleep. None of us will sleep. We're in the ward now, and I don't have the reclining chair anymore. I sit stock straight in a rolling desk chair and wait for Liam to fall asleep, but he refuses.

Under this dirty florescent light time is irrelevant. All these children have lost their sense of time, and my own failing ability to grasp the meaning and measurement of time is what separates me from the other adults. I am neither nurse nor patient. I am a phantom observing everything, but barely participating. I am the scenery and a bystander as Liam and I drift further from our sense of self.

Behind me, Charlie plays with a toy in his crib. He doesn't realize he is dying. I can't stop realizing that the rising tide of death just one bed over is drowning me tonight.

Charlie is blond like Liam, only Liam's skin is sky blue because his heart and lungs are so inefficient. He is always short of oxygen. Charlie's skin is the color of summer corn because his liver and kidneys failed. He is swaddled in those familiar purple hospital pajamas that Liam just outgrew.

Charlie was made to wait too long for a heart transplant. Now he has a dead baby's good heart, and every good thing Charlie was born with is now broken. I turn away and burn with guilt because I don't have the strength to watch this child die. I can do nothing right by these boys, so at midnight I head back to the Ronald McDonald House with the security guard. I try to sleep, but I lay in bed and think of Liam and Charlie.

Denver Ronald McDonald House, Wed. April 12, 2006, 7:30 am:
Jim left to sit with Liam. I stay in bed, armed with the remote and let Moira watch far too much Disney Channel in her Pack and Play. I'm so tired, and I love The Wiggles for letting me sleep. Around nine o'clock I drag myself out of bed to get my poor child breakfast and change her sopping diaper. Moira will be two in June, but she seems so much older in this place.

Three days ago both of my kids were patients at Children's Hospital. Moira was in the emergency room on Sunday with rotavirus after thirty-two hours of retching in the small Ronald McDonald House guestroom. I asked Jim's mom Karen to bring Febreeze to kill the smell, but it's Wednesday and our room still stinks. I did nonstop laundry for two days, and I didn't sleep.

Today Moira eats dry Cheerios in the communal dining room and drinks a cup of milk for the first time since Friday. Jim rushes in, upset that I wasn't in our guestroom to answer the phone. I'm so confused.

"I've been trying to call you. Liam needs another surgery!" he pants because he ran here from the hospital and up three flights of stairs

As Jim bends to catch his breath, I sigh, "Oh shit . . . oh shit."

Jim tells me that Esther, our surgical nurse, discovered Liam's sternum separated in its steel wires, like sticks bound in twine shifted out of place. All I can see is me marching Liam in staggering laps as his ribs floated loose in all that juice. My child was literally sawed in half, and I, like a war criminal, made him march.

I return to the hospital while Jim stays with Moira.

CICU, Wed. April 12, 2006, 10:00 am:

When I walk in the CICU, I pull back the curtain around Liam's bed. He is delirious and begs the phantom over his bed to take him away to the Island of Sodor to play with Thomas the Tank Engine. Maybe that's his idea of heaven. Maybe he just wants to be Liam again.

Liam doesn't know I'm there. I wish he would say, "Mommy, come here."

Instead, he just whimpers. His wound from the last open-heart surgery seven days ago weeps a clear liquid, like tears, but sticky. Jillayne, our day nurse, takes cultures.

I call Liam's grandparents from the hallway. Someone has to take Moira, again.

Liam and I hang on this trapeze for hours. My son twists in his delirium and pain, and I swing over him, rubbing his forehead, hoping to catch him before he falls away entirely. We know surgery is imminent, but before Liam slipped away to play with Thomas in his mind, Jim convinced him to take a few bites of a Rice Krispie treat. Liam wouldn't eat for two days. That huge accomplishment has delayed surgery by five hours.

Finally, another cardiac anesthesiologist comes to me with another clipboard, and I sign Liam's life over for the ninth time since he left my body thirty-five months ago. The world-class surgeon, Dr. Lacour-Gayett, appears from nowhere, leans into the bed, rubs Liam's cheek and murmurs, "I'm so sorry, I'm so sorry," in a soft fatherly voice.

It's as if I'm not there with them, and I've never heard anything more terrifying than that Frenchman's whispered apology.

I'm shutting down.

Liam can't stop cringing and whimpering. The pain of his separating chest is tearing him from his dreams, burning off the cloud of drugs. At my insistence, the attending doctors have doped him up all day with double the opiates recommended for a thirty-pound child. But my small son still whimpers. There aren't enough drugs in the world to make the hurt stop, so Liam sounds like a dog struck by a car, each breath literally rattles his bones and stops my heart cold.

I shut down a little more. I am a fading light, but I won't leave Liam's side until we reach the operating room doors. Then Liam is gone. It is 5:00 P.M.

Denver Children's Hospital, Surgical Waiting Room, Wed. April 12, 2006, 7:30 P.M.:

The cafeteria is closed. Jim and I ordered Chinese takeout. We eat beef and broccoli and sesame chicken in the waiting room as the sky slowly darkens the windows.

My mom took Moira an hour before the surgical team took Liam back to the OR. Jim and I are childless again.

All the familiar strangers went home for the day. The TV that runs all day every day is finally silent, and the white-haired ladies in blue smocks that staff the desk took their knitting home for the night.

So many long hours on so many different days of Liam's life, Jim and I camped out in this room waiting for our son. During the day, we can look out and see the older part of the hospital that houses the administrative offices, the valet parking circle, and a blue letterbox. Tonight, I only see my pale face, distorted by the strange and silent darkness, as this room loses its familiarity. A child's heart surgery is not meant to happen at night.

Denver Children's Hospital, Surgical Waiting Room, Wed. April 12, 2006, 10:00 P.M.:

Before they rolled Liam back to the operating room, the surgical fellow, Dr. Kosic, told me it would take forty-five minutes to reset Liam's sternum. It's been five hours.

All day long the docs and nurses kept saying, "No fever. Can't be an infection. No fever."

According to Dr. Lacour-Gayet, it *was* an infection, an infection so deep and so violent that another ninety minutes and a bomb would have detonated and all my worst fears manifested. It takes an adult one minute to circulate all the blood in his body. Liam weighed thirty-two pounds the week before, so maybe fifteen or twenty seconds after the sternum infected his heart was all the time required for his heart to pump septic blood to every vessel in his being.

Ninety minutes and thirty seconds from an ending to a life just shy of three years. I would have had the bereavement room for the remainder of our stay. No new parent could dislodge me, only the coroner, only the end of the road. But thanks to Esther, Liam's story goes on. She caught it just in time before my son's skin and bones poisoned his heart and blood with two strains of staph and one strain of strep.

Dr. Lacour-Gayet, assisted by Dr. Kosic, struggles to find the right English word to describe Liam's tattered sternum. He turns and looks at her, shrugs, then settles on, "ratty." The inside edges of our son's dissected sternum were left ratty from the infection that chewed apart his bone from inside the wound. So, Dr. Lacour-Gayet stripped the dead tissue down to healthy bone before irrigating Liam's heart and chest cavity and resetting the whole mess. The process was so violent that the thoracic duct and lining between Liam's digestive tract and lungs was ruptured and will seep fat for months while he loses more weight.

The surgeon's description is clinical. He is direct. He offers us words we shouldn't know but we recognize, "corrupted," "necrosis," "dislodged," and "infection." These words are sterile, but his tone seems nervous, almost giddy.

Then this world-class, super confident, nerves-of-steel, Parisian heart surgeon who saves babies' lives for a living says the words that will ring in my ears for the rest of my life, "We were *so* lucky."

Anything that was left of my conscious presence in the room has left the building, the city of Denver, and the state of Colorado. I am gone. My real self might have been an astral projection atop a mountain in Utah, but I have checked out. It will be years before I come back to this moment. It will be years before I cry.

I spend the rest of the night babbling to the cadre of nurses and Dr. Kosic about our childbirth experiences. I desperately pretend that all this intense attention on my son doesn't mean what it clearly means. I pretend that this surgeon really wants to shoot the breeze instead of owning that she's standing vigil over my son whose chest she just closed. I pretend this wasn't a major heart surgery because I never saw this one coming. Tonight I willfully deny how close we came, how close we still were to Liam's death, and the manifestations of my fears. The threat has not passed, and it's too soon to open my eyes.

CICU, Thurs. April 13, 2006, 9:00 am:

Liam wakes with six chest tubes shoved into his torso. By noon, the attending doctor will clear the room and cut another star shape with a scalpel for a seventh tube because Liam's right lung collapsed. The nurses pronounce Liam a chest tube record holder, but there's no blue ribbon for that.

To understand these chest tubes, imagine a masked man took a scalpel and slit seven x's under your ribs and then shoved a garden hose in each hole, pushing each hose until it made contact with a vital organ. Then the hose is literally sewn into your skin to keep in place.

Liam's old chest tube holes, the ones that were there the night before, were cut out, stripped of infected skin and sewn shut. The old holes pucker like the gathered openings of drawstring bags, sprouting little black stitches like purse strings. The skin around Liam's old sternal incision was cut away like the ratty parts of his bone.

For the first time in the five times Liam's chest has been spread open, he sports primitive Frankenstein's monster stitches instead of the clever inward stitching that leaves a fine white line. These sutures tug at Liam's skin and leave an even pattern of horizontal white ticks down his chest that he will wear for the rest of his life, however long that might be. Seven tubes, eleven holes, thinned out bone, Frankenstein's whipstitches, and my child is more disfigured than ever, but he's not dead.

Liam is not dead today, so I cannot complain.

He is so small. He's a little teapot spouting hoses draining blood, water, and fat. Liam is wretched. Jim and I are wretched. Moira is playing with her cousins, unaware that her brother almost died last night. I'll get her back on Friday. I won't let her be away from me this time.

Liam and I will not walk together for weeks. When he finally walks again, he has trouble with muscle control from being immobile for four weeks, so I walk no farther than the bathroom or to tag team Jim so I can take over with Moira at the Ronald McDonald House.

For five long weeks, Jim and I are tethered to Liam's bed, passing each other in the orbit of the Children's Hospital to exchange Moira for Liam and Liam for Moira. We are a satellite family, never coming together.

Home, Thurs. May 3, 2006, 4:00 P.M.:

We finally bring Liam home for good. We went home a week ago, the day before his third birthday, but he was quickly readmitted for too much fluid on his lungs. He marched right back to his bed in the Step-Down unit, as if he had never been home.

At home a PICC line runs super antibiotics through Liam's left arm straight to his damaged heart. A special diet keeps fat out of his lungs, an oxygen cannula up his tiny nose keeps those lungs inflated, a triple adult dose of diuretics keeps the same lungs dry. I'm not quite sure what spark of resolve keeps Liam alive, but I am in awe of my son.

It took almost five weeks of extraordinary measures, not the three we expected. It took five open-heart surgeries to keep Liam alive for three full years, not the three we expected. I will never promise my child anything. I don't dare. I have lost all sense of expectation.

All that remains is hope.

2

Blissful Ignorance

Greeley, Colorado, 1991-1994:

Jim and I met as teenage crewmates at McDonalds. Against the thick stench of McDonald's back washroom, home to the trash compactor and the grease bucket, we fell in love.

Our hands were gloved in salty cuts, our feet shod in cheap black shoes so grease-sodden that every third month the right sole cracked with a pop when we went up on our toes to reach for a Big Mac on top of the pass. We knew with that first pop the left sole would follow by the end of the shift, and we'd be out $12, two and half hours of wages, for our next pair of work shoes. On this greasy dance floor we were friends for a year, dated for two weeks, and began a life together that flowed far too quickly into eighteen years.

Our first apartment was in a quality neighborhood. One night, while watching a show on our thirteen-inch TV, we heard, "Come out with your hands up!"

It sounded so cliché we assumed it was someone's television. Our assumptions shattered when a SWAT officer tapped on our window and told us to get down and stay inside. The Evans police department busted our next-door neighbors for making meth in their bathtub. Their little girl was taken to God knows where, and all she left behind was her nail polish graffiti on the laundry room window and the memory of her wandering around in the dark parking lot long after she should have been in bed.

Eventually that apartment complex was approved for state assistance, and the government paid the landlords more than fair market value for the neighborhood. We were forced out when our rent nearly doubled to what welfare paid. We were told we made too much money to stay, all of $900 in monthly McWages. We were the working poor.

Our second apartment was much smaller but nearly as expensive as our first. Our new neighbors included more college kids than single moms, and marginally fewer drug dealers.

While living at Brentwood Park Apartments, Jim and I married. It was early autumn 1994. I was twenty and he was twenty-one. We were oh-so-totally grown up and mature, buying each other cartoon character watches for our wedding gifts. I gave Jim Snoopy, and he gave me Sylvester the Cat. Our sugary white cake was a gift from a woman I babysat for when I was in high school.

We hosted our reception in the same church basement/gym where I took P.E. and ate lunch for nine years of parochial school. The cavernous peach "reception hall" preserved the odors of generations of sweaty middle school boys and the adjacent musty basement. High above, near the graying acoustic ceiling, wasps circled their nests in the caged florescent light fixtures. The gym was $25; the wasps and the church wedding were free.

The gym was the perfect setting to conclude my childhood and begin a marriage. Jim and I played a mix tape of our favorite songs on the boom box Santa gave me when I was thirteen. A DJ or band would be as out-of-place as a catered meal, but this pauper's party was all we could afford.

Our earliest years were full of retail jobs, aimless drives in the Rocky Mountains in the sunburned silver '81 Honda Civic, and little direction in daily life. But those nights of watching *Saved by the Bell* marathons and binging on Ben & Jerry's Phish Food were our golden moments. Life was simple. Life was good. Reality wasn't biting yet, but it was about to bite and bite hard.

Less than a year after he walked me down the aisle on my wedding day, my dad told his four kids that he had terminal cancer. I was twenty-two when my dad died at forty-eight. Three years later, my best friend Mary died at twenty-five. I dealt with my grief in my mid-twenties by focusing on college and graduate school and constantly planning my future to avoid dwelling on my losses.

After Mary died, Jim and I naively believed the worst was behind us. With seven years of marriage to our credit, we decided we were ready to have kids. Unfortunately, my body wasn't ready to cooperate. We started trying the summer of 2001, but it took more than a year of failed attempts before I was finally pregnant.

I couldn't understand why it took so long, given my family's history of high fertility. I was in the sweet spot of my childbearing years. As a college graduate and homeowner, I counted on a solid stash in my karmic bank account with dividends for personal responsibility. After all, I wasn't one of those teenagers who got pregnant before she was ready, only to become a bitter, resentful, or negligent parent. Nor was I a selfish forty-something boomer with poor prioritization skills who tried to have it all and forgot about kids until the last minute. I was impatient and, therefore, thrilled to be delivered from frustration with a positive pregnancy test after only one month of charting my basal body temperature.

Awash in my sense of Gen-X entitlement and big ideas of what the universe owed me, I celebrated all that was coming to me now that I was finally pregnant. I would use a midwife! Maybe a doula! Look at me! I was a textbook baby maker, now that the baby finally made its way to where it was supposed to be. I bought all the books, signed up on all the baby websites, and was ready to rock on with my mommy-to-be-self-righteous-satisfaction. Bad things only happened to women who did it wrong. Not me, I did it all right.

Those heavenly days of being pregnant for the first time! Everyone in my adult education class at Colorado State buzzed with sweet excitement, all for me. On our many field trips to adult learning centers around the state, my classmates made sure I had water, food, access to the bathroom, etc. I relished being the spoiled darling of the day. I loved the attention; it was finally my turn. It was like falling in love. I was swept away with my first pregnancy.

That first trimester was a true honeymoon period. Ten weeks in, the midwife, Tina, couldn't hear the baby's heartbeat through Doppler or through my belly. To ease Jim's and my worry, Tina did a transvaginal ultrasound.

We saw our child for the first time. A tiny gray lima bean held in its center a bright flashing light. That was the heart, and it shined like a diamond on the monochrome screen of the dark ultrasound room. We nicknamed our tadpole Flipper, like the dolphin, and danced out of that appointment with our first photograph of our baby.

Everything was going great that fall until Jim's cousin, Mandi, who was also pregnant but due in December, learned her baby had a birth defect. Mandi's baby was diagnosed with omphalocele, meaning his intestines were not enclosed in his abdomen. Everyone else seemed so relaxed about it, even Mandi, but I was devastated.

Mandi and Eric had a plan at this great hospital in Denver with these great doctors whose names I didn't pay attention to. The doctors would simply give Mandi a c-section a little early, and fix her son. The baby would be fine. Everything would be fine because the doctors caught it early and could fix it. "Fix it, fix it, they could fix it and make it fine, fine, fine." that was the refrain of the day – fix it, fine. It didn't matter that it was broken because it could be fixed.

While the rest of our family seemed to graciously accept Mandi's misfortune, focusing instead on the optimistic "they'll fix it" mantra, I was heartbroken for her. They could fix her baby maybe, but they couldn't fix the theft of Mandi's plans and expectations. I numbly imagined how awful it was to go all the way to Denver for c-section and to subject her first child, her newborn baby to immediate surgery. That wasn't "just fine" to me.

Even as I pitied poor Mandi, I scheduled my Lamaze classes, daydreamed about waking Jim in the middle of an April night or maybe May. Flipper was due April 29. Would it be diamond or emerald?

I fantasized about our exciting drive to the hospital and debated whether or not I was tough enough to avoid an epidural. I was so warm and safe and smug in my cocoon of certainty that since this bad thing was happening to Mandi and Eric, nothing bad could possibly happen to Jim and me.

I created a math-magical rule of numbers and proximity in my head that told me, as badly as I felt for Mandi, her random misfortune was my insurance. My deep well of sympathy was double indemnity.

December came, exchanging the daylight for holiday lights. I finished my last classes at CSU, took my final finals, and registered to complete my thesis before my baby came. I would graduate a few days after Flipper was due. I was on top of things and on top of the world. All my plans were coming together so nicely.

Life couldn't have been better. Work was going well, and Jim and I registered for baby gifts and neutral bedding with a cute jungle animal theme. We got all kinds of little baby mementos for Christmas. It was a swirling golden time of the greatest expectations.

On Dec. 26, Mandi delivered her son Trace as scheduled. He was taken into surgery a few hours later and, thank God, her baby really was fixed. On Dec. 27, I went to Presbyterian St. Luke's (PSL) along with my mother-in-law Karen and my sister-in-law Jenny to see Mandi and her baby, who was making a solid recovery from his surgery.

When we arrived, being one of only two non-blood relatives in the waiting room, I was repeatedly bumped by higher priority guests. The NICU had a two-visitors-at-one-time limit.

I was five months pregnant, not uncomfortable or unbearably sleepy, and everyone was interested in my baby-to-be as we waited en mass. I was entertained and entertaining and excitedly distracted by talking about my ultrasound planned for the following Monday.

Someone said that Mandi cried while waiting for her ultrasound. She just knew something was wrong. I was impressed by her psychic connection to her baby. My psychic lines must have crossed with another woman's child, because everything told me I had absolutely nothing to worry about.

I waited, and waited, and waited, and eventually everyone saw Trace and Mandi but me. Just as my turn neared, the VIP great-grandparents blew in, and I was bumped again. I never did see Mandi or her baby that day, but in the several hours I waited, I became familiar with the blue and mauve tones and aqua green accents in the NICU waiting area.

Still, even with the squishy couch, good company, and its "We believe in Miracles" tagline bobbing by on buttons pinned to lab coats, this was a foreign place to me. I wasn't disappointed to get out of the hospital and have a late lunch. Pregnant ladies get hungry.

Because of my HMO-ish PPO insurance plan and the fact that I was twenty-eight, the midwives didn't want to give me a twenty week ultrasound like the "What to Expect" ladies and all the preggo-mommy message boards insisted was par for the course.

The insurance company paid for that first one at ten weeks. It's a one-shot deal unless the doctor/midwife deems it "medically necessary" and codes it accordingly. It's a rule of numbers, not unlike the one I played to assuage any worry for Flipper since Mandi's baby found the problems first. My midwives told me I didn't need another ultrasound, and I believed them completely.

Nothing bad was going to happen to me or my Flipper, but I can't stand surprises. I hate waiting for Christmas presents, I won't tolerate suspense in movies, and I lose my mind when my ipod gets set to shuffle. I cannot abide not knowing exactly what's up, and you do not ever want to take a vacation or plan a party with me. It can't be coincidence that there are five A's in my name and my blood type is A+. Being a snoopy, controlling, flawed Pandora type, I had to know if Flipper was a girl or a boy.

During my pregnancy, I drove the five-minute commute home to eat lunch every single day so I could watch two episodes of *A Baby Story* on TLC. Like those people on the show, I paid lip service to the "we only want a healthy baby" line. But Jim and I both wanted a girl..

Years before, when I ran the Montgomery Ward Children's department, my favorite part of the job was displaying the frilly holiday dresses. I worried I might be disappointed if Flipper was a boy and I was forced to go with the tracksuits. I was unapologetically shallow. I didn't know any better. Caught up in my moment of impending motherhood, I just enjoyed the ride.

Still, I had to know whether Flipper was a boy or a girl. The suspense was killing me. On the midwives' second "no," I slyly mentioned Jim's first-cousin-blood-relation was having a baby with omphalocele, and maybe they should do a check since that might be genetic, right?

Oh yes, I played the birth defect card from Mandi's unfortunate hand so I could shop for my baby before it arrived. No, of course I am not proud of it. However, to my dying day I will be glad of it.

We were medically approved for one more full coverage ultrasound. Still, the midwife knew our ulterior motive and suggested we wait until week twenty-three when the baby was bigger.

December 30th was our big day. Our appointment was late morning, and we had lunch plans to celebrate our great discovery. Whatever sex Flipper was, our baby would be great! We brought nothing but optimism into this appointment.

I had a commitment after the appointment to return a narrow black proof book of family pictures we'd taken in November. I was already a week late returning it, and the trip to the studio was an excuse to investigate the cute cafes and bookshops in the neighborhood. The afternoon was ours, and I filled it with expectations of adding pink items to my Target registry. I was planning and expecting, always planning and expecting.

I held my bladder for hours and grew excitedly uncomfortable waiting outside the ultrasound room reading the *Working Mother* magazine with Rosie the Riveter on the cover. That issue listed my employer as one of the best companies for working moms because they gave new moms breast pumps. Mine was already at home in Flipper's spacious closet.

Finally, the other couple came out of *our* room. My turn! The routine exam began with warm goop on my belly. It didn't take long before our son made his maleness known. Overwhelmed by a wave of love, I saw that baby with his reptilian spine, his tiny skull and looming eye sockets, and his little baby-man-parts on the screen. I didn't want a girl. I only wanted him, that baby, our baby, and so did Jim.

Flipper was suddenly and forevermore Liam, and any thought of girls disappeared as our glee washed over the room. We watched our son in his grainy alien world inside my own familiar body and brimmed with love, wonder, and not a few tears of joy. No doubts, no second thoughts, nothing existed in that moment but love for our little boy. Nothing ever felt so pure and true or so right in my entire life. It was a perfect moment, and I cherish it all the more for how brief and fleeting it was.

We were having a boy, and at the peak of my blissful ignorance it never occurred to me, other than my bursting bladder, that this exam was taking a long time. I'd never had a complete ultrasound before, so it didn't seem strange to me that Karen, our ultrasound tech, kept making me shift around for the better part of an hour.

Finally and mercifully, Karen sent me to the bathroom to see if Liam would move. The fact that she muttered "I just can't get a good view of his heart" more than once set off no alarms. I had no idea that was extraordinary in any way.

Karen should seek a second career as a professional gambler. With her poker face, she'd be a millionaire. We were beyond oblivious to what was coming. Pregnant ladies hear what they want to hear.

3

My Death and Resurrection

Jim and I rolled down the hall from ultrasound room to the midwives' office with our fabulous fetus photos. We called both grandmas to gush about our boy. Liam! Liam! Liam! He, he, he! We were having a boy and everyone who crossed our effusive path was made aware of the gender of the child I carried. You'd have thought we were the first people to ever procreate.

Like a powder-blue freight train driven by a maniacal stork, we chugged in for our appointment as if it was no more than an inconvenient station stop on our way to our glorious destiny as Liam's parents. We were cow-catching every person in our path with entirely too much information.

Once we checked in, a nurse weighed me and took my blood pressure and then tucked us into a corner exam room to bask in our joy. We waited for a midwife we'd never met before. We waited so long that shadows replaced the sunbeams. We observed the fading view on two sides of the building, made a couple more cell phone calls, giggled, waited, looked at our pictures of Liam, and waited some more.

We began to wonder if they'd forgotten about us or gotten busy with another patient. Maybe a woman went into labor during an office visit. We made sport of it because we were too happy to be annoyed. It never once occurred to me that anything was wrong - that anything could even possibly be wrong. We were so young eight years ago.

Rachel finally crept in like a timid rabbit. Perched on the exam table with my back to the door, I didn't see her enter the room at first. I looked over my shoulder and watched her slink slowly around the bed, sigh, and sit on a round medical stool. Rolling up to me, she put her hands on my knees, then took my hands in hers and said, "I have some really bad news."

I don't think the pause between Rachel's first words and her next was more than a few seconds, but time stopped.

I was in free fall with Midwife Rachel's exclamation of "... really bad news." I hit rock bottom with, "Your baby has Down Syndrome and a severe congenital heart defect. . . static . . . neuchal fold . . . static . . . Hypoplastic Left Heart Syndrome . . . don't look it up on the Internet, it will only scare you . . . static . . . you should still go on your vacation this week . . . static . . . you might want an amniocentesis. . . . static . . . none of our doctors are available, they're all gone on vacation."

Jim and I both cried. In shame, we retreated downstairs after our previous display of "it's a boy" shenanigans, like vaudevillians realizing they crashed a wake. Everything we had been was now wholly inappropriate. We stumbled out the door to find the air outside.

In the parking lot the day that literally and figuratively started out so sunny had grown overcast. Most of the afternoon slipped away while we were in the corner room, and it was dead winter. I grabbed a naked young tree in the cold air and sobbed uncontrollably. I'd gone rubber-boned as I absorbed the chilling vinegar of Rachel's pronouncement.

Tears streamed down Jim's face as he caressed my back. An elderly couple walked by us, their faces awash with pity. Their expressions made me sick to my stomach, and the heat came back to my ears. I felt frozen everywhere else as we retreated to the car.

The narrow black proof book was still in my seat where I left it, like a bookmark for my life. My life I left in the blue Saturn was on a different planet from the one we now inhabited. Jim wanted to go home. I refused. I absolutely could not go home. Going home made this real. I willed myself to return the proof book to the photographer. I had promised, and it was already late.

Jim said they would understand, but I had to take it back. I didn't think they would understand. *I* didn't understand. I offer no explanation for that compulsion. Though she was only the messenger, Rachel stole my life away from me, and I was determined to finish this one thing that I'd set out to do that day. It was now too late for lunch and we couldn't comprehend food. We would not shop for baby clothes. Everything else was shit, so I had to return that book. It was the only thing I had left to do. It was all I could do.

We drove through town to the highway. I called our moms and retracted all of our good news through sobs. . . on voicemail. I imagine them both off telling their work friends about the new grandson, how excited we were, and how we kept saying we wanted a girl, but they're so happy now. After all those years together and wanting a baby, "Jim and Amanda are so happy now."

Only now we weren't happy at all. Not a drop of happiness remained in my body. It was as if I was brimming with it and a nuclear explosion detonated, incinerating every drop of my joy in my flesh with a flash. All that remained was an ash shadow of that glowing happiness from a couple of hours before. It took all my energy to not blow away.

I was unintentionally cruel that day, making Jim drive me thirty miles and back to return a stupid proof book and telling two grandmothers to expect a broken grandchild on voice mail. I still see them, our own mothers, returning to their desks, checking their messages expecting congratulations but hearing me sobbing and incoherent, stealing back all their joy.

I was the instrument of aftershock lying helpless in the rubble of my own life. I've never found the strength to ask anyone else about that day, to apologize for my insensitivity. It never occurred to me that there was collateral damage as I carried the time bomb in my own body.

When we hit the cloverleaf to exit I25, I wailed like a banshee, "I don't want a retarded baby!" and instantly felt guilty and evil for saying it. This poor baby that I wanted so badly only hours before and years before that did nothing wrong. Liam didn't change anything, but everything had changed.

For years whenever I found myself cresting the incline of that exit, I was seared again with guilt for rejecting my child in that one wicked moment. It's been eight years and I'm still trying to take it back. My empathy lapsed for our mothers, but I never stopped thinking of our child.

We parked a few doors down from the photography studio, and Jim waited in the car. I'd pushed him to the limit. Jim took me this far, but now he was fixed to his seat. Maybe he called his mom, I don't remember. I was a negligent wife and a wild animal in pain. I was desperate to get that proof book out of my life, as if returning it would set everything right. It was insane.

I was insane.

In defeat, I walked through a hallway lined with gorgeous pictures of pregnant bellies caressed by paternal hands, naked newborns on their father's hairy forearms, smiling infants, and gleeful toddlers. When I finally made it to the counter, I was in tears again. No one was there, so I shoved the book on the desk behind the counter hoping they would find it.

Just a month before, I'd studied those baby pictures, relishing the time when I would bring my own baby back in the spring to create our own photos to hang in our own house. I relished how after being so good, doing everything right, and dodging the cold threat of infertility, it was finally my turn. I had the goldenrod price sheet at home, a souvenir from when I thought I could plan my own life and set expectations. That time was now over.

I hastily retreated down the hall of shame and held my hands to my face like blinders to block those photos from my periphery. I quickened my step. They were like evil faces staring through a window in a horror movie. All those perfect babies sneering at me and my broken boy, "You'll never be like us. This isn't yours anymore." But, it never really was.

I folded my rubber self back into our car, instantly exhausted. I had been running on adrenaline and now was flooded by sorrow.

The December sky was growing dark as we drove home. Jim took the dogs out about the same time the phone started to ring. I suppose it rang all afternoon, driving our dogs to distraction. But I made us take our time getting home. I wanted to stop time.

Everyone knew, everyone called, my mom called twice. The first time I re-explained what I didn't know or understand.

My mother said, "I'm so glad you didn't find out until after Christmas, you were both so happy at Christmas. I'm glad you had that."

I folded like Gumby, sliding down the door to the floor, and whispered hoarsely, "I don't think I'll ever be happy again." I shut my eyes. "I have to go."

Against Rachel's advice, we hit the Internet and learned about Hypoplastic Left Heart Syndrome (HLHS). It scared the shit out of us, and for the first time I learned there are things far worse than Down Syndrome. It made me hope for Corky from that TV show *Life Goes On* instead of the tiny white coffin trapped in my head tearing apart my soul.

My mom called again. She wanted to come over, she kept asking if I wanted her to come over. I didn't take the hint. I didn't want her to come over. I didn't want anyone to come over. I could not bear a house full of mourners. Who was dead? Our two parental bodies were still breathing, all three broken hearts were still beating, but something was clearly dead.

The day we learned of Liam's massively defective heart and impending mental limitations, I said, "Fuck it," and took a warm bath. I hadn't taken a bath in over a year. I stopped soaking in favor of showers when I read that warm baths make it harder to get pregnant. I didn't take them after I was pregnant because soaking in hot water wasn't good for the fetus's heart—seriously, the heart.

I didn't drink diet soda, alcohol, caffeine, etc. I ate well, slept well when I could, and generally followed the "What to Expect" book like a Bible for the cult of the pregnant. I did everything right. I only gained the bare minimum weight, and I was careful to get the right nutrition. I took vitamins for as long as I refused myself a bath, and it did me absolutely no good. A crack whore knocked up by a heroin addict with AIDS would give birth to a healthier child than ours, so I ran a bath.

I forgot myself for a few minutes in the warm water and thought, "I should shave my legs," but my razor was nowhere to be found. Jim took it while the tub was filling. When I asked him why, he looked at me so sadly and said, "I was afraid you might do something."

Jim was afraid because he knew that when I was fourteen I'd been on the edge of suicide, and if anything could drive me back there, wouldn't this be it? But I laughed out loud, because as horrible as this day was, and it was truly the worst day of my life, I felt no desire to end my existence, much less by disassembling a Daisy razor.

In that one moment of inappropriate laughter, I realized that as dark as things were and as scared as I was, I had survived a worse mental state as a teen and emerged stronger. Truly, my suicidal teen phase held no catalyst as obvious as what I now faced. Yet, I trapped myself in a private hell at fourteen because I couldn't see any way out at the time. With no social skills, no coping skills, no self-esteem, and no recourse as a child, I was lost. Now I was twenty-eight. I wasn't a little girl any more. Yes, I was terrified for my son, but I was not afraid of myself and I didn't want Jim to be afraid for me either.

This night, fourteen years later and a lifetime stronger, fearing for my baby's life, I couldn't see the way forward, but I knew in that instant, as surely as I knew I would never kill myself, that there was a way. I would do whatever was necessary to save my baby. No matter what Liam was like I would love him unconditionally. I already did but it took my brain a few hours to catch up with my heart.

I would survive this conflagration. I might not know the exit in all the smoke, but I was going to find the way for Liam, for Jim, and for myself. I arose from that bath like a Phoenix from her ashes. A naked, bald, badly-beaten, scorched and mangled Phoenix, but I was ready for a fight. The prototypical pregnant lady was dead, but a Heart Mom was born.

4
Areas of Specialization

The day after I died inside, New Me made phone calls. I wasn't satisfied to wait for my amnio until the local doctors returned from shooting at elk or skiing. All my web research indicated it took as long as three weeks for results, and I couldn't bear to wait another week to start that clock.

I was persistent, and the midwives found me a kind doctor in Denver who I will adore all the days of my life. Dr. Wexler not only doesn't take Christmas vacations, he was one of the physicians who originally got amniocentesis approved by the FDA. Dr. Wexler taught genetics at CU Medical School in Boulder - score!

He also kindly wrote me a note to fax to Travelocity to get most of our prepaid travel expenses to a friend's Las Vegas wedding refunded. Against Rachel's advice, we cancelled our travel plans, and had no intention to "relax."

After killing my cordless phone batteries nagging the midwives to get that appointment, I laid on the couch with my dogs tangled in my legs. Together the three of us stared vacantly into the fireplace as it consumed flickering bits of my dreams. Jim was upstairs doing more heartbreaking research about HLHS. The doorbell rang. The dogs freaked out. I had to get up.

Opening the door, I was greeted with flowers sent by my coworkers, specifically my co-pregnant buddy Lex. The night before I'd rattled off a semi-coherent e-mail message to work about how my ultrasound went and why I was not coming into the office the next day. The gesture of flowers was sweet and made me feel a little less lonely to know that our devastation was being felt in ripples beyond our front door. Misery loves company best when it keeps its distance and sends flowers. The flower man left, trailing a "Happy New Year" behind him.

The day was nearly over and it hadn't registered that it was New Year's Eve. This strange year that brought me out of the deserts of infertility, into the promised land of prenatal elation, and left me stranded in the rubble of my expectations was about to come to its whimpering end. And the year to come in just a few hours might leave me . . . what exactly?

In that snowy moment on the fading edge between years I realized we have orphans, widows, and widowers, but there is no moniker for a woman or man who loses a child. Bereft doesn't quite cut it. You can be bereft of your dog. What would I be if this baby, if Liam, died? What would my condition be in a nameless state?

How would I manage it if he lived? How long might he live? I was thawing from shock to an icy baptism of inquiry. What next?

New Year's Day arrived like a whisper in the snow. Our moms were adamant about coming with us to the amniocentesis, so we made arrangements to meet them the next morning. For them it was like viewing a corpse; they both needed to see their children in the flesh to move from the denial stage and claim their share of the communal grief.

Around 7:00 A.M. on Jan. 2, we met the moms, who between them birthed seven healthy children without incident, and rode to South Denver with Jim at the wheel and our moms in the back seat.

Dr. Wexler's office/family business was founded by his wife. Their son, Mr. Wexler, counseled Jim and me about the relative infrequency of chromosomal defects. While our mothers waited outside, Mr. Wexler reviewed the types of abnormalities and the terrifying list of trisomies. 18 is even worse than 21. Trisomy 21 is Down Syndrome and the trigger that brought us to this appointment. Mr. Wexler also reviewed the screening process and the time it took to culture and analyze the cells. The high point was that it would only take ten days for our results, not three weeks like I'd expected.

At the end of the session, we accumulated serious evidence to doubt not only Rachel's emphatic diagnosis of Down Syndrome, but her very ability to determine such a thing from a basic ultrasound. Also suspect was the hasty conclusion that HLHS and Down Syndrome happen together. In reality, that is beyond rare.

We found seeds of hope in the incredible odds against Rachel being right about Liam. The Wexler's institutional statistics were more accurate than my horribly failed "Jim's cousin's birth defect misfortune + our proximity = nothing bad will happen to us" math-magical disaster ever was. Then I had the amnio.

An amniocentesis is essentially paying a doctor copious amounts of money to stab your swollen belly with a nine inch needle, with a slight chance of miscarriage, because there is strong reason to suspect that something is terribly wrong with your baby. You're quite literally taking a stab at the truth in a desperate hope that the odds are in your favor.

Wait! It gets better, because there is also a full bladder and lots of pushy ultrasound probing against said full bladder to make sure the needle doesn't damage the baby or your vital organs.

I, however, won the booby prize, for as soon as that amazingly long needle pierced my uterine wall, the muscle seized up like a bear trap and bent that sucker in place. My uterus was as protective of Liam as my heart was. Dr. Wexler slowly twisted, wiggled and withdrew a wickedly curved and slightly stuck needle. I carried a nagging muscle memory for days from that single contraction.

On his second attempt with a shiny new straight needle, my mom and Jim each held one of my hands and I looked away from the needle and tried to breathe deeply. As if I could control my involuntary muscle spasms by pretending to relax.

The second time a needle went through my belly, Dr. Wexler successfully withdrew enough cells to culture and eventually tells us definitively whether or not Liam had Down Syndrome, or anything worse.

Dr. Wexler shared a priceless and humble wisdom that day. I kept asking him what he saw in Liam's heart, and he told me, "The only person who can answer your questions is a pediatric cardiologist. I'm good at what I do and they're good at what they do, and that's your next stop."

I asked who I should see, and he said that they "have a bunch of good ones at The Children's Hospital" and to work with my doctor/midwife in Fort Collins to set that up.

I would be remiss if I didn't address the frequently raised question regarding amniocentesis, which is, "Unless you're determining whether or not this is a genetically abnormal baby so you can decide to keep or abort it, why would you do an amnio?"

It never occurred to me to abort Liam. I needed to know what he faced, what his condition would be when he arrived. I could not wait until he was born to know it, even less than I could wait to know if he was a boy or a girl. I couldn't stand the five month suspense of "maybe he'll be mentally retarded and have other health issues, or maybe he won't." I can't imagine how anyone could tolerate that mystery. I needed to prepare myself for what life would be like when he arrived.

The ten-day wait for results was painful. I was back at work by then sitting at my desk ever so far from the ladies' room, waiting for Mr. Wexler to call me. I was getting bigger and more uncomfortable by the day, and I *really* needed to pee, but I refused to leave my desk lest I miss his call.

Finally, in desperation, I called the Wexler's office. Mr. Wexler, the doctor's son, put me on hold and came back a few minutes later. "Mrs. Adams, your son has no chromosomal defects. He does have a y chromosome, so he's definitely a boy."

I was so completely over gender at that point that I simply offered weak smile to the telephone receiver for the boy statement. I melted to silent tears for the first part. "No chromosomal defects," I sighed, "Thank you so much."

I continued to ramble a litany of thank you's until Mr. Wexler convinced me to hang up the phone.

Jim wasn't at his desk when I called, so I left a message with the good news and told him I *had* to go to the bathroom and would call him back. Then I flew down the hall to relieve myself of tears and my bladder. All the way back to my desk I stopped to tell friends at work my good news. When I sat down again, I realized, "What about the heart?" and mine sank.

The heart was now the matter at hand. Rachel went on her own vacation after our first visit with her, so we turned to Tina, a midwife we'd seen before. Rachel never called us, and Tina didn't know where Rachel had left off. Tina was tasked with finding us a pediatric cardiologist. After three days of waiting, I called her, and she told me she couldn't find one in Fort Collins.

Today, eight years, two thousand miles, and millions of dollars later, I can laugh at that, but at the time it didn't occur to me that there would be no dedicated pediatric heart practice in a town of 140,000 with no medical school. The weirder thing is that it didn't occur to her. Congenital heart disease (CHD) is the most common of all birth defects and the most fatal affliction facing newborns not only in the USA, but the world over. You would think a woman who delivers babies for a living would be more informed. It's shocking how few are.

Frustrated with my clinic, I turned to my friend the Internet, which led me to the American Heart Association. The only person I could find in the Colorado office with a listed phone number was Louise. Louise was coordinating the 2003 Heart Ball, but she was my only lead, so I called Louise.

Providence was smiling at me. I've since met many AHA employees who coordinate events, and not one of them could tell you the fundamental difference between congenital heart disease and adult cardiovascular disease. But at the time neither could I, and neither could Louise. Fortunately, Louise was a mover and shaker who knew not one but two pediatric cardiologists. I don't think she knew much about their jobs, but she had their direct phone numbers. I finally connected to my son's future doctor through the Heart Ball lady. Thanks Louise, wherever you are!

The first cardiologist to return my call was Dr. Henry Sondheimer at Denver Children's Hospital. I told him that we were originally told HLHS, but that Dr. Wexler said there was transposition of the great arteries and the left side was fine, and that's all I knew, but Dr. Wexler said we need to see someone, and my midwife didn't know anyone . . . I'm sure he was laughing at my breathless incoherence with his hand over the phone.

Dr. Sondheimer was sweet and gave me the number to the lab to schedule our echocardiogram, (also called echo, an ultrasound of the heart). He answered my questions, indicating that if Liam had any of the things I mentioned, then he'd need open-heart surgery by his third day of life.

When I asked about where we would have Liam, he said, "Oh you just have him like you planned up in Fort Collins, and we'll airlift him to Denver after he's here." Kind of like you might say, "Oh, I'll just drop off these library books on my way to meet you for coffee, don't worry, I won't be late."

Scared but hopeful, I scheduled my ultrasound at Children's.

Then Dr. Smooth at PSL returned my call. The first thing he said to me was, "You can have your baby right here at our hospital, then you'll just be right down the hall from him when he's in the NICU." Smooth!

Seriously, work this equation: emotional pregnant lady who knows her first desperately wanted baby is going to have to have open heart surgery at birth. All things equal in her mind, does she want to A) have her baby snatched away, loaded on a helicopter, and then wait until she is discharged by her hospital to see him over an hour away, or B) be able to walk down a hallway to see her child? It was staggering how quickly the situation I found so pitiable for Mandi a few weeks before now sounded so palatable to me. I canceled at Children's and made my appointment with Dr. Smooth's practice. It didn't take too long before we were there, and waiting . . . .

I couldn't pee before the echo (yes this is a theme and a very visceral biological memory), but I sat in one of the few chairs available in the waiting room staring at an aquarium full of very wet fish. The room looked serene with the fish and the sedate colors, but the screaming little girl on the other side of the wall grated my spine. Her lack of cooperation with her cardiologist in the echo room was causing us to be more than an hour late for our turn at bat, which wouldn't have been that bad except I hadn't used the toilet in over four hours.

That child screamed and screamed and screamed, but we took comfort in the dozens of children coming and going and the fact that we couldn't differentiate the "heart kids" from their healthy brothers and sisters. We hoped that whether Liam screamed his head off or passively enjoyed the fish tank, that we would have a living child to take to cardiology appointments one day.

Finally, we went in, but Dr. Smooth was not there. We saw his colleague, who came to be known by our entire clan as Dr. Doom and Gloom, or Dr. Doom for short. Dr. Doom rushed us to the table and went straight to work. Before long, he was visibly frustrated with my inconvenient anterior placenta and the poor views it allowed.

After a while, he sent me off to the bathroom so Liam would turn. Despite Dr. Doom's lengthy and forceful probing of my uncooperative belly, I grew sleepy in the dark room where the only thing we heard was his occasional grunting in frustration with the tool or the patient. Then, just like that, he was done.

Dr. Doom sketched a crude drawing of Liam's heart, which I still have tucked away in my basement somewhere with the EPT pee stick. A company or organization makes this little red book that they give pediatric cardiologists. It includes about thirty-six pages of heart diagrams that show all the "known" heart defects and what they look like compared to a normal heart.

Pages are titled Atrial Septal Defect (ASD), Transposition of the Great Arteries (TGA), and Tetralogy of Fallot (TOF). Then, in the back there is a blank page for people like us - people who are totally screwed. Seriously, they just should title that page "Oh, you are so fucked."

Essentially, you could take eight of the preceding pages and superimpose them, and still not quite have the craptastic malformation that only God in His infinite wisdom or sadism could have dreamed up and called my baby's heart. Untenable arteries, severe hypolasia (way too small parts), no tricuspid valve to speak of, which meant Liam was missing his right ventricle. Big ass holes between the upper chamber, (my words, not Doom's). It was bad news all around the organ. Liam's tiny unborn heart was a train wreck and a time bomb all in one. Dr. Doom made brief mention of termination, but I ignored his pause in conversation until he moved on.

"He will have three open-heart surgeries," Dr. Doom proclaimed. "The first one will be when he is two or three days old. If he makes it through that, the next one will happen when he's about six months old. The last one is done around age three or four."

We asked about transplant, but Dr. Doom insisted they would try the surgeries first. We meekly asked if Liam might get better before he was born, but Dr. Doom was brusque in his reply. "It can only get worse."

We asked about having Liam at PSL as Dr. Smooth sold it to me. Dr. Doom told us to go down the hall to make an appointment, like we were troubling him for directions to a bus stop. We stopped asking questions.

I didn't dare cry in front of Dr. Doom, not because I was brave, but because I was afraid of him. He was colder than the ocean-blue gel he squirted on my swollen belly. He didn't want to see us again until thirty weeks, so we left that very dark room, walked past the aquarium, and turned down the hall to the Obstetrix office.

We walked into the OB clinic, and I told the receptionist that cardiology sent us over to make an appointment. She gave me forms on a clipboard, and I started to say something like, "Our baby is going to have three heart surgeries," and I freaking lost it.

The clipboard flapped in my hands with the attached pen flying wildly from its coiled plastic tether. Disconnected from reason, I wondered if the pen was drawing on my clothes. I wasn't thinking about anything solid. I was breaking down like chunks of an ice wall into the ocean. My body and mind were divorced. I shook so hard that Jim was frozen solid by the sight of me.

A doctor came out from behind the counter and put his arm around my shaking shoulders, pulling Jim in to our group hug and said, "We will do everything we possibly can to help you and your baby."

I will never forget the warmth and sincerity of his words and the giant surge of hope that I took from him. His name is Dr. Porreco, and but for my last ninety minutes of labor he would have been with me until Liam's birth. I still write him once a year to thank him because he said exactly the right thing at exactly the right time to help Jim and me stay the course and planting the seeds of hope that have sustained me.

The lessons Dr. Wexler taught us were reinforced at Obstetrix. Only perinatologists, level 2 ultrasounds, amniocentesis, and laboratories can definitively diagnose Down Syndrome. Everyone at the practice was aghast that we were told Liam had Down Syndrome based on a routine ultrasound by a midwife. It wasn't true, but Liam's heart defects were all too real.

Another lesson Dr. Wexler introduced, and the perinatologists confirmed, was that only a pediatric cardiologist can diagnose a specific congenital heart defect. Rachel was definitely striking out with her guesses.

For the remainder of my pregnancy I took every other appointment in Denver, at PSL with the same doctors Mandi raved about, and I went to my appointments in between with the hometown midwives until my last month.

When I finally saw Rachel again in her rotation, she was shocked that Liam didn't have Down Syndrome when I told her. She honestly asked me if I was sure about that, as if I might have been confused about two abdominal stabs or the "no chromosomal defects" report that, once "jacketed" and mailed to my home, became one of my most cherished possessions.

I was annoyed because she never called us back like she had promised to do. She clearly hadn't checked the chart before she came in to see me, either, or she would have seen Dr. Wexler's report. She would have seen medical evidence that she was wrong instead of questioning my understanding of the past month.

During the same appointment, when recounting all the appointments and information I'd learned over the previous weeks, I began to cry. Rachel told me that if I couldn't handle it that termination was a possibility. I stared at her dumbfounded and finally managed to say, "I'm at twenty-seven weeks, is that even legal?"

Rachel didn't answer my question. I don't know if I was more shocked or angry. I'm ambivalent about abortion, necessary evil under certain circumstances and all that. But it was never an option for me or for my baby.

With termination mentioned a second time in a few short weeks, I was flustered that these people who were supposed to be taking care of me and Liam bore no faith in our fight. I was livid that they seemed to think me weak because I was sad that this was happening but didn't abort and walk away. I know they have to present the option, but they don't have to encourage it or make you feel stupid for not wanting to terminate.

Besides, who the hell were they to judge me? Did they think that I couldn't fight for my child's life if I was going to cry about it? I still don't understand where they were coming from, but they didn't know how far I would go for my child.

I never saw Rachel again, but I met three other families in town whose babies (two boys and a girl) were born the same spring as Liam, and all were sent for amnios after Rachel declared "Down" on them. Not one of them had it. I also learned from an employee at that clinic that, less than a year later, that Rachel wasn't working there anymore.

In retrospect I prefer to believe Rachel was in over her head rather than a sociopath leading all these families to risk their pregnancies with unfounded amnios. Still, in one of four of the cases I know about, she called a heart defect, the wrong defect, but at least we were forewarned. I don't know if that redeems her, but it may have saved Liam's life, so I can forgive her. Still, I would never let her treat me for another pregnancy, or even a hangnail. By this point I was becoming a specialist and a doctor-snob, and it was only getting worse. Funny thing happened on the way to the OR. . . I started out thinking that too many doctors gave in and did c-sections in America. I started out thinking midwives and home-births were cool. I started out questioning epidurals and pitocin. I started out thinking I knew it all, and with one medically "unnecessary" ultrasound I was transported to a world of extraordinary specialization where everything I had known and wanted no longer applied to me.

5

A Baby's Story

During the first half of my pregnancy I rushed home every workday to watch *A Baby Story* and eat lunch off my coffee table to the accompaniment of begging dogs. After the diagnosis, I lost my appetite for it. I stayed at my desk through the lunch hour and read tribute pages to babies who died from their heart defects while I sobbed into my baloney and cheese, until I had to stop doing that.

I did meet a few moms on line. Julie and Traci were both mothers to little boys living with severe congenital heart defects. They gave me hope that Liam would survive long enough to be like their sons.

I also met Susan and Lucy whose baby boys had more similar defects to Liam, but both Jack and Joel died in infancy. Still, these grieving moms were so warm and caring and consoling, that all these years later I'm still in touch with them. I'm in touch with all four of these mothers. Gage and Atley are big boys with full lives. Susan and Lucy went on to have more children, but nothing ever replaced Jack or Joel—nothing ever could.

These real women offered me comfort.

I was on restricted activity during my last month of pregnancy. The doctors didn't want me to go into labor early because a baby with a heart like Liam's should be full term to have any real chance of surviving that first massive open-heart surgery. Some smaller babies make it, but most preemies with heart defects are at even higher risk. I left work at the beginning of April, and with all that free time and feeling more resolved about my situation, I thought, "OK, I'll just watch this one episode," of my old favorite. Big mistake.

The subject mommy was a daytime soap actress who married a cop and was expecting her second baby. She endured "such a hard time" delivering her first baby that she was electing a c-section in case this baby was big like her first one. Her second baby wasn't big at all, he was barely seven pounds, but it was all dramatic and sad and blah, blah, blah - it pissed me off.

Subsequently, every episode I watched pissed me off, and I used to absolutely love that show. Now it made me sick and angry.

Every time I'd watch the couple go to mommy-to-be-yoga or Lamaze it would remind me of the night Jim and I went to our first scheduled Lamaze class right after the diagnosis and told the instructor we couldn't stay because of Liam's heart and I'd probably need a c-section. Then I did a waddle of shame out of the circle of happy couples with their fluffy pillows and intact expectations.

I don't know why I went. Maybe I figured that if I didn't show up I wouldn't get a refund. I did, and suffered a lot of things then that I probably didn't need to do or suffer, but I was clueless and suffering regardless.

I hadn't learned to play my "sick-baby" card to get out of situations over the phone instead of in person. Doing so would have been admitting how bad it really was. I never wanted people to pity me. I just thought I'd deliver my news and leave, but always got weepy. I hated crying in front of people, so I worked on that. I had to toughen up, at least publically, if I was going to get through this pregnancy.

Still, I saw all these people with all their unbroken lives on the floor in the clinic rec room, or on TV telling their beautiful Baby Stories when Jack and Joel were dead, when Liam honestly might die. It hurt me so deeply, and I hated them for it.

I no longer found the charm in a couple planting a placenta under a new tree in their yard. Instead, I was planning costly cord blood storage on a Hail Mary that someday it might help Liam survive when his heart failed completely.

One family I followed in a CHD web forum ran out of options. Their daughter wasn't going to make it, so they ordered the doctors to unhook everything. They quickly cleaned her and dressed her for the first and last time. Then, they took her to the hospital courtyard so she could be outside once in her life before she died. That little baby died in the warmth of her mothers' arms while the April sunshine froze the moment. That was her baby story.

That might be my baby story.

To then see people on "reality" TV complaining about a long labor, oozing about how great it was to finally get their boy after three girls or the other way around, or whining that they didn't get the good birthing room at the hospital with the hot tub. It was too much for me.

Every mom who cried about how disappointed she was that she had a c-section while holding a healthy child in the comfort of her own home pissed me off. They had no idea how fucking lucky they were. They could have been sitting in the grass while that child died. They could have woken after getting their baby through a huge surgery only to find their son dead his second night home from the hospital. That happened to a friend. That was her baby story.

Who were these people on TV, and why was my reality so far removed from theirs? What had happened to me? Why was I so different from them? I was just like them a few months before. Maybe I hated these people because I loathed myself. I didn't know where my anger originated, but it was deep, corrosive, and ceaseless.

Now that I was a Heart Mom, I realized that babies all around the Internet were dying, in Pennsylvania, Alabama, and Texas, and everywhere in between. Babies were dying all the time and had always been. No one knew. No one seemed to care. Now I was terrified that my baby would be one of them. I stayed offline most of that last month. Mostly it made me sad and I couldn't read any more stories of baby death when Liam's arrival was so near.

I was lazy and fat and full of heart burn and heartache, but I did go shopping the week before Liam was born and found a few little outfits that didn't need to go over his head because I was warned that raising his arms would cause him post-operative pain. Everything I looked at took open-heart surgery into consideration, snaps and zippers only. I couldn't pick anything that pulled over the head, no matter how cute it was.

It was surreal to be in public. People saw me at full term waddling about in my giant purple corduroy overalls. They would congratulate me and smile at my big belly. It was like I was Barney the dinosaur, so cute and approachable. But then I'd tell complete strangers that my baby had a heart defect and would need open-heart surgery as soon as he was born, that he might not make it. I didn't bite their heads off, I just broke their hearts.

This was like when I went shopping for a dress to wear to my dad's funeral. Grief and fear put people off. But from the inside, in my own cloud of pain, I didn't see it clearly. Blurting is like bleeding; you're cut deeply but blind to the mess you leave behind.

Liam was due April 29th, toward the end Dr. Porreco asked when we wanted to deliver within a two week window of his due date. My birthday is April 23rd, and I was terrified if we shared that day and he died, I would want to die too.

I also wanted Liam to have his own birthday. We chose April 28th mostly because it was as close as I could get to full term, and it was a Monday so the hospital would be fully staffed and Liam would receive everyone's full attention.

Sunday morning came with no dogs to take out, no ferret to feed, no responsibilities but to get our stuff in our mom mobile and head to Denver. Just our luck; they weren't ready for us. . . but they put us in a labor room and let us watch TV until they could get our room ready. At 5:00 A.M. the following morning, I awoke to the sun peeking in my window and a soaked bed. My water broke. I made it until about 10:30 before I gave in and accepted the epidural. I got it, and then everything ground to a halt.

Meconium came through my dilating cervix. To prevent Liam from aspirating his own stools, I got a major-fun uterine flush. Then I got it again. It hurt, even with the epidural, and after the second violation I just wanted everyone out of my room so I could take a nap.

Finally, I dilated enough that at 5:30 P.M. my nurse let me push. A half-hour later, Dr. Porreco left for the day, and another doctor I didn't know, Dr. H., came on. Seriously, I don't know the name of the man who delivered my son, it all happened so fast. Dr. H. kept checking on me, and after almost ninety minutes of pushing he warned me that if Liam didn't come soon, I'd be having a c-section.

I was ambivalent. I wasn't in any real pain, but I was exhausted. Between 6:55 and 7:00 P.M. Liam's heart crashed big time. He was in distress. The room was suddenly very full, and a clipboard was thrust in my face. Dr. H. said, "You can push this baby out, but he won't be alive when he gets here."

Not knowing me from any other would-be mother, I suspect he anticipated a vaginal delivery battle. He needn't have worried; I was resigned to a c-section months before. I didn't care what happened to me as long as they got Liam out safely. My thoughts were something like, "Well then, what the hell are you waiting for?"

I signed the surgical consent form as my bed was rolling to the OR at 7:00 P.M. and Liam was born at 7:05. Thanks to the anesthesiologist upping my epidural as they pushed my bed down the hall at breakneck speed, the surgery was not painful.

That said, I felt every bit of it, the shaving, cutting, pulling, tugging, and sewing. It was kind of like when your foot falls asleep if you sit on the toilet too long reading. When you get up know your foot's still attached and you can sort of feel it, but it's not all there. I felt Liam being torn from my body, but I was too numb to feel pain.

In the five minutes between my ride to the OR and my son's first cry, eighteen doctors and nurses assembled in that room, prepared to take my baby. Jim and I made twenty. With the birth of Liam we had Blackjack. We were so lucky.

When I finally heard him cry, I wept with a hope so powerful it was a jolt that ran through me like electricity and remained like the prickling hum that vibrates your bones after a shock. As soon as Liam was out of my belly, my body buzzed with the fervor of hope and longing for his survival.

I met my baby for the first time with my ears, the same ears that flushed with blood when my hope was stolen. But now they rang with joy, filled with the voice of my child. In the wake of Liam's beautiful voice, I stole back my hope and never let go. I could never have done that without him.

I wasn't strong enough to hold Liam on my own. The nurse rested him close to me so I could see and touch his tiny face. In the few too-quick pictures we have it almost looks like I'm holding him, but I could barely feel my arms and felt like I might fall off the table. In the rush, I gave Liam a fast kiss, told him hello, and he was gone with Jim and an entourage of doctors and nurses before I even said goodbye.

6

Three Choices

The very moment Liam's life began he was swept away from me and thoroughly examined. As I tilted my head back, I could see a swarm of doctors and nurses clustered around Liam, inserting an intravenous line in his umbilical stump and loading him with prostaglandin before he was tucked safely in the Level IV NICU— one of only three in the state of Colorado in 2003.

Jim followed them out in his matching blue uniform, leaving me alone with my own army of faceless doctors and nurses. They finished putting my uterus back together and rolled me to recovery, where I shook uncontrollably for over an hour. The whole time my teeth chattered and I begged, unsuccessfully, to go back to my room. I wanted to sleep, but I also wanted to get off that surgical bed where I felt like I was laying on a balance beam while convulsing.

I was chilly at first, but the nurse kept giving me warm blankets (if I ever win Lotto I'm buying one of those hospital blanket ovens and building a house around it). It was the drugs and the significant blood loss that made me shake so fiercely. I didn't know how much of my blood pooled behind the stealthy blue curtain they draped above my ribcage to hide the carnage at my pelvis, but I was incredibly weak.

Eventually the recovery team released me to my room. I don't remember when they did it, but they also put me on oxygen. My nurse then spent the next several hours injecting me with epinephrine to stabilize my blood pressure. I only noticed the injections because the blood pressure cuff kept going off by itself and would beep annoyingly and rudely squeeze my arm. After that, a nurse would enter my room like a shadow against the hallway light, and I'd feel an icy flush in my IV. I was entirely oblivious there was anything wrong with me.

I was delirious, but I had no narcotics except the epidural. The oxygen was dry and scratched my nose and I kept sneaking it off, but my pulseoxometer would rat me out. The nurses would rush in and put it back on me, until I convinced them to give me a mask instead so I could get "blow-by" oxygen. I promised to set it next to my face.

As the night progressed two nurses rushed in to consult on my blood pressure and give me more epinephrine. I asked Jim if those stewardesses would give us more peanuts in case he was hungry. I tried to negotiate with them to leave me alone, even suggesting my friend's husband could fix their obnoxious alarms that were clearly broken. I slept a little here and there, and then I woke with a start.

For the first time since 10:30 the previous morning, I fully and clearly understood what was going on below my waist. A wide and gaping hole was hastily carved through in my belly, a child torn out, and then it was all just sewn shut like filling a muddy hole. I had been ripped apart, and now I felt it.

I moaned and Jim called for a nurse. I don't know what was in her syringe, but the nurse-angel who came in the dark room left a black bruise the size of a silver dollar that marked my thigh for more than a month. I slept until Jim woke me at 7:30 A.M. to go see our baby.

I won't lie; after the sunlight first registered on my eyelids, the next thing that I knew was serious pain all over my body. I hurt more than any time in my life. Still, I got myself into that wheel chair. I rode down that Promised Land of a hallway Dr. Smooth sold me that winter. I sat in a rocker with a pillow propping up my arm, and I held my child.

I, like everyone who saw Liam, was amazed that he looked so normal. I felt his nose and his cheeks and his face. I unwrapped him from his receiving blanket and touched his little thighs and the crooks of his elbows. I ran my finger along the side of his tiny neck and under his perfect baby chin. I pulled off his tiny cap to behold his honey colored halo of curls. Oh, his nose, his perfect, beautiful little nose was delicious to my hungry heart.

I did all the things new mothers are supposed to do when their baby is handed to them for the first time, but we experienced delays. Liam had lived a whole life without me for the past twelve hours.

The night before Liam's father, four grandparents, and his aunt, all held him before his mother. Everyone cut in front of me. I, the girl who lives to be first in line, was forced to wait my turn to hold my first child. Then I was met by a hovering nurse who wanted to put Liam back in his bed the minute I picked him up. She criticized me for unwrapping him to look at him, and made me put his hat back on him.

The whole hospital staff was used to preemies that no one could ever hold. That's PSL's niche. They rarely saw babies with hearts anything like Liam's; few people ever do. That first nurse was extra nervous, and she made me nervous.

Liam was so beautiful. He liked the pacifier. He was nothing more than Liam in a tiny white snap-front t-shirt. I was in love, but I was also in pain, and I felt sick and dizzy and tingly where my epidural punctured my spine. I desperately needed to lie down. But they would never let me take him with me. I had to go, but I didn't want to go. I couldn't hold myself up. I felt so much guilt and shame, but I was desperate to lie down.

I felt even sicker and guiltier when I asked Jim to take me back to my room and he asked me incredulously, "Seriously, you've only been here for twenty minutes. Don't you *want* to see Liam?"

I stalled a little, but then I couldn't stay upright any longer. I dreaded how far it would be in the wheelchair to my room. Jim pushed me back but announced defiantly that he was going to go back and sit with Liam. I felt like a traitor wife and a bad mom only thirteen hours into motherhood. Yet, I could hardly sit upright. My middle and my back hurt so badly that it made my head hurt and the room spin. To add further insult, I was fuzzy and nauseous, and on the verge of tears. As tired as I was, I was too upset to relax when I finally got into bed.

I lacked the strength or self-awareness to suggest that hey, I hadn't eaten anything but ice chips since dinner more than thirty-six hours before, endured hard labor, pushed for ninety minutes, and then had my midsection torn open, lost buckets of blood, my blood pressure and my blood sugar were both significantly low considering the exertion followed by massive surgery, and oh yeah, a human being was yanked out of me, all in less than five minutes time. Then I slept inconsistently for maybe five hours total, and maybe, *possibly*, I wasn't in the best physical condition. Instead, all I felt was guilt, and all I could do was apologize to Liam, to Jim, and to myself. I felt I'd let everyone down.

I was barely back in bed before Dr. Doom came calling. He was annoyed that Jim wasn't there, so a nurse went to collect him from the NICU.

Now that they'd had a look at Liam's heart without my own body in the way, it was clear that Liam was worse than Dr. Doom expected. We had three choices: transplant, surgery, or the alternative. Dr. Doom discouraged us from surgery and recommended a transplant because Liam's case was so severe. According to Dr. Doom, even if Liam survived surgery at our mile-high altitude that everyone else finds so charming, his lungs would certainly fail from the stress of it. The surgery was also more dangerous than a transplant. The last alternative was to go with "compassionate care," where "at least you could take him home."

I was in a semi-delirious state of pain when Dr. Doom first approached, but this announcement snapped me into a surreal clarity like pure oxygen or outer-space. It wouldn't be the last time adrenaline worked as a pain reliever.

We cried big sopping silent tears. We choked on our grief. We could form no words; there were no words. Dr. Doom looked at us exasperated and snapped, "This isn't easy for me either!" A nurse interrupted and suggested we take more time to think. She was one of the many angels that filled up the maternity ward.

Dr. Doom made noises about seeing other patients or something. I didn't care where he went and hoped he'd never come back. We went inside ourselves and went over the options. We feared losing Liam to the complicated surgery, and it was hard to forget the sad little transplant baby I'd watched on TV the night before Liam was born.

But when we said "hospice," out loud for the first time, Jim said softly, with tears in his voice, "But it's Liam, he's Liam, and look at him."

And though we couldn't look at him because he was trapped down Dr. Smooth's insurmountable hallway, we saw Liam with our hearts, and we knew we would never let him go without a fight. He wasn't but a half a day old, and he deserved a chance to fight. We never got further than saying the word before taking it off the table.

Instead, we picked curtain number one, and the magical idiocy of America's health care system in all its glory was about to unfold before us.

In the year 2003, Denver Children's Hospital performed a high volume of successful pediatric cardiac transplants. They had recently recruited one of the best pediatric cardiothoracic surgeons on the planet. United Health Care was the insurance provider the very employees of the Children's Hospital carried themselves. But despite all these things, UHC would only allow their pediatric patients (including Liam) to receive heart transplants at four hospitals in the USA. Even though Denver Children's Hospital was across the street from PSL, it wasn't on the list.

In the hopes of an exception, we went through heart transplant boot camp with the transplant coordinators from The Children's Hospital. They told us it would be an eight-month wait for an O+ heart. We learned all about the cancer risks, the rejection risks, the random extra facial and body hair, the infinite laundry list of scary risks, but we took them all on believing transplant was our only hope.

Within two days of our decision, UHC declared they would not grant us an exception. Our four choices were Los Angeles, Cleveland, Ann Arbor, or Boston.

We turned to Dr. Doom for guidance, and he told us they were "all the same." So, we chose Los Angeles for distance and the frequency and price of flights from DIA to LAX. In spite of our fear and confusion about where to go, I'm grateful for the way things turned out. I believe Los Angeles is truly the City of Angels and they were calling us there to deliver our misdirected miracle.

On January 1, 2004, eight months after Liam was born, around the time he might have received an O1 heart, Denver was added to UHC's approved pediatric cardiac transplant centers. Of course.

7

To Live or Die in LA

Once we decided to take Liam to Children's Hospital Los Angeles (CHLA), arrangements progressed. When I talked to the Cardiothoracic Intensive Care Unit (CTICU) attending physician over the phone he was shocked that I asked if we could wait until Monday to transfer Liam. Usually, people were tearing him a new one about how long it takes. But Liam was stable for the moment, and I wasn't quite ready to be released when the plans were set in motion.

The week Liam and I were at PSL, I willed myself to stay in the NICU no matter how much it hurt my body. My spirit couldn't take the pain of being apart from him, and this meant I frequently missed my pain medication because I wasn't in my room when the nurses came by.

I wasn't taking care of myself because I couldn't think of myself. All my thoughts, hopes, and energies were focused on the tiny child whose naval IV dried out and now sported a "unicorn" horn of an IV out of his forehead. I was riveted to my child, and would only leave his side to pump milk and occasionally go to the bathroom. I was the sidecar to his motorcycle. Liam was running the show.

I didn't eat anything but beef broth for a couple of days after Liam was born, graduating to pudding. All I did was sit around in the NICU. Once in a while, when I almost fell asleep holding Liam in the rocker, I'd give him back to the nurse and slip away for a nap. But in my room the loneliness and fear would grip me and it was a fifty-fifty shot whether or not I'd sleep. If I did sleep, invariably, someone always came in and woke me up.

Jim was always with Liam, too. In fact, he never left, and ate even less than I did. We held Liam without pause, as if it would keep him from leaving the world. Jim held him whenever I didn't until the nurses made us put him back. Jim slept in the pull-out sofa in my room, and he never left the building until the day I was discharged. We dug this foxhole and were in it together.

In the days leading to transport, we had Liam baptized by one of the hospital chaplains. The hospital broke their own rules and allowed a large crowd of our relatives, including Mandi, who'd spent so much time in this place before, into the NICU to witness the event in person. I don't think there was a doctor or nurse in the PSL NICU who thought Liam had a snowball's chance. When Jim told Dr. Smooth we were going with transplant, he said flatly, "Well, good luck with that," as if we told him we were trying out for the Olympic gymnastics team in our present condition. It wasn't encouraging.

Finally, the chaplain baptizing Liam said, "We all need to be here for Jim and Amanda in their time of loss."

She said "loss" not need, and that set the tone for our last few days there and fired my desire to escape with both Liam and my scraps of hope to Los Angeles.

I was supposed to be discharged the Friday after Liam was born, but that day I felt an intense pain in my right side. The attending doctor ordered an ultrasound of my liver and took blood gases, but it was all normal. The attending OB/GYN kept me an extra day to be safe. I learned a few years later exactly what that pain was when it led to an ambulance ride and the removal of my gall bladder. But at the time there were greater worries than my mysterious pain, which did pass. I was discharged on Saturday night, very late on Saturday night.

I dressed myself for the first time in a week and waited for the nurse to bring discharge paperwork. While sweeping my room for personal items, my eyes landed on the acrylic baby cart. It cradled all manner of sweet things— a tiny hat, measuring tape, pacifier, all in a little bed for a newborn baby to bunk with his mother. This one never cradled my baby.

I took the hat and the pacifier with me because I figured I would be paying for them either way. It didn't dawn on me for a few years that this cart caused me five days of additional pain. I pushed myself past it every time I winced out of bed en route to my wheelchair. But the physical barrier was nothing compared the visual impact.

Seeing that cart in my room, consuming valuable space, reminded me that Liam wasn't with me. Things were nothing like I'd planned a few months before. The bassinet was the plastic ghost of my dead expectations that haunted me in my miserably lonely room.

I wish I possessed the presence of mind to have that cart removed during my stay, but I left instead.

We held Liam and kissed him goodnight. Back in the familiar parking garage where our new car sat for a week, I reached down to fasten my seat belt and my eyes locked on Liam's baby carrier in the back seat.. I stared blankly and remembered the little green snap-front "going home from the hospital" outfit with a tiny lion on it that I'd bought in April. I sighed, pulled off my glasses, and mopped up a few more futile tears.

The outfit and the baby carrier were coming home with me, but Liam was not. I was tired of crying. I was annoyed with myself and my weakness. What was this but one more small theft committed by Fate? As long as she hadn't taken Liam, I had no right to lament going-home clothes or the hospital standard-issue baby pictures no one ever takes in the NICU.

We would send no formal birth announcements for William James Adams, born April 28, 2003, at 7:05 P.M., weighing seven pounds seven ounces, and twenty inches long to family and friends. We would be lucky if we made it through the coming days and weeks without funeral bulletins.

Rather than worry about what he would wear home from the hospital, I worried if he would ever leave it alive. As we backed out of the parking space, leaving Liam for the first time in his five days of life, I stubbed out the last cinders of my expectations and felt a cold building from inside my bones.

We slept in our own bed for the first night in a week, and we were on the road by 6:30 A.M. Sunday morning and at Liam's side until midnight.

Ironically, the Ronald McDonald House called and said we finally had a room. We were shipping out the following day, so we told the clerk to give the room to someone who needed it more.

As we left Liam for the second and final time, the attending in the NICU came to get our child and our consent. The doctor needed to do a "cut down" to place a central line from his arm to his heart for Liam's life flight the next morning. I made a comment about how I wouldn't want to see that, and she said she wouldn't let me see it even if I wanted to.

The last time I saw Liam that night a lone doctor was strapping my baby in yellow restraints to board on the other side of a window to place a scar into the sweet softness of his left wrist that I can see with my eyes closed. That was Liam's first scar, and my first surrender to informed consent.

The Monday morning Liam was airlifted from Denver to LA, we were back at the hospital before 7:00 A.M. They didn't even kick us out for shift change. We held Liam until the flight crew showed up. I didn't care what the nurses might say since we would cease to be their problem soon, but they didn't challenge us. To us it was a beginning, to them it seemed like an ending.

The Children's Los Angeles (CHLA) flight crew came with EMTs in an ambulance from the airfield. They offered either Jim or me the jump seat in the plane, but I couldn't possibly handle it since I was still in a lot of pain from the C-section. Jim could have gone, but he didn't have any extra clothes.

Then there was the problem of how would I even get home from the airport if Jim went on the jump seat. I was on restricted activity, heavy pain meds, and I couldn't drive yet. I wasn't even allowed to carry anything heavier than my purse. So we walked Liam to the elevator in his fancy flight for life incubator. The flight crew told us we could go down to the parking lot all the way to the ambulance doors with them, but I couldn't. *We* couldn't. There was so much we could not do.

Liam was leaving us. We had to say goodbye and we had to do it here. He took his first elevator ride, first car ride (in an ambulance), and first flight, all without us. If I took one more step toward that inevitable separation, my heart would break completely in two.

I trembled seeing Liam in that plastic box that looked too much like a Wonder Woman's invisible coffin. But I didn't allow myself to cry until that elevator door closed. I did not dare show those angels who brought us hope how much they tore the very heart out of me when they took my baby away. There were no choices, there should be no resentments. They were heroes and due no guilt.

I pumped one last time to relieve myself. We stopped by the Labor & Delivery area to see if the on-call doctor would give me a new Percocet prescription. She hadn't been on call the week before. She didn't know me or Liam. She reviewed my chart then looked down her nose at me and said, "It's been seven days since your C-section. You should be feeling better by now and not really needing the Percocet anymore."

It was clear she didn't want to give it to me, like I was a junkie that came in off the street. I told her I didn't think I would need very much, but I had no time to rest. She hesitated.

Jim gave her a hard look and said, "Our baby was just airlifted for a heart transplant, and my wife has to walk through the airport in the morning and get on a plane to Los Angeles." I can always count on Jim when my own words fail me.

The doctor relented and scribbled off a surprisingly generous prescription. Then we got the hell out of PSL. We should not be there without Liam. He was the whole reason we were ever at PSL. My baby was no longer at the end of Dr. Smooth's promised hallway. All those promises floated off in a misty jet stream over the Rocky Mountains.

On the way home, I went to a specialty store to buy nursing bras. When we went in for the fitting, the clerk asked me why I didn't bring my baby. I didn't cry when I told her. It was what it was, and I went on with buying my new bras. I was doing OK, until I got on my phone.

Back in the car, I called the insurance company on my cell phone to find a doctor for my follow-up care in LA. The agent gave me three names. I called the first and the line was out of service. I called the second and the woman who answered asked if I was an existing patient. I told her no, I lived in Colorado and was coming to California. She was beyond rude and told me the doctor would not see me. I tried to explain my situation. I had a C-section a week ago, my child was in the air on his way to wait for a heart transplant, and I needed to be seen by a doctor. But she was immovable.

She was so cruel.

Her doctor would not see me. I felt like the hell beast when Gandalf put down his sword and staff and said, "You Shall Not Pass!" She was so definite, and I was so desperate.

I hung up and cried. Jim wanted to pull over and call her back, but I told him to let it go. I didn't try the last number. I didn't have the energy to tell my story again that day. I would go to Los Angeles and figure it out.

We had no food at home, so we ate at a Wendy's on I25, and it hit me so hard that Liam was gone. I can't drive past that Wendy's, even now, without remembering May 5, 2003. That moment of looking out the window, staring at the blue sky over the Rocky Mountains and missing my son on his way to the coast is seared in my memory like a brand. That brief separation and the longing for my child defined me in a way that would impact all of my choices.

Later that day our families came over to help us pack for a long stay in California. At home, I sat on the floor of Liam's nursery sorting through his many things, picking through hope in the form of tiny onesies and wee little socks.

I was right next to his crib, but I couldn't stand to look in it. I asked Karen to put his baby carrier in it. It became a collective, like nesting dolls of empty places where my baby should be. I could have popped my stitches and pulled out my empty womb and thrown it in the seat and then shoved my heart inside of that, but my heart was already in California, and my womb was busy weeping. I didn't have the physical strength to pull myself off the floor without assistance, much less do anything more dramatic than whimper. And even that I would not do with a crowd in my house. I sucked it up.

We had every reason to believe that we would be in LA for a year or longer. The doctors expected it would take eight months before an O+ heart might even be found for Liam, if at all. Then recovery and close supervision would follow. We believed we'd return to home and work eventually, like the family I'd watched on the Discovery Channel. My manager said I could work from LA, but for now I was on maternity leave, so I left work behind. We were steeling ourselves for every possibility.

That night, after our family left, I wept my soul raw in Liam's nursery until I left everything I had in his lonely room. Jim helped me get off the floor. As we turned to our own bedroom for our last night at home, we closed Liam's door. Silently, I prayed that the next time it opened we'd have our baby. I truly didn't know if I could bear to ever open it again without him.

Tuesday morning, my mom dropped us off at the Frontier counter at the airport. I didn't bring a baby carrier because I didn't know if, when, or how I would be getting home, or if Liam would ever come home alive. I didn't need any extra baggage.

On the plane one of the flight attendants was moved by our journey and made us a flower out of a cocktail napkin. I kept it for a long time. I kept every angel pin, note, card, dried flower, every little scrap of hope that came our way on our journey. Like rungs in a ladder, I might need them again to break my fall.

When we deplaned, Jim's second-cousin Gary was waiting for us at the baggage claim. Gary drove all the way from Bakersfield to meet us at LAX. At the time, I had no idea how far he'd come or what traffic he'd battled to meet us there in time for our arrival. We got in his minivan and headed for Sunset Boulevard. It took forever.

Anyone familiar with Southern California isn't surprised by the time it takes to get fifteen miles, but I hadn't pumped for close to six hours, and I was on a three-hour schedule. At this point Liam was eight days old and my milk was well established. I was in even more pain by the time we finally found the CHLA parking garage.

We went down a loooong hallway to the front desk, and they sent for a volunteer to take us upstairs to see Liam in the Cardiothoracic Intensive Care Unit (CTICU). Seeing that I was barely making it, the volunteer got me a wheelchair, where we rode up the elevator to the second floor.

They waived the two-person rule for Gary, and we finally saw our baby again. Though it was only a thirty hour separation, it seemed like we missed everything. We missed him so much. Liam was our Odysseus in this journey, and we were lost without him.

The CTICU was so incredibly different from the NICU in Denver. The NICU was dark and silent and the beds were so tiny. Even though the babies in the CTICU weren't much older than the preemies in the NICU, the beds were huge, the lights were bright, and the noises never stopped. It was a constant hum of ventilators and beeps, beeps, beeps, short ones, long ones, alarms over every bed. Within days I would recognize every conceivable beep in this place and learn to tune out the ones that didn't belong to Liam. I knew which ones mattered because they always brought a nurse the few paces back to our bedside. In the years that followed I would dream about this symphony of high-pitched alarms, but this first day in LA left me shell-shocked by the cold florescent light and the constant noise.

By the time we saw Liam, I was way beyond needing to pump; I was leaking and damp. And wouldn't you know that the desk attendant couldn't find a key for the pump room. Then Dr. Badran came to Liam's bedside and started to explain things. The key was still missing, but when Dr. Badran realized I was going on eight hours of milk accumulation, she fondly recalled when her daughters were babies, and offered to loan me her office if they couldn't get me in the pump room.

The attendant found me a parent sleep room across the hall where I could use my own pump, and Dr. Badran patiently waited for me to go relieve my maternal urges. After I returned, Dr. Badran explained that the cardiologists were shocked by how good Liam looked when he arrived considering the complexity of his condition. They expected him to be on a ventilator or at least on oxygen, but Liam was breathing the same air we were.

She went on to say that transplant wasn't a good option for Liam. Given the severity of his defects, he was unlikely to survive to eight weeks of age, much less the eight months we would need to get a new heart. Dr. Badran said that her colleague, Dr. Starnes, would evaluate Liam on Monday and would likely perform a surgery called the DKS - Damus Kaye Stansel or "modified Norwood." We'd never gotten that much detail from Dr. Doom, and Dr. Badran wasn't even done yet. She started to draw pictures.

At one point she said, "I don't understand why you are even here considering they just hired a surgeon in Denver who could do this with his eyes closed." Thus began my secondary education in medical politics and insurance nightmares.

Dr. Badran explained and re-explained Liam's condition and the surgery to Jim and me, but I was distracted and exhausted, and she could tell. At one point she said, "It's really important that you understand this."

Honestly, at that point I understood nothing any longer. I was trapped in someone else's dream and had no tactile hold on reality. The social worker came and went. She was trying to get us into the Ronald McDonald House behind the parking garage.

We learned things, we held Liam, we melted into puddles in our hard office chairs. The social worker reappeared to tell us we got a room, but we needed to arrive by 3:30 to check in. Gary was still with us and drove us to the Ronald McDonald House (RMH).

I collapsed in our room while the nice man who greeted us took Jim and Gary on a tour of the place so we could find our way around. I'd run myself ragged for more than twelve hours after doing hard labor on the edge of a C-section only eight days earlier, and I'd barely claimed four hours of sleep each night since. It was too much for my body and my mind. I needed to stop.

I first sat in a pale blue chair upholstered in a pattern of Sleepy, the Travel Lodge bear and put up my feet on the matching ottoman. When I caught sight of the two full beds covered in the same bear print, the gravitational force pulled on me like Jupiter as I gingerly climbed onto the nearest one.

I laid on my right side and stared out the window at the spring sky. It was May 6th and warm in Southern California. I lay very still and listened to the children playing down below on the RMH playground, the drone of Sunset Boulevard's heavy traffic, and the occasional car on Fountain. At least twice I heard helicopters, and I faded but never slept. As exhausted as I was, I was like an electronic device that hums when plugged in even if it's not turned on, always ready to run.

Eventually, Jim came back after convincing Gary to head home before the traffic got "bad." What? It got worse?

We unpacked a little and then made it downstairs to have community dinner. One of many wonderful things about Ronald McDonald House is the people who volunteer to bring full meals in for the families. That night they served burgers and hot dogs, and the best chocolate cake I've ever had. Until that day, I'd never eaten cake at sea level, and while I can tell you many wonderful things about Colorado, our dry mile high cake doesn't make the list. This cake was soft and moist and chocolaty with a creamy fudgy frosting. It was comfort on a fork, and I had two pieces.

As we sat at a table for four, I looked around the dining room and noticed how many families knew each other. We knew no one. A woman was walking around with her plate ready but nowhere to sit. She looked lost, exhausted, and so painfully sad that it hurt me to see her adrift, so I waved her over to our table.

Jane was at CHLA and the Ronald McDonald House for a month, maybe longer. Her son, Jamal, was born very premature, so his home was an incubator in the NICU, a ventilator. More than anything, Jane longed to just hear his voice, to hear him cry just once.

She gave us the inside scoop about locking up our food and taking the shuttle van that loaded at the back door and dropped at the door of CHLA—especially at night. Some RMH guests were mugged in the Von's grocery store parking lot that filled short distance between Fountain and Sunset across the street from CHLA. Ah, welcome to LA.

I told Jim I wanted to take the shuttle van back to see Liam after dinner because I didn't want to walk that far tonight. Once back at the hospital we stayed until after 11:00 P.M. It had been a long, exhausting day as we made our way back to the RMH. We never once called it "home."

We came to Los Angeles expecting a transplant, and we already knew a transplant was simply exchanging one lifeline for another. We'd still be hanging over a cliff waiting out Liam's life because a donor heart wouldn't last forever. The surgical option bought us more time for modern medicine to blaze new trails, but it also rescued us from the torment of waiting for a donor heart.

Before Dr. Badran held out surgery as a viable and preferable option to transplant, the only way Liam was going to live was if another child died. In our helplessness waiting for another baby to die so Liam could have a new heart, I had to spin reality, or else feel cruel for wanting my own child to live.

Most likely, if Liam did receive a donor heart, it would have come from an abused baby whose brain was damaged but whose heart kept beating, despite the absence of love. Maybe a child would be killed in a car crash. Either way, the tragedy of others on which we gambled to maintain our hope was almost too much to bear.

Then there was the issue of supply and demand. Crib death babies aren't usually found quickly, so they've been dead too long to donate their hearts. There are few other ways for a baby small enough or healthy enough to die in order to save Liam, since most newborns who die are killed by their heart defects or heart surgeries. The odds were against Liam ever receiving a match. All I could do was hope that if, by chance, an angry man would shake the life from his own child, that the non-complicit mother would be big enough to give away the unbroken parts of her shattered life. That was my best-case scenario.

To cope, I pretended I was waiting for grace, not tragedy. The sad fact is that the two are traveling companions. Either way we looked at it a baby was going to die, either a stranger's or ours. Maybe both.

When Dr. Badran first told us the hospital didn't want to list Liam for transplant because his long-term odds of survival were better with surgery, we were genuinely relieved. Even as we waited, we talked about how if Liam didn't make it and if his other organs were good enough, we would donate them, without question. Even if it was only his eyes. It was such an ugly space to fill, the limbo of waiting for one death to save the life of my only child. The Norwood/DKS surgery was a welcome escape from a no-win situation.

Yet it would be a week between Liam's arrival and Dr. Starnes' return. That week was less depressing because we had the hope of surgery, but it was excruciating because there was the matter of whether Dr. Starnes would actually agree to do the surgery. The cardiac and CTICU attending doctors and nurses acted like surgery was imminent, but they also offered frequent disclaimers that Dr. Starnes was the final decision maker. They saw no reason why Dr. Starnes wouldn't do Liam's surgery, but until he committed, all bets were off. We were in a different limbo.

It was gut-wrenching, and we tried to get them to commit and save us from our anxiety. The nurses would say things like, "Well, if I had to I'd say I'm ninety percent certain he will want to do it, but again, there are no guarantees."

I learned over the ensuing years that babies like mine are considered career makers or career breakers if you don't have the skill or the nerve to handle them. And it's not only the surgeon's career, it's the hospital and anyone affiliated with the cardio thoracic surgical program.

There were, and still are, plenty of surgeons and hospitals that wouldn't touch neonate Liam with a ten-foot pole, much less a scalpel, because he was such a hard case. So hard a case, that even though Dr. Starnes did plenty of cases just as difficult, no one would put his name on the line without his consent. I get that now, and I feel beyond blessed that we were in a place that would even consider taking the risk on the only thing that mattered to us.

Other than the "Will he/won't he?" aspect of our wait, the week leading up to Liam's surgery was long and repetitive. It was a lather-rinse-repeat week. We knew we couldn't be in the CTICU from 7:30-8:00 morning or night because of shift changes and privacy laws, so we always shot for getting there right at 8:00 A.M.

We would ride the shuttle to the hospital, eat instant oatmeal at the RMH or breakfast in the cafeteria, then go upstairs and sit with Liam, get updates, and hold him until shift change, when we would either eat at the cafeteria or go back to the RHM to see if there were community leftovers from the sponsored dinners. Then we would go back and stay until 11:00 P.M. or slightly later. During our entire time in the CICU before Liam's surgery, all of televisions in the unit were constantly running. The TV filled the space where none of us parents had words to offer. We couldn't talk about where we were, and we couldn't name our fears, lest they find us.

When we would finally relent and go back to the Ronald McDonald House, Jim stood sentry at the parking garage entrance for the shuttle van while I rested on a bench in the long hallway between the lobby and garage.

While waiting, I looked up at the looming wall in front of me filled with photographs of patients and practitioners. Liam's nurse, Mark, was on that wall. Next to the hospital caregiver photos was a collage of financial supporter plaques. I stared at those plaques night after night, making a game of "find the celebrity." We *were* in LA, right on Sunset Boulevard. The only supporters I remember were Danny DeVito and Rhea Perlman. It was an Easter Egg hunt of finding the famous amongst the merely rich. Eventually, the shuttle would pull up to the parking garage exit, and I'd stagger out to get in the van for the three-minute drive back to the Ronald McDonald House.

Back in our room, I pumped before I slept, set the alarm for three hours later, woke up, pumped, and went back to sleep, and then pumped again when I woke up three hours later. I got less than five hours of sleep each night, but not because my newborn was waking me up. He was so far away across a parking garage and a universe I could not bridge.

One night after sterilizing the hoses to my breast pump and reattaching them, I looked up in the mirror and thought very guiltily and quite sincerely, *I was only there for sixteen hours today.* I felt like I literally abandoned my son to produce milk to feed him and sleep a few short hours. I believed I was such a bad mommy.

When I finally made it to bed, where Jim was already sleeping, I would lay on my left side, facing the wall and hear my heart pounding in my ear like a drum pulsating and mocking me. Boom, boom, boom - you will not sleep. Boom - boom - boom - your baby doesn't have your heart. Boom - boom- boom - you can't give it to him. Boom - boom - boom you cannot win. My own heart mocked me with its healthy rhythm and cruel beat.

The only thing that would make my heart stop in my chest and silence its taunting in my ears was the sound of helicopters landing on top of CHLA or Kaiser across Sunset or City of Angels Hospital down Fountain. The rescue choppers were so close, and each time I heard one I thought, *That helicopter carries crisis. A family's life together is coming undone to the beat of those helicopter blades,* and I would say a prayer for the new neighbors while the well of misery deepened in this strange vortex of hospitals in the shadow of the Hollywood sign.

More often than not, I lay awake until there were only forty minutes left before the alarm clock went off. Then I gave up, got up, pumped, and reset the alarm. I felt guilty being anywhere but the hospital, and I never once relaxed in laid-back California.

The day before Dr. Starnes' glorious return and Liam's first open heart surgery was also my first Mother's Day. Jim, sweet as ever, got me a card, but there were no flowers and hardly any mention of it at the Ronald McDonald House or in the CTICU. We were all mothers, but this Hallmark holiday was incidental, like Christmas in a foxhole.

No one could easily call us in the CTICU, and though I probably had messages at the RMH, I don't remember anyone acknowledging the day. I was painfully aware of it. The irony would have hurt if I weren't already so raw from the savage screams of my baby who was always so docile and sweet.

Liam was literally starving before our eyes. The doctors switched Liam from bottle-fed breast milk, to breast milk through a nasal gastric tube, to no breast milk at all. Instead, he received IV lipids and fluids to keep him alive. By his sixth day at CHLA Liam was getting daily kidney, liver, and heart ultrasounds. My baby was on the precipice of multiple organ failures, and his body thought it was starving to death.

To conserve energy and keep the blood going to his vitals instead of expending it on digestion, the doctors and nurses would not feed my baby, or let me do it. Even though I would guiltily sneak away to pump, the sound of his primal screams filled my breast with more milk and my heart with more pain. It all made perfect sense to my brain, but my nerves were shot.

That last day, we took a photo of Liam's bare, unmarked chest. We held him as he screamed and screamed, and my chest ached inside and out. The pacifier was an insult. The only way I could effectively comfort him would hasten his death. By midnight it was a moot point. Liam went on NPO (an acronym of the Latin *nil per os* or nothing by mouth) for the morning's surgery.

We finally put him down tightly swaddled, and his nurse Judi put a vibrating device beneath him to calm him. Maybe it worked, or maybe he was numb and exhausted, but we left Liam sleeping. That was my first Mother's Day gift.

We got the last shuttle back to the RMH that night, and neither of us slept more than two hours. We were back at 5:30 A.M. We didn't bother with the shuttle, and though Jim flew several paces ahead of me, I staggered up the hill to the parking garage entrance, and we went to Liam. I held him, and held him, and held him. Then we met Dr. Bushman.

Dr. Bushman is a pediatric cardiac anesthesiologist and a highly specialized human being. He kindly explained what they would do to Liam during the surgery, and was very patient with us. While I held my baby tight, he was still talking to us at the foot of Liam's crib when Dr. Starnes quietly pulled up a chair and politely waited to be introduced.

To hear his staff talk about him, I had visions of Adonis or Zeus, enormous and glowing like a god. But I think he was smaller than Jim, who isn't a physically imposing man. Regardless of physical attributes, Dr. Starnes's size is in his lifesaving skills. He is a giant among men.

He brought paperwork for us to sign. I asked about future surgeries, and his reply was gentle, "Let's just get through this one, OK?" That scared us a little.

At one point, lost in the details, Jim and I both heard him say there was a twenty percent chance Liam wouldn't make it through the surgery. Jim choked and spat back, "Twenty percent! No one has told us that before now."

Dr. Starnes told us very slowly and clearly, "There is a twenty percent chance your son won't pull through the surgery today, but if we don't do the surgery THIS morning, there is a one hundred percent chance Liam won't be alive this weekend."

Decision made. That was informed consent.

Nurses and respiratory people, and all manner of pre-op activities fluttered around us as we held Liam until we couldn't hold him anymore. I handed him over to Jim about fifteen minutes before they came to take him away. I didn't know I wouldn't get Liam back, that I wouldn't hold him again that day or for several days. I didn't know at that moment, that I would soon leave this room and not know if I would ever hold my living child again at all. Had I known how close we were to handing him over, I might have never let him go.

A transport bed appeared like an unwelcome guest, and Jim reluctantly handed Liam to our nurse, Mark, who placed our baby in the bed. It was like Abraham placing Isaac on the altar, but we did not wield the knife, and this altar was acrylic and stainless steel on wheels. All that was left was prayer.

We walked out to the hallway with Liam and kissed him over and over, rubbed his tiny head, and wept goodbye as Dr. Bushman and the nurses rolled Liam to the left. We waited until he went through the OR doors. Then we turned right into the dungeon of a waiting room to begin our time in purgatory. Either we would get a heavenly miracle or begin our descent into the hell of mourning our only child.

The surgery was amazingly fast. The Damus Kaye Stansel (or modified Norwood operation) is one of the most complicated surgical procedures known to mankind. Imagine a walnut or a strawberry in the palm of your hand with coarse hairs coming off of it. Now imagine trying to cut into that strawberry without destroying it so it can be put back together again. Imagine trying to split those hairs and re-combine them to make new hair. Liam's heart was no bigger than his fist, and he was less than seven pounds after his "diet."

The surgery must be fast because the baby's entire body is put into a hypothermal state, meaning that his tiny infant head packed in ice and his blood removed and rerouted through a machine so his heart can be stopped. Liam was as close to dead as a person can be, all so that we could keep him from dying.

For the first surgery there is no scar tissue, no doorman to slow down opening the chest, no delays to work around old surgeries. It is as cut and dry as nuclear science—either you do everything perfectly, or you destroy someone's entire universe.

Yet, as fast as it was in the OR, the waiting room made time stand still. It lacked TVs, books, magazines, windows, food, or water fountain. It was devoid of all links to the outside save a sale ad for a discount store. It was alarmingly similar to the DMV, except we were all alone.

Our sparse bit of human contact was Liam's nurse, Mark, who updated us once or twice and prepared Liam's space for recovery. He would now be closer to the nurses' station instead of the back corner, where we started. It wasn't because Mark was simply being kind—he was moving Liam to the spot where crash carts and fast access were easily at hand.

Little more than two hours after we let Liam go, Mark came back to tell us the surgery was a success. Shortly after Mark left, Dr. Starnes debriefed us with surgical details. Jim jumped over the connected chairs to hug him, while I fell into my seat and exhaled. We couldn't see Liam for at least an hour or two while they stabilized him. They suggested we go eat. With the early morning surgery, we hadn't had breakfast. But first, we called family in Colorado from the waiting room. Then, we went downstairs to eat and wait. Only, we didn't know what we were waiting for.

8

What I Never Expected When I Was Expecting

After his DKS surgery, Liam was swollen and waxy. A cotton panel of gauze floated over his chest like a cloud, covering the area where we expected to see stitching. Underneath the gauze there were no stitches. Rather, his sternum was still spread like a gaping mouth in his chest and his heart could be seen pumping on the other side of a translucent Gortex patch that kept his insides inside. I only saw an orangish-pink flutter in the shadow beneath the gauze.

At one point Jim saw the bare truth, but it was too much for me to see my child with his chest wide open like a sideways smile with ribs for teeth and his heart flitting like a pink tongue. Liam was on a ventilator that breathed for him, forcing his broken little chest to expand and contract even as his ribs were separated from each other.

Once the initial shock wore off, I counted twenty-one different drugs going into stacks of IV valves before entering Liam's puffy little body. I touched his tiny foot and was instantly reprimanded. Mark told us not to touch Liam, not even his hands. It might distress our baby, and he could not be stressed in the state of hovering between us and the angels.

We were not to talk to Liam much either because the sedation was for his best interests. He wasn't quite done dancing with death, and we were not allowed to interrupt until the music stopped, one way or another. Reaching into Liam's medically induce coma to break into his fog with our loving voices might cause him to falter. I can't fathom the pain that would have broken through if we disrupted his stasis, his body still taken apart, each artificial breath shaking his unhinged ribs. I don't know which was worse, being told not to touch my own child or the fact that doing so could cause him to crash. All of Liam's being was focused on survival, and we were simply intruders and distractions, not his parents, not the people who loved him more than life.

We chose this for him.

In our gallows humor at this ghastly separation where our son was veiled in a limbo of precious and precarious moments, we nicknamed him Baby Borg. In retrospect it seems cruel, but we were as much in a fog as our child.

In his two towers of life-saving drugs, the only thing missing was the prostaglandin that kept Liam alive up until this point. What's prostaglandin, also called PGE? It's a hormone that a mother's body makes while she carries her child that keeps a hole in the baby's heart and a connecting blood vessel open to exchange the mother's oxygen with the fetus. Once the baby is born, the large concentrations of PGE leave his little body and the blood vessel clots. The hole, no longer needed, closes up, and the child becomes entirely dependent on his own lungs (that are no longer aquatic) to oxygenate his own blood.

Liam's heart was so dysfunctional on delivery that the prostaglandin kept the ducts and holes open, so his blood would mix about, not fully oxygenating, but not suffocating him either. PGE can become toxic over time, and Liam's time was running out by May 12th. This was all a dramatic attempt to reset his clock.

Liam's primary pre-op problems were that his aorta (the big artery that takes blood out of the heart and brings it to the system that delivers it to the whole body) and his pulmonary artery (the artery that brings depleted blood out of the heart and to the lungs to re-oxygenate) were backward. In and of itself, that's a bad defect that requires a high-risk surgery to put them right. With a highly skilled surgeon and no additional defects or extenuating circumstances, that one defect can be "corrected" in one surgery.

Liam was not a candidate for correction because on top of the reversal of the arteries, the aorta itself was only ten percent of the size it should be. It's kind of like expecting a drinking straw in your drink and, instead, getting dental floss. Then literally on top of the aorta is the aortic arch which feeds blood to the arms and brain. Liam's aortic arch had a severe coarctation (think kink in a hose). Like the transpositioned arteries, the hypoplastic aorta and the coarctation are each life-threatening heart defects on their own that necessitate immediate surgery after birth.

Liam's heart never formed a tricuspid valve. The tricuspid valve is the door between the right atria and the right ventricle and it allows the spent blood a body used to oxygenate cells to move from the entry chamber to the exit chamber and back to our lungs through the pulmonary artery (which, in Liam's case, was his useless aorta).

Since Liam had no doorway (tricuspid valve) for the blood to get through, he never formed a functioning right ventricle, and the only way that the blood leaked into that itty bitty aorta that wasn't supposed to be there in the first place was through a blessed series of Swiss cheese-like holes in the walls inside of Liam's heart that allowed a small trickle of blood into the aorta. Since there was never adequate blood flow there, it never formed properly.

Liam received all of his oxygen from me in utero and all those little extra holes and vessels that made his prenatal heart work inside my body then enabled a mix of oxygenated and depleted blood to run through his tiny body after he was born. With PGE, we kept everything open and mixing until Dr. Starnes could redirect the blood flow traffic in that surgery . . . the DKS—and if you can imagine trying to put right that unique three dimensional jigsaw puzzle God made in my son, you understand why one in five babies didn't survive this surgery, and why Dr. Starnes in all his normal looking flesh, seems like a god.

I could try to explain the DKS, but the truth is, more than seven years later, I don't entirely understand it. Dr. Starnes basically cut away and reconnected and rerouted Liam's heart. He re-plumbed it, but no one could ever "fix" it—too much was missing and too much was malformed. They couldn't just go to Lowe's and buy junctions and brackets to make it work like a normal heart.

Dr. Starnes worked with what he had, and he gave me back my Baby Borg wrapped in artificial tubing inside and out. Liam received grafts inside his chest that cost $10,000 in 2003 money, only to become medical waste in subsequent surgeries. Liam bore tubes running drugs in and tubes running blood, fluids, and urine out of him. Every secretion was carefully weighed, every input cataloged. Liam began his existence in my temperature charts and he clung to it in a bizarre display of record keeping that looked like high school chemistry gone mad. Life and death was weighed in milligrams.

In those first forty-eight hours, the nurses begged us to leave. Our nervousness and our sorrowful fear weighed on them too. They were also genuinely concerned for our well-being, and they knew better than we that our hovering wasn't good for Liam, or for us.

We decided to take a nap, and then we decided to go see a movie across the street from CHLA at the Vista Theater. It is an impressive old movie theater with handprints outside and memorabilia all around. So strange to stand where Johnny Depp and Sarah Jessica Parker once celebrated their movie opening for Ed Wood and be entirely unimpressed. Typically that would be thrilling for me, but I resented it. I didn't want to gawk at their signatures in concrete. I wanted to gawk at our "Baby Borg" where resistance to the storm that left him full of tubes was futile and hope was all we had left.

We watched the X-men sequel, and while I disappeared into the escapism of the film for brief flashes, my mind always scampered back across the street. It was like being half asleep on an airplane, I was neither here nor there.

We returned to Liam's bedside briefly only to see that they wanted us gone again, so we went to the subway and visited the walk of fame. I was still sore and slow, so we stopped at a diner, and I ate an official Cobb Salad at its birthplace. It might have been fun if we weren't so scared the hospital would call with bad news.

We took a photograph of Arnold Schwarzenegger's handprints outside Grauman's Chinese Theater. Dr. Starnes performed open-heart surgery on the man who would later that year become the Governator. Other than that the same hands had been on his heart as Liam's, we didn't care about Arnold.

After those first forty-eight hours elapsed, Liam's heart was still swollen, his chest still open, and we were still terrified. Finally, a surgeon in training closed my son's sternum, but we had to leave yet again because it was a "bedside surgical procedure," and there were gowns and draping and sterilizing, etc. In our exile, Gary came back down from Bakersfield and brought his mom, Jim's great-aunt Peg. They did their best to distract us by taking us to the beach for the day and to Disneyland for dinner. For all the kind diversion, I wasn't pleasant company at the happiest place on earth because I needed to pump, and the battery pack wasn't working right. All I really wanted was to get the hell out of Disneyland and get back to the hospital to see my baby on a ventilator and pump my breasts before they exploded all over Mickey Mouse. Poor Gary, the two times he spent in my company I was a total bitch in physical agony.

We did get back to the hospital, and I did pump while Gary and Peg visited Liam. I felt badly when they had to go. I'd been bitchy while in my amazing boob pain— and really, how does one explain that to people who are trying to treat you to a nice dinner at Disneyland and offer a bit of a respite? But they were gone, and we were there alone again with Liam. The waiting continued.

Liam's swollen little heart took three days before the muscle contracted enough to fit back in the cavity of his chest and the doors of his split sternum were closed for now. Another day passed before they could pull the tube from his nose and throat and allow us to share the same air. In a few more days, the nurses fed Liam with an NG tube and he had food in his stomach for the first time in more than a week. Each day was a lifetime, and each accomplishment was a step toward true survival. We spent endless hours on the edge of our seats as we fought for every small movement forward, away from death.

Line by line, tube by tube, that disaster of a newborn heart patient began to look like my baby again. It was five days before I could hold him again. It was weeks before he would re-learn how to drink from a bottle. It would be years before I could blink, terrified Liam would disappear before my very eyes.

9

A Simple Plan

The morning of Liam's DKS surgery, I tried to pry some knowledge from Dr. Starnes about Liam's future and the other two surgeries Dr. Doom had mentioned while I was still pregnant. He gently told me, "Let's just get through today."

I don't think I registered the risk that morning, not really, not deeply. In my way I refused to accept that Liam might truly die on May 12, 2003, or that night, or in the days following. I had to focus on the future because the present was too much for me to process at the time. Cerebrally, I knew it, but I didn't feel it. I was too numb, and focusing on what came next made it seem like we had less to overcome in the here and now.

Yet, everyone else was rightly focused on the present. So over the weeks Liam was in the hospital, I could only verify that he would have three open-heart surgeries in total. My previous internet research and future activities revealed more.

Liam's first surgery, the modified Norwood or Damus Kaye Stansel, was the riskiest because he was so small, so weak, and so brand new. That surgery was much more complicated than the rest because of all the cutting and reconstruction on such a tiny heart.

Liam's second open heart surgery would be the Glenn. The Glenn is essentially half of the Fontan (the third surgery). Originally, the Fontan included both procedures in one, but they learned that for most patients spreading them out into two surgeries was less risky for the patient. That's right, two open heart surgeries is less risky than one because it's such a huge surgery.

So the Glenn entailed dissecting Liam's superior vena cava from his right atria (which after the DKS was just a single atria because the wall between the left and right was surgically removed). Then that enormous vein is sewn to his pulmonary branch artery to feed his left and right lungs directly. Before, his lungs were fed by an artificial shunt between his subclavian artery and his right pulmonary artery. Before the Glenn, Liam's mixed blood (half oxygenated and half not) was sent back to his lungs to get more oxygen. The Glenn would send more spent blood directly to his lungs, improving the efficiency of his heart and sending more oxygenated blood to his body.

After the Glenn, Liam would have the Fontan. The Fontan entailed removing his inferior vena cava from his heart, grafting it to an external artificial (Gortex) conduit, and grafting that to his pulmonary branch artery. This would mean that all of his de-oxygenated blood would now be sent directly to his lungs, and his heart would be a single pump focused exclusively on sending oxygenated blood to his body.

Some Fontans are done differently, and the blood flow is tunneled through the heart instead of outside of it. There are also occasionally fenestrations (openings) applied to the conduit where the conduit is sewn to the side of the heart and a hole cut between the conduit and the atria to allow blood to slosh back into the heart and relieve pressure on the lungs if the lungs can't handle the change in capacity.

After all of that, Liam's lungs would receive all of their blood passively through drainage instead of through the rhythm of his malformed heart. It was good because his heart would last longer, but it wasn't the way the body is supposed to work. These surgeries are palliative, not curative, and they opened a world of potential complications. There were also diagnostic heart catheterizations that no one told us about until we had to schedule one. But like Dr. Starnes said, we had to get through that first day first.

And we did get though that first day, and the two that followed, on little more than fear and adrenaline. The days and weeks we spent at CHLA were defined and laborious, but they blend together in the muddled distance of my memory. The distinct moments were profound, like the day we returned from lunch to find Liam's bed missing and him with it. I have no words for the confusion and panic that seized me. Upon seeing my expression, the nurses jumped up and said, "Don't worry! He's just against the other side of the wall."

We walked right past Liam, not seeing our own son because we were so well-trained in HIPAA. We didn't stare at other families or look at their kids. It never occurred to us to do anything but make a beeline for Liam's bed, our little piece of turf in the chaotic mélange of patients and practitioners in the CTICU.

Liam was now de-tubed enough, de-medicated enough, progressing enough to move to a less critical space in the CTICU. He wasn't out of the woods, but he was in a sunnier clearing.

A few days passed and we ended up upstairs in the step-down unit. At every hospital I've been to, the step-down unit is always at least one floor above the ICUs, so you go up to step down. The large room held four babies, and the intensity was much lower. There's a reason they call them the intensive care units. Step-down was much more relaxed.

We finally started changing diapers and working with the bottle. We were blessed with Darcy, a lovely nurse whose kindness helped us feel more comfortable when, after Liam's first three weeks of life, we finally got to feel like new parents. Mind you, we were far from typical new parents. We handed over every single diaper to be weighed, worked with an occupational therapist to try to teach our baby how to suck again, learned how to lift our baby without yanking out his external pacemaker wires and oxygen tubing. But we were new parents all the same. We were all making progress. Eventually, the external pacemaker left, too, and we were tethered only to oxygen, which would remain a prominent fixture in our lives.

Liam was four weeks and three days old when we were allowed to leave CHLA, but not LA. Under doctor's orders, we stayed with him at the RMH across the street for three days before they felt he was healthy enough to survive the flight home without incident. Before we could lift off, I arranged oxygen at the RMH, oxygen to the gate of LAX, oxygen on our flight home, oxygen at the gate of DIA, and oxygen at home for months and months to come. The oxygen relay race took days to orchestrate, and cost $200. A bargain.

On the Friday of Memorial Day weekend 2003, we went to the heart clinic the morning of our flight and were cleared for takeoff before going back to our room and packing up for our flight. We'd been surrounded by so much caring, patience, and empathy. Then to ruin it, an asshole shuttle bus driver was annoyed that we took so much care strapping in our newborn son for his first ride in a vehicle that was neither an ambulance, rescue copter, or chartered life-flight jet.

You would think the idea of picking people up outside of a Ronald McDonald House would soften a person, but who knows what lies beneath the unkindness of strangers? We rode out past CHLA and headed to our future, uncertain as it was.

At LAX, we were all flying one-way. All the transplant plans pleasantly thwarted, we had to re-ticket far sooner than we expected. However, thanks to Mr. Bin Laden and Co., one-way fliers were thoroughly checked, including Liam. While at the first check point, a British man, very much in a hurry, started shouting out to the TSA lady helping us, who very promptly and sassily told him, "Look at this tiny baby. He had open-heart surgery and I'm helping him now. He has real problems, wait your turn, sir!"

I was half shocked and half grateful that she recognized this wasn't easy for us, and even though she had to process us as a potential security threat, she wanted to make it as easy as she could. It was a nice counterbalance to the shuttle bus driver.

Finally at the gate, we relaxed into waiting. In the months of specialist visits and the weeks in the hospital, we'd become experts at waiting. Being a Chatty Cathy by nature, I started a conversation with the young woman whose chair backed up to mine. She asked about Liam and I shared our story.

She held back tears as she said, "I was feeling so sorry for myself because I've been bumped off of three flights today and have been here since 5:00 A.M., but look at what you've been through."

I smiled at her. "It's OK, no one should have to go through this, and getting bumped three times really does suck."

It was the strangest thing because I felt she wanted me to say just the opposite, like, "You're right, you stupid bitch, buck up!" But I couldn't. She was trying to feel our pain, and people exerting true empathy rather than simple pity are rare.

Empathy is ethereal. Empathy is a genuine attempt to transcend yourself and feel what others feel. It's the selfless act of jumping into someone else's free fall. Pity, on the other hand, is visceral. Pity is a petty shield we throw up that reflects how pathetic other people are in our own eyes. I hate pity. I don't want people to feel sorry for me and Jim, or for Liam. We are so lucky.

I would rather people want to help us, to want better for us, and to understand that we are bigger than what has happened to us. I want the world to know that my family is no less human because of our challenges. If anything, our struggles through darkness make us more human.

The girl at LAX saw that. She gave us empathy, and I wanted to give it back. Though at times my ability to do so has often been frozen by a harsh anger I didn't want to own, and sometimes I've felt nothing because of it. On this day of homecomings, I had it to offer, and that was a mutual gift.

Once on the plane, we realized that Jim and I were split up. It got worse. The oxygen they provided was for an adult. The tubing was for an adult. Liam was a newborn. Even if we could have configured the tank to fit to the neonatal oxygen cannula that came off Liam's original oxygen tank, the one we were forced to leave at the gate, the modulator for the adult-sized tank had a lowest setting of one full liter. That much oxygen would have left our child brain damaged by the end of the flight. Liam was so tiny that he only needed 1/8 of a liter of oxygen. Instead, we arranged an impromptu blow-by. It was entirely unscientific, utterly terrifying, and our first act of medical improv to be performed at forty thousand feet.

We were the last people on the plane because the flight crew wanted everyone seated and out of their way when they enabled the O2 for Liam. So everyone within earshot (which was quite a crowd) got to hear what was happening with the tubing trouble, how sick our baby had been, how sick he still was, etc. When that situation was resolved and the flight attendants moved on to other things, I returned to my seat eight rows back.

As teary eyed passengers watched me, so tired and defeated, march down the back of the plane, at least six people offered me their seats so I could be closer to my baby. I ended up in the seat one back and across from Jim. By the time the plane landed, Liam cried several times. As new parents, we were so embarrassed for causing so much commotion, but many passengers' faces were flushed with understanding. We were so clueless and unforgiving of ourselves.

Jim's parents (Bill and Karen) were meeting us at the airport, along with the oxygen we'd arranged from the distributor in Loveland. In this Post-911 era, we were told only one grandparent could get a gate-pass to meet us, and the other would have to stay behind in baggage. We waited until every other person was off the plan to get our carry-ons and turn off the oxygen, so it came as a huge shock when *both* grandparents boarded our plane with an oxygen tank in tow.

The flight crew had spied them while they stood at our gate watching our fellow passengers disembark. They weren't hard to spot with a tank of pressurized gas in an airport. Apparently, while we were still in the air, someone on the plane had called ahead to the gate and made sure that the United ticketing counter sent them both back through security. More than one person was listening, and at least three people cared enough about us to make a difference. So these two grandparents, who only got to spend a few hours during six strained days with their first grandchild before he was swept up in an odyssey of survival, got that much closer, that much sooner, to hold their grandson that much longer. It was these series of kindnesses from strangers and friends that smoothed the pavement over our rough road.

As soon as we left the plane, I couldn't believe I was in Colorado. I couldn't fathom that my baby was here, alive, being held by his proud grandparents. When I got home I was finally going to be a Mommy. I prayed to get home safely. I rolled my eyes as I imagined that after all we'd been through we'd get hit by a truck on the way home.

10

Dear Random Stranger, Please Don't Diagnose My Child

Settling in at home meant eventually going back to work. As luck would have it, I was called back early. I'd planned to burn my vacation time and stay out twelve weeks, but my manager called me at eight weeks asking if I could please, please, please come back to work. Things hadn't gone well in my absence. Yeah, things weren't exactly a cakewalk in LA. Whatever, I was too shell-shocked to compare war stories and had a mess to clean up at work despite my sincere attempts to prepare them for my absence. I wasn't so much indispensable as they were ill-prepared, and I had to own part of that, so I went back to work.

I negotiated a part-time work-at-home arrangement and got a nanny for that time. Life at home was an adjustment.

As long as Liam was at home, things were pretty normal, but when we took him out, things got interesting. Taking him between floors on our home meant switching him off the big oxygen tank and hooking him up to a portable tank. This meant swapping the valves, making sure the amount stayed calibrated correctly. Too high, and we blind our child or cause brain damage; too low could cause heart and lung damage. We were living the damned if you do, damned if you don't existence.

Leaving the house was equally precarious. Walks were better because we could stick the O2 in the bottom of the stroller instead of carrying it, but getting in and out of the car was a pain in the ass. Once calibration was worked out, we had to get Liam in his baby seat and carry the oxygen tank over the opposite shoulder of the arm holding the carrier, lest it should slip and smash our baby.

There were the stares, and the "Awww, poor baby" refrain that followed us everywhere we went, like our own theme song. Then there were the random strangers who came up and touched Liam. But the worst were the lay people who liked to diagnose him as a preemie.

Now, don't get me wrong, I saw enough preemies at PSL to know it's a critical state, and I'm not diminishing it. I had lunch with two good friends at different times during my pregnancy who both recounted their marathon hospital stays with their preemies, the brain bleeds, and the clear and present danger. But Liam wasn't a preemie. He was a full term baby who did not surmount the challenge of maturing to the point where he could begin his life at home. Liam's diagnosis led him not to a ventilator or an incubator for weeks on end to finish growing his lungs and immune system. Rather, his half-heart would never grow back, and his chest would be ripped apart to spare his life.

Yet, these people who knew nothing about Liam were no different than I was six months before. We were all ignorant that babies ever need heart surgery. Everyone just said, "Oh," when I enlightened them, except for one.

One evening we finished dinner at Red Robin and were on our way out when a skinny fifty-ish thin, prim woman clad all in denim held the door for me as I went out. I thanked her as we passed by.

She saw Liam's oxygen, and asked, "Oh, is he a preemie?" to which I offered my canned open-heart-surgery reply, and honest to God, she said to me, "Well, then he's probably better off."

I went numb with shock. The woman went inside and I stood there with Liam's oxygen tank in one hand and Liam in his carrier in the other entirely off balance. For a flash, I burned with the desire to chase this woman down and say, "WHAT? Why don't you come with me in a couple months when he has it again! And in a few years when he has to do it AGAIN! If he's still alive in a couple of months or a few years!"

This intrinsic and fatal flaw in Liam's heart led my son to have his newborn brain packed on ice, chest sliced open, bone sawed through, heart cut up, while suspended between life and death in a crap shoot for survival. Liam's diagnosis arrived at a ventilator, it did not start there. All that Liam suffered was taken on only to have a chance to do it two more times, or so we "expected." That this woman could casually claim that Liam was "better off" than a preemie was an insult to my intellect, my reasoning, my very soul.

In reality, the odds for most preemies are far better than Liam's odds ever were. So, every time a stranger saw Liam on oxygen and asked, "Is he a preemie?" I cringed, breathed out my nose, and said, "No he had open-heart surgery."

My experience with that woman at Red Robin was my first sweeping, "Damn, people REALLY don't get this!" moment. I'd known times where it was weird to go from the hospital battleground where Congenital Heart Disease (CHD) was the cornerstone of people's careers and families' battles to a world where no one knew what CHD was. But until that moment, I refused to really admit to myself that there would be more surgeries or there would be no more Liam, and that was why the preemie questions dug at me so deeply.

This woman made me face my looming truth through her ignorance, and it stung like a bitch. She wasn't the bitch; the truth was, and damn, it hurt. On the steps in front of Red Robin, I knew we had to go back to the hospital, and I wasn't ready.

Later that summer, I was having dinner with my in-laws and the waitress kept eying Liam in his baby carrier with his oxygen. I knew, the way you know that car in the rear view mirror is about to hit you, that we would not get through dinner without the preemie question.

I even warned Bill and Karen, "If she asks me if he's a preemie, I'm going to say, 'No, he's a life-long smoker.'"

Then she asked, and I responded, and she looked stunned like a deer in headlights. I felt guilty; I still do.

Yet, every time a stranger misdiagnosed Liam, it undermined the seriousness and cruelty of what happened to him. It was like they were holding out this tantalizing preemie-made-good, ready to start his life, put it all behind him promise, and it could never be kept. The fight was not over. We weren't reaping the rewards of an amazing recovery. We were treading water until the next wave hit.

It wasn't the fault of the lady at Red Robin, or the waitress at Coyote's. It was that the whole world was ignorant and we were all part of it. I was equally ignorant until this happened to me. No, it was more than that. They were more innocent than ignorant. How could they have known, and who was I to judge? But I did judge. I burned, and I ached for the innocence I lost when I learned how these horrible disfigurements of the human heart could steal the life of a child—my child, my Liam. My innocence was lost and my identity was twisted. As I rebuilt my life and my identity as a mother, the only thing my fractured worldview saw was ignorance. I hurt deeply, harbored resentments, and bled flippancy.

In my frustration and my tendency to blurt, I was becoming an apostle to the world, proselytizing about CHD. The conversion happened so gradually and out of necessity, that I was oblivious to the role I was about to create for myself. Necessity is the mother of invention, and sorrow often sows the seeds of hope.

11

Catalyst

Before we left CHLA, I asked the attending cardiologists in the CTICU who we should see when we got back to Colorado. In the chaos of our hard-fought, but temporary, victory in saving Liam's life, we learned so much. We figured out pretty fast that Dr. Doom did not possess the attitude required to foster such a tenuous miracle.

Our referring doctor suggested we see Dr. Henry Sondheimer. This was the same Dr. Sondheimer I spoke with on the phone while I was still pregnant before I was bewitched by Dr. Smooth into thinking that I could manage this nightmare, or ever have my way with this situation.

I spoke with "Dr. Henry" on the phone to coordinate details, and he laid into me for getting myself in this mess in California when I should have gone to Denver Children's in the first place like he told me. I wanted to shout into the phone, "You lost me with airlift!" But in reality, that seemed silly considering a Lear Jet brought Liam to LA.

Nope, I didn't say that, but when my nerves were stretched just far enough, I said, "You're right, it's over now, let's get on with it," and that was that.

The morning after we came home, we took Liam to see a pediatrician, literally doctor's orders, to make sure he had handled the flight all right. It was a Saturday. By Tuesday Liam and I were on our way to Denver to see Dr. Sondheimer, the first of dozens of hour-long drives we'd make to the Children's Hospital that year. -

By August of 2003, we were at either the pediatrician or the cardiologist each week, sometimes both. Since Liam was my first and only baby, I couldn't fathom how extreme the frequency of those appointments was in relation to a healthy child. Even though he was sick, I still knew we were at the doctor a lot.

Obviously I knew Liam was sick. As if the oxygen tubing, tape on his face, scars hovering above his veins and chest, and all the medicine didn't remind me several times a day. But Liam was such a sweet and joyful baby who loved to eat and responded to music, that he seemed perfectly normal to me, even though our situation was not.

My favorite thirty minutes of the day were bath time. Off with the oxygen! For that glimmering moment we savored our baby splashing his tiny hands in the water, peeling stick-up ducks off the tiles, and laughing his broken little heart out.

I rarely saw Liam's tiny baby fingers because we were constantly covering them in scratch mittens to prevent him from yanking the oxygen tube from his face that tethered him to life. When we gave bathed him, his hands and face weren't obscured by the mechanics that kept him alive. When Liam was in the bathtub, other than the scar of scars, he looked like a real boy, and he was.

In our little yellow duck-filled bathroom we bought into the fantasy of being a normal family. After the bath, Liam snuggled in layers of warm towels on our bed and I sang and cooed to him, delighting at how he reciprocated. Jim and I cuddled him and touched his soft blond hair. Such a normal moment was so unusual and precious for us—stolen and then gone.

I put lotion all over Liam's wriggling little body, paying special attention to his tender cheeks that were shredded and raw from taping the cannula on and his tearing it off. I put a glaze of vitamin E oil on his chest scars. The after-bath fun ended when Liam's persistent blue pallor got bluer and the oxygen was no longer negotiable. All his blood was mixing in his inefficient heart. Without the supplemental oxygen Liam wouldn't get enough for his body to grow. Eventually, his heart would fail. Oxygen wasn't an accessory, nor was it optional. We enjoyed precious few minutes of tube-free time, and I cherished every second of it. I still do.

I struggled between the reality of all this medicine in our lives and the weekly Apria oxygen tank deliveries. I worried about what a healthy baby would or should typically be doing developmentally those first three months. More than that, I worried incessantly that Liam would die on our watch.

One day Liam was lying on the floor in our living room in his Boppi Pillow when I ran upstairs to use my bathroom because the chain in our powder room toilet broke. I came back down a few minutes later and his entire right ear was pooled with blood. I thought he was bleeding out his ear, that he had a stroke or was dying. I thought I lost Liam on my way back from the bathroom, and then I lost my mind.

I rushed to him and realized he'd torn his nasal cannula off in spite of the scratch mittens and tape. The tape took a strip of Liam's soft skin with it. In a healthy child that small scratch wouldn't cause the blood bath Liam took. But Liam's skin was so raw and sensitive. Compounding the problem was the oral syringe of baby aspirin we gave him every day in order to thin his blood so his artificial shunts wouldn't clot and kill him. That blood was proof of the lengths required to keep Liam alive. As the blood pooled in the curve of Liam's ear, it seemed to glare at me to remind me that I could never take a moment for granted, not even to pee.

I cleaned Liam and held him tight for a long time on the floor with tears of anger for the insurmountable strength of my fear and my own weakness. I cried tears of relief that we averted those fears for now. I cried only and always over Liam's shoulder. I never let my son see me cry.

My anxiety over a scratch on Liam's face and the guilt I felt for going to the toilet was simply the price I paid for his life. I couldn't question it. I had no right. To question the price of the gift was too dangerous. Liam's life might be rescinded for my ingratitude.

Instead of feeling angry, I was simply afraid. I relapsed into a behavior from third grade when Michelle Wood swore at my slumber party that if we said "Bloody Mary" in a bathroom mirror three times in the dark, Mary would materialize and murder us. For a year I wouldn't close the bathroom door, much to my mother's annoyance.

After Liam's bloody scratch, I simply propped Liam on the Boppy pillow in the hallway within view from the bathroom and never closed the door. Using the bathroom became a coordinated effort, but what else could I do? I couldn't hear him bleeding on the baby monitor.

As the days progressed and Liam grew, I developed questions faster than new anxieties. No matter how long or how hard I looked online, I found nothing definitive and few things that reassured me. I'd gone to one of our favorite haunts, Barnes & Noble, and desperately sought books on CHD—nothing. Not one book in the enormous store. Amazon.com wasn't much better. Truth be known, no one had what I needed.

So I turned to the internet. I emailed a few moms I found on websites and forums. Stephanie T., Monica R., Laurie B., Amy H.E., Heather A., Sharon D. and Julie P.B. were the first Hypoplastic Right Heart Moms I'd met. I wrangled them onto a Yahoo group so we could compare notes, and on August 15, 2003, I had my second "baby," my very own support group for a defect that wasn't even in the book of heart defects.

Kendra, Sharon, Kim, and Barbara soon joined. Before we knew it, there were dozens of moms who came out of the woodwork, all with hypoplastic right babies or toddlers, all dazed and confused.

"The group" was in its very first day of existence when Liam had another cardiology appointment. We hadn't been for a couple of weeks, so Dr. Sondheimer ordered an echocardiogram and chest x-rays, etc. Then, he came in and said, "So you know another surgery is coming, right?" Yes, we'd been told. He then said, "So when are we going to do it?"

I said, "We were told [at CHLA] he'd need it when he was six months old," like a school kid answering a quiz question. A silent pause while reality took effect. "Do we need to do it sooner?" I asked.

To which Dr. Sondheimer, always so upbeat, responded through a smile, "How's next week for you?"

As if we had a choice, as if we ever got a choice after we chose to fight. Once you choose survival over surrender the conditions are never up to you.

12

Back So Soon?

Liam's blood oxygen saturation was dipping below seventy percent even on supplementary oxygen. Most people are at around ninety-eight percent. Most babies are at one hundred percent. Liam was bluer than blue, he was downright Smurfy. He was also bigger than the doctors expected him to get with the defects he had, which meant he was outgrowing his heart. We had to come back the next week for Liam's first heart catheterization.

CHLA hadn't done a heart cath before the DKS because it was too risky for a newborn on the precipice multiple organ failure. They were running out of time in Los Angeles, and surgery was nonnegotiable.

In Denver, the surgery coordinator scheduled Liam's heart cath for Tuesday, August 18th. Liam's second open-heart surgery was scheduled for Monday, August 25th. Just like that.

Liam was having the Glenn, a surgery we didn't expect until he was six months old, and here he was, not even four months old. The Glenn is where I learned about the vena cava. It's the giant vein that runs all our used-up blood back into our hearts. The superior drains the top half and the inferior drains the lower half. It all drains into the right side of the heart, the side Liam doesn't have, to pump to the lungs to get more oxygen.

My father's superior vena cava was encased in an inoperable malignant esophageal tumor the size of a softball. Dad was forty-eight years old when he died. My son's superior vena cava would shortly be completely dissected from his heart and reattached to his pulmonary branch artery, bypassing his defective heart entirely. Liam was to embark on his second foray into the masterful art of cardiothoracic re-plumbing, but my baby was the plumbing project.

We thought we had three more months and time for baths and cuddling. We'd grown foolish enough to once again think we knew what to expect, to think we were allowed the privilege of expectation.

My exact words in an e-mail I sent the following week were, "It's going to be hard for us when we get home because it will be a little while before we can get back to where we were with holding him and practicing rolling over, etc."

All my fears about Liam's potential developmental delays were about to increase exponentially. Because things were so rushed, we had to squeeze a heart catheterization in before the surgery. So, the day of Liam's heart cath we were on stand-by for the hospital to call us once they confirmed they had the facilities available. Liam was not allowed to eat at all that day. The hospital called early that morning, and we drove to Denver around 8:00 A.M., and waited. With no breast milk or even water for over twelve hours, Liam was a very hungry little caterpillar.

For the first hour or so after checking in, we tried to entertain Liam. Jim did the usual schtick that always made Liam laugh, and it worked for a while. We hung a webbed ball from the ceiling-mounted IV tree and spun it around. Our improvised mobile entertained him, but only for a while. Liam's hunger was just too big for our baby. By the end of our second hour of waiting, Liam was inconsolable and screaming for food.

It was one thing at CHLA, when Liam was tethered to a bed with IV lines and a nurse standing over us. For all of Liam's first month of life, when and if he ate was determined by his doctors and nurses, not me. In that environment, I responded to their charts, not to Liam's actual hunger. Whether at PSL or CHLA, it was not my job as a mother to give Liam comfort on demand. We weren't allowed to comfort each other.

In LA, Liam's hunger came on gradually, so I never truly mothered my child in that environment. Before I ever took him home from the hospital, my job as his mother was to sit and wait. In this hospital in Denver, I was reassuming that role, and I resented it.

Now, after having him to myself at home for two months, the best I could do was sit in this dark little side room behind a curtain with my screaming child cuddling against my leaking chest, smelling what I couldn't give him. I felt that same old helplessness, and yet it was completely different this time.

In California, my breasts ached because I was new to this. In Colorado, my heart broke because it was getting old fast. I yearned to give Liam something, anything to calm him. The once desired pacifier was again an insult, the cuddling smelled like food. I felt like such a horrible human being, dragging my child here to be cut into and wires run up his legs into his heart, to injure his body in preparation to violate it entirely. But before the torture could begin in earnest, I teased his hunger with my own smell.

I hadn't eaten either. I was making so much milk, over 1,600 calories a day worth, and I was starving, but I wouldn't eat if Liam couldn't. His crying and the darkness of these windowless banks of pre-op beds made me dizzy, sleepy, and numb.

Why didn't they hurry up? They were two hours behind. In my hunger and frustration, I was eager for the nurses to take my baby away. When I realized what I was thinking, I wanted to vomit the cold air from my empty stomach.

I didn't mean it! I mentally uttered a fast retraction in between yearning for deliverance from my stress. I willed myself not to break down completely. I didn't mean it—I didn't mean that I want to let them do this. I took it back, but the thought had already formed. Over the top of my exhaustion, hunger, and disorientation descended a toxic cloud of guilt.

They had to do it. We had to consent to it, but I never wanted it. I only wanted Liam to stop crying. Still, I would have rather given him the milk he so desperately craved than give him to doctors who were going to drug him and cut him.

The nurse finally gave Liam his sedative, and he slurped it down greedily. I handed my groggy baby over to the nurse and meekly followed her down the hall to the door of the cath lab. After she went in with our child, we kept walking down the hallway past the lab until we saw no people or motion, so we could cry privately. That was our M.O., we always kept moving.

After we got ourselves together, Jim and I claimed a pager from waiting room staff, should they call us back before we finished breakfast at the Red Wagon Cafeteria.

We ate and promptly traveled back upstairs to wait, wait, wait, and wait some more. I spent half of 2003 waiting in hospitals and doctors' offices. Unless it involved withholding food from Liam, waiting was painless, and the time didn't matter. He was always worth the wait.

Liam's heart catheterization was where we first met Esther. Esther is a goddess, an angel, a tiny woman whose long black hair is almost always tucked up in a surgical bonnet, which coordinates nicely with her scrubs and lab coat. Like Dr. Starnes, she was a person whose stature belied the size of her skill and talent.

Esther took us in, made sure we were in all the right places at all the right times, and took care of us the entire time we were at the hospital—that first time and every time that followed.

The day dragged on in recovery and threatened to never let us go. Liam was a tiny baby with a crazy heart under general anesthesia. The doctors had trouble accessing his femoral arteries in both legs. They cut down one side of his groin only to give up and cut down the other. Eventually, when those stitches were ready to come out, they were so tight our cardiologist paged a surgeon to cut them out of Liam's skin. Our chunky little baby was scared for life with a pair of matching lines on either side of his crotch.

More trouble came with placing an IV, so they put one in his head. In our love and desire to save his life, we had subjected Liam to extraordinary physical abuse. Oh sure, it's not technically abuse when it's medically necessary, but all those stitches and blood on my baby broke my heart again. His blood is forever in my memories and on my hands.

Eventually, we learned our doctors were contemplating coiling "collateral venous growth." Later, I learned more about this from my

HRH support group. Basically, Liam's body was trying to undermine what Dr. Starnes had done by growing veins between his heart and lungs in a desperate search for oxygen. But in doing this, the growth undermined the artificial system that Dr. Starnes had started and Dr. Laour-Gayet was about to enhance. Dr. Chan and Dr. Chang decided against the adding platinum coils to starve off the collateral veins that day in case Liam needed those them later.

During our debrief, Dr. Chan, the senior cath specialist made a comment about the Fontan surgery, the third stage of Liam's treatment path when he turned three, as being the "bridge to transplant," which freaked us out. We thought we'd taken a detour to *avoid* transplant land, and it now sounded inevitable.

As our anxiety built up we freaked out to Esther in the waiting room about the previous "Bridge to transplant" comment, she made sure we talked to Dr. Chan before we left. He told us that not all Fontan patients get transplanted, and that the term "bridge to transplant" is a historical term for the three surgeries we were facing with Liam. Historically, the surgeries bought time, but now surgeons were trying to optimize them to get children well into their thirties with those three surgeries. That was comforting, but shadows remained in our heads now that transplant returned to our vocabulary.

The day stretched out past 8:00 P.M. before they would finally discharge us and we could take our baby home. When they pulled the IV from Liam's head, it bled out heavily and took time to clot. We finally got home well after 9:00 P.M., exhausted. That was technically Liam's second heart surgery. Sure, they hadn't cut his chest open, but they shoved wires in his heart, and that's heart surgery with all the stroke and infection risk included.

We returned Friday, August 22, for pre-op for the second act. The phlebotomist took blood, but I waited outside. I've got to give Jim credit, he held Liam for that blood draw. Not to worry, I'd had my share of holding Liam down while he was stuck with needles, but I just didn't have the heart for it that day.

The cardiologists did another echocardiogram, and we had to have "the talk" with the surgeon. Despite everyone's best laid plans, I learned that nothing ever happens on schedule in a hospital, especially where Liam was concerned. The day stretched from four to seven hours, and eventually we met up with the life-saver.

Dr. Francois Lacour-Gayet. A name worthy of a sentence. When we first met him, he'd been in the US for less than a year and was difficult to understand. Yet, even in my muddled state I was riveted to every word he spoke.

He told us that compared to the Damus Kaye Stansel (DKS or Norwood) surgery Dr. Starnes performed, the Glenn would be straightforward and much less risky. He told us how fortunate Liam was to do have done well with the DKS, as it was one of the most complicated procedures that could be done. Lacour-Gayet is an expert on surgical difficulty and started the Aristotle Foundation to help assess surgical risk, so he knew his numbers.

It was reassuring to know that the Glenn was safer than the DKS had been. Still, we signed papers, again, acknowledging a five percent risk of *Liam's* death, *Liam's* debilitating stroke. It was Liam's name was on the papers and then I wrote my own. We handed the clipboard back to the surgeon, and then he was gone. We took our baby home from the hospital for the third time, for the weekend.

The morning of Liam's Glenn, we drove up early from Fort Collins. I remember so clearly pulling Liam out of his car seat in the parking garage. He was wearing his "Dinosaur Rescue" romper we bought a month before. It was one of our favorite outfits on him.

This would be the last time I'd lift him up from under his arms for eight weeks. It was the usual acrobatics trying to get the baby out of the car with the oxygen attached. Once they admitted Liam, we had to bring the oxygen back to the car. They had their own supply. Everything from home, even the oxygen was becoming foreign.

It was August 25th, and the first thing I did after we checked in was call to get on the Ronald McDonald House waiting list. Then we surrendered ourselves to the pre-op room. The nurses gave us a gown and we took off Liam's "Dinosaur Rescue" romper, his tiny brown shoes, his baby socks, and his blue and yellow pacifier, and I shoved them into a plastic draw-string bag with the hospital logo on it. I pulled the cords tight and wondered if my son would be alive to wear these clothes again and how far we would have to go before we would be home again.

The surgical team took Liam's vitals, after which we cradled him and tried to comfort him until the nurses came in to give him some Versed (a sedative). I was grateful the meds would keep him calm and remove any memories of what was about to happen in the OR. Hungry, he gulped it down and didn't even notice the taste until it was gone.

Jim and I sat behind a curtain answering the typical pre-op questions — when did Liam last eat, how many teeth had he lost. Who were they kidding? He didn't even have teeth yet. Then, like Dr. Bushman had done a mere fourteen weeks earlier, he allowed the nurses to come in and take Liam from my arms, where he was happily snuggled and drunk with Versed. His head wobbled as the woman in scrubs took my child against her chest. Emotionally spent, I had to look away as they walked to the OR. Would it have been any easier if we could have walked down the hall with him as we'd done at CHLA? Sometimes there simply aren't any right answers. Or any answers at all.

Liam's surgery began at 8:30 A.M. We gathered the bag, our own things, ourselves, and escaped down the hallway to cry a little bit before joining our family in the surgical waiting room around the corner.

By the time we dug into the donuts my mother-in-law brought, the surgical team had already sawed through Liam's chest for the second time in his life.

We practiced the high art of waiting. Today, I mix memories of all the times we waited in that room on the second floor of

Children's Hospital with little gray-haired volunteers in blue smocks paging parents to take calls from the operating rooms, cath labs, and other invasive treatment rooms.

For the second time in seven days we were here, and this surgery took a lot longer than the one at CHLA, despite being "less complicated." Scar tissue and the complexity of his first surgery contributed to the length of the second. Dr. Lacour-Gayett was working around the "extraordinary" and "brilliant" work done by Dr. Starnes. Starnes and Lacour-Gayet must belong to a mutual admiration society. They each had nothing but compliments for the other, which added to our confidence in both.

It was late afternoon when we finally saw Liam. He was still intubated and bright purple from his rib cage to his scalp, making his pale blonde hair look like a golden crown on a plum. His puce color was the result of the new flow of Liam's superior vena cava, now dissected from his heart and reattached to his lungs.

Liam's inferior vena cava still fed into his heart. The superior now drained passively into his lungs as a straw dripping into a hungry mouth. At one point the shock of his new irrigation system sent our purple son's oxygen saturation dipping down to forty-four percent, even on the ventilator. It was the first forty-eight hours all over again, with all the panic and tension those hours entail.

Blood products were pushed into Liam's central lines, drips going non-stop, and though his chest wasn't open like the last time, this was scarier. This time, Liam was more than a tiny bundle of possibility that my womb wept and convulsed over losing. After two and a half months at home with him, Liam was the smiling child who filled my life. He was more than a hope or a promise, he was a person—a person in pain and a person at risk. Liam was my little person, and the fear of losing him now was different than the fear of losing him in California. Statistically the risk now was lower, but it felt more present, more tangible. I had an image of life without Liam now that I'd had a taste of life with him.

His blood pressure was elevated by all the changes to his anatomy, his heart rhythm was off, and he was on an external pace maker. I was genuinely frightened, but I couldn't be frightened away. I stayed by his side as long as I could stay upright. I'd been on high alert since 3:00 A.M.

By 11:00 P.M. we staggered off to sleep in a parent room we'd secured from the Volunteer office. The bed was like a wrestling mat. It was full-sized, but the hospital only had twin-sized sheets. Two sheets were pulled horizontally across the bed. We woke up twice from people trying to get into our room. We woke up several more times due to the insanity of the ill-fitted sheets swallowing our legs.

The next morning, Jim and I showered in the parent bathroom. The door didn't lock, so we stood guard for each other. We ate breakfast in the cafeteria before shift change and moved through the hospital until we came to rest at Liam's bedside, where we stayed like statues until nature called or we were kicked out for a procedure or shift change.

The time spent being riveted to our child gave us the opportunity to ask questions and learn as much as we could about the lines and medicines going in, the fluids coming out, the what, when, where, why, and how of our mysterious child. We never missed an opportunity to soak up new information about Liam's heart, his care, his changes—it was all ammunition and fuel for hope.

If we heard something we didn't like, we asked ten more questions, seeking points of clarification, seeking answers that would help us create a context and understand where we were and where we needed to go.

On Liam's second day in the CICU we were able to get a room at the Ronald McDonald House (RMH), and by the third day, Liam was doing better. Everything (echocardiogram, blood gases, chest x-ray, skin tone, etc) looked good, except his heart rate, which was low, and his oxygen saturation, which was either quite good or not at good all. I felt like a rubber ball bouncing all over the room.

The doctors weren't particularly worried about Liam's inconsistencies and indicated both variances are standard effects two days out of surgery. We waited for his heart to adapt to the changes that nature never imagined.

Then things changed. After a good start at recovery, Liam's little heart wasn't quite up to full speed. His sinus node in his atrium weren't working right. The nodes send the electrical signal for the upper chambers, atria, to contract in time with the lower chamber's ventricles. Liam only has one atria because his was surgically altered and one ventricle because he was born without the right one. Even so, Liam's heart rate should have been 120 - 160 beats per minute. It was 59 - 65 bpm. This was not good at all.

The rounding doctors said Liam's heart rate should return to normal after the surgical swelling decreased. That should have happened within the first three days post-op. We were five days out.

The CICU staff discussed alternative medicines for Liam on day six. If the nodes didn't kick back in, we would discuss a "permanent" pacemaker to replace the external one that sat in his bed and ran into his heart.

The pacemaker terrified me. One of our roommates at CHLA, Danielle, was born on my twenty-ninth birthday, five days before Liam. Danielle had HLHS and hadn't been diagnosed until she was born. I could not forget how frightened her parents, John and Violet, were the day Danielle was rushed back for a pacemaker because she wasn't recovering well.

Worse than Danielle's surgery, was the slow and measured sound of Violet's voice on my answering machine thanking me for my letter, but Danielle had died before her Glenn. Her message was followed by the sound of us both crying softly in my living room, her on the machine from a thousand miles away, me standing over the machine with my face in my hands.

Pacemaker was another word for decline. It was a direct hit to my hope, and while it seemed inevitable in Liam's life, we wanted to delay it as long as possible. We wanted as much mileage out of his heart as we could get before changing the battery.

We asked friends and family to pray that Liam's heart would start up again. We struggled in the tedium as we helplessly waited and hoped for Liam's heart to beat correctly, only to worry that it never would.

13

One Angry Mother

It took a few days but eventually the staff moved us upstairs to step-down. We found ourselves in another four-bed corner room, not dissimilar to the way beds were arranged at CHLA. In Denver, circa 2003, the step down unit wasn't comprised entirely of cardiac patients like it had been at CHLA. These other patients came and went so quickly, sometimes two in one day. We seemed to be the only permanent fixture a room where everything, including the children, was on casters.

A Southeast Asian immigrant family with a teenage daughter moved in against the Northern wall. I don't know which country they came from, but neither of the parents spoke fluent English. Their older daughter had a degenerative disorder and couldn't walk, and could barely talk. Only her family understood what she said, but she rarely spoke.

I wondered what they endured to come to America for their share of the dream only to end up here with me, and Jim, and Liam. I ached seeing this family in crisis, but we were all together in our crises. We were a new breed of boat people.

One particularly long day, I sat at Liam's bedside for hours on end, waiting for the on-call cardiologist to answer the questions we'd been asking the non-cardiac nurse. I was tired and scared. The talk about drugs to help set Liam's rhythm right and permanent pacemakers was just talk. We had no decisions, no answers, and no plan. Jim had been staying overnight with Liam and catching up on sleep during the day at the RHM. I was on the day shift.

Alone and adrift, I felt so lost in that dim room on 3N, even though it was daytime. I sat quietly winding up musical toys to distract Liam from his pain. I gently bounced his elevated baby seat and attended to him as much as I could with his pacer wires and oxygen attached. Then, she came in.

I heard her in the hall before I saw her, this woman in a fuchsia suit with costume jewelry and her click-clack heels. Her made-up aging face and highlighted hair could have graced any bench or a bus selling real estate or insurance. Click Clack had that Glamour Shots look. She flew passed me in my dumpy pink hoodie and dingy jeans, and made a b-line for the family against the North wall.

Click Clack knew this family, maybe from their kids' school, maybe another place. I don't know, but she knew them, and she oozed a toxic pity that people in hospital fogs don't need. She offered her chit-chat and the younger, healthy daughter translated to her parents. Then, Click Clack lit a spark that set off my tinderbox of raw nerves.

She went on and on about her own daughter and how when said daughter was in college she went on international student exchange and had to have her wisdom teeth out, "in Germany, of all places!" She honestly said that.

Click Clack lamented about how she had to secure a last minute ticket to fly there to take care of her poor twenty-something daughter, not much younger than me. This adult woman with her wisdom teeth was Click Clack's example of how she understood "exactly" how hard this was on this family huddled around their broken teenager.

Only this family would never see this girl become an independent young woman. She could no longer feed herself, and she would certainly never study abroad in Europe.

Click Clack's own daughter's pain, her compulsion to travel thousands of miles to be at her side, her poor, poor little girl with her painful tooth extraction. It was all the same to her.

Here she was with this family whose daughter and hope was wasting away in a cold bed in the heat of August. Down the hall in the burn unit were children quarantined from their own mothers in unimaginable agony. Upstairs the kids with cancer were fighting to survive the poison that cast them into the roles of androgynous ghosts that haunted the halls dragging their IV posts. And then there was Liam, four months and one day old, and so sensitive to pain with electrodes strung into his heart, and I couldn't even hold him. He seemed more than an ocean away even though he was in the bed right in front of me.

This whole time my back was to Click Clack, and between us an ugly hospital curtain and a vacant space in the floor that would soon house another tragic bed. But her voice echoed through that empty space, and I'd had all I could take, and I couldn't takes any more.

Tears erupted and raced down my face. Angry, angry tears at this woman who dared bring adult dentistry into this den of medical misery and unspeakable loss. The nurse saw me red and running with tears and asked what was wrong. I lost it completely.

My diatribe ran out in incoherent gasps and gulps about wisdom teeth and how my baby was laying here and might need a permanent pacemaker, and how I didn't know if he would even live long enough to ever get any teeth at all, and were we ever going to bring him home again?

The nurse looked stunned and said, "But this family's daughter is very ill," as if I was talking about them, and I moaned loudly, "I'm NOT talking about *them*!" That's when she asked if I wanted a clergy person to talk to me.

I mumbled, "Sure," but then I pulled up the side rail of Liam's crib and left the room. I stomped down the long hall past the anorexia unit, sobbing until I snaked through the building to the parking garage near the outpatient offices. I knew the bathrooms by the parking garage were never busy, so I went in and cried out my anger until I felt embarrassed. Then I was angry at my embarrassment because, at the time, my anger seemed so just. . . I cried until I was overcome with guilt for leaving Liam in that room. Then I overcame my shame and went back.

After my tantrum, the first public outburst I'd had since Liam was born, and without the benefit of Ben or Jerry, I sat at Liam's bedside and stewed. Click Clack was gone, and I was embarrassed, not for Click Clack, or the nurse with no answers, or the clergy person that never came, but for the family whose guest I had likely forced to a hasty exit.

To placate my guilt for any embarrassment I caused the family, I imagined they were as happy as I was to see her gone. I didn't know where they came from, I didn't know where they were going with their sick child, and I don't know how much I'd affronted their culture. I didn't mean to do any of it, but the damage was done.

As conflicted as I feel about how off base this woman was, she wasn't talking to me, wasn't visiting me, and it was more that she hit my time bomb of nerves that had nothing to do with anyone else in the room.

I blew out the door in a selfish, angry, huff. While I can forgive myself, I still feel badly for what my actions might have done to that family, for the collateral damage of every parent in that room tied to a child whose presence on earth was a tenuous as Liam's. None of us needed any more drama than we found by being there in the first place, but that invasion of the mundane was the spark that lit my fury.

I always regretted my actions for the sake of the families in the room. Only now, all these years later, can I regret my drama for Click Clack's sake too. I bet she hasn't forgotten me, and I can only imagine her memory of me at my absolute worst.

She didn't know any better. How could she? She was simply trying her best to relate, but she was a bunny teasing a pit viper. I had so much venom wrapped up in my grief, and I was still grieving. Click Clack bore the brunt of a huge eruption, and that was no fairer than the circumstances that put me in that room with her in the first place.

Ignorant, insensitive, yes she was both of those things, but so was I. She didn't deserve my anger because in the end it wasn't about her, it was about the grief and the fear. She stepped on a coiled up snake, and for that I AM sorry.

My anger at strangers and friends who didn't "get it" was more about the feeling of being lost at sea in an ocean of souls and not bonding with any of them because my grief was so much stronger than I was. It was alienating. I felt alone, but I retreated further because it hurt too badly to reach out. I didn't know what else to do, so I either retreated or lashed out. I was so angry at no one in particular and in my raw state I grew angry at everyone. It was madness, it just was.

The anger over having a very sick child and nowhere to place it causes a lot of chaos in a person's life. If someone molested or injured my child, I would be angry at *that person*. That pain would be equally deep and that anger would be equally as corrosive, but it would have a natural target. Who can I be mad at about Liam's heart? No act was committed, but the destruction was real, and there was no one to blame.

Clearly it was not Liam's fault, he was simply the victim of his own heart. Not God, too risky. Not myself, because that way leads only to self-destruction and paralysis, and the science doesn't support it.

Jim and I have both blamed ourselves at various points. Jim blamed his genetics because his brother has a less dangerous heart defect. I blamed my weight when correlations appeared in the press. But neither Jim's genes nor my weight were definitively responsible for Liam's heart defect. I know enough about statistics from grad school to know that correlation is not cause. Besides, we were both ignorant of those correlations until they were staring us in the face, long after Liam was a reality.

No one owns the blame, and so there is no one to absorb the anger. No, it's not Click Clack's fault either, but certain people can get under the skin and pop the ugly angry blisters – the effect is messy. The anger is real, the target is unidentifiable, and everyone gets hit. It's not fair, but what is?

Then there is the fact that Liam didn't die. If he had died, people would expect me to go through the stages of grief. I would have expected and allowed myself more space to grieve a death that actually happened. But I was grieving a death that still might happen. I was aggrieved that Liam's life that could never be what I thought it would. I grieved the life Jim and I expected to share with our son, the life we expected to give Liam in that small space between knowing he was a boy and knowing he was broken. I grieved my loss of power to be the mother I wanted to be. It wasn't only that my anger held no target for blame, my very grief was always in question because I was supposed to be so grateful that Liam was even alive.

No one, especially myself, allowed me to grieve because we were so lucky to be in the fight, and we had so much fighting left to do.

Still, that shameful meltdown day wasn't quite over. After waiting in that room for more than twelve hours, sans two escapes to pump, my twenty minute tantrum, and one or two trips to the bathroom, starving, tired, thirsty, ashamed, holding my bladder, and annoyed, the doctor we'd been waiting for finally graced us with his presence.

He flipped through Liam's chart, mumbled, and headed for the door. "Not so hasty, if you please!" would have been my appropriate response, but it was more of a Neanderthal grunt and whine of exasperation.

The nurse looked over her glasses and said, "I think they've been waiting for you."

Jim was back by then, and we asked about pacemakers and drugs, and he seemed annoyed that we delayed him. Then he said, "Wait and see," and I must have blurted a rude retort. We had a tense moment.

Finally, I broke the Mexican standoff and said, "I know you're busy and have other patients, but this is *your job*. You come in everyday, park your car, go to work, talk to friends, eat lunch, see these kids, and then YOU GET TO GO HOME. We don't know if we will ever get to go home, we don't get to go home tonight. Instead, we sit here all day in this one spot waiting for you to come and answer our questions. We don't even leave to eat in case we might miss you. We can't go to the bathroom unless the other one is here to wait for you in case we miss you. I'm sorry you think we're being impatient, but all we ever do is wait."

The doctor softened a little and said they would try caffeine tonight, and he put orders in with the nurse. Maybe it would stimulate Liam's heart enough that his rhythm would stabilize and we might get off the pacer. So, I got what I wanted—a plan. It wasn't much of a plan, but it was a step forward, and that helped me sleep after a full day of going nowhere.

Days came and went, and the caffeine helped enough that they took the pacer lines out of Liam. On Labor Day, the doctors surprised us at rounds by telling us we could go home. Even though Liam's heart was still weak, it was finally beating "regularly," which was more important than its weakness. We left the hospital with our son and new drugs for the weakness, and a couple more to prevent pneumonia and swelling.

The swelling subsided, and Liam's sinus node conduction returned. We had to see Dr. Sondheimer that same week and once a week for the foreseeable future, as if there was such a thing as a foreseeable future. Still, the doctors were hopeful that Liam's heart would improve as he had more time to recover from the surgery. A pacemaker and a surgery to "install" it was still a possibility, but no one was rushing to make that irreversible decision. On the other hand, we rushed out the door as fast as we could.

14
Picking Up a Fourth Passenger in the Game of Life

While we were in the CICU in August and September for Liam's Glenn in 2003, at least one nurse was constantly walking, holding, or feeding Baby Joseph, a roommate who had traveled much like Liam had the first time, thousands of miles on his own to find hope. Unlike Liam, no one followed Joseph. His parents couldn't afford to come and had another newborn baby at home who was being breast-fed. Joseph was shuttled halfway across the country to have surgery and recover all alone. He left us all brokenhearted.

One day, we left Liam's room to talk and walk visiting family to the parking garage. When I got back to the room, a volunteer was holding Liam, and I was livid. Not at the volunteer or the nurse who called him for help in a room full of crying babies, but at myself.

The volunteers were there for the stranded and abandoned children, children like Joseph. I left Liam for fifteen minutes, not for a death-defying surgery. I set myself apart and above from the parents who weren't there all day, every day, even as I felt guilty for going back to the RMH to sleep at night. I was full of myself.

When Joseph joined us in the step-down unit, watching him sit there eating cheerios alone in his highchair, I said, "I can't believe his mother could let him go, even if she had another baby. I would have left the healthy baby at home."

Oh, sweet Irony. Every time in my life that I get judgmental and arrogant, my guardian, Irony, is there to remind me to mind my own damned business. What a picture perfect memory of when, despite seeing my own baby through two open-heart surgeries, I still lacked the humility to leave well enough alone. Within sixteen months I'd be wearing Joseph's mother's shoes and I'd wear them on opposite feet, but walk in them no better than she did.

I hope wherever Joseph is today, that he is a happy eight-year-old and has no memory of those lonely days when parents in two states ached for his exile. I hope for his mother's sake that she has all the love I could not spare for her before I knew what it really meant to choose between your children.

When Liam got home from the Glenn, his head ached constantly because of the strange changes to his blood pressure caused by the redirection of his blood flow. Now instead of an inefficient and overtaxed pump (his heart) the spent blood in Liam's upper body drained downward to his lungs and the pressure was building up in his head.

The change in pressure made his head throb with too much blood volume, so we elevated his crib to keep his head up. Eventually, he adapted and returned to his happy little self in a few more weeks. They were very long weeks.

We went home, and Liam spent autumn healing. By the beginning of November, his sternum had healed and his wounds became scars. From fall until spring, Liam endured painful monthly Synagis shots to prevent RSV. RSV is respiratory syncytial virus, and it hospitalizes even the healthiest babies every winter, scaring lungs and causing lifelong asthma in some, death in others. RSV would be deadly to Liam's compromised respiratory system.

Despite the monthly shots, life went on. We had a fabulous first Halloween with Liam in his little bat suit. We did family photos, and in the very beginning of November, Liam got off of oxygen! It was a fabulous moment for me, not only because there would be no more Apria man who had seventeen octogenarians on his route and one tiny baby that caused him to enter our house under a veil of pity, but because of the appointment itself.

We had a medical student. I truly love medical students. They are always the smartest and most ambitious kids in their elementary, middle, and high schools. They're the smartest kids in their undergraduate programs, and they are just the smartest things that ever walked the earth. Most of them are friendly, bright, eager and full of questions, but not this medical student.

This medical student took Liam's pulse ox and it was, for the first time since we left sea level, over eighty. Jim and I were dancing with our little blue baby, but she looked at us like we were crazy. We said, to each other, not to her, "Maybe Dr. Sondheimer will let us get rid of the oxygen."

This medical student frowned and said, "I don't think so," in her most condescending voice, which called Dr. Doom to mind.

We cast off her wet blanket with joy and elation when Dr. Sondheimer came in the room, looked at the number, and threw his thumb back like a hitchhiker. "Loose the oxygen."

Double bliss! The biggest part, besides losing the oxygen, was ditching the tether that brought painful and unwelcome comments from strangers, and kept me from being able to pick up my child with ease. The bonus bliss was the look on this girl's face when she realized, possibly for the first time in her life, that she didn't know everything, and maybe there are numerous lessons in life that haven't found their way into a text book. She huffed through the rest of Liam's exam, but we beamed.

As November brought shorter days, I noticed that my milk was down to about twenty-two ounces a day. It was exactly enough for Liam, where a mere two months earlier I was making eighty ounces a day. I figured this is what people talked about with their milk drying up, and I kept pumping every four hours to try to keep those twenty-two ounces.

My period was late, but it was late the previous month, and I figured it was more of the same. I waited about seven days, and remembered that I had an extra pregnancy test in my filing cabinet at work from the late cycle the month before. I decided what the hell, and brought the test down to the women's locker room when I got to work that morning. Instantly, a glaring and bright plus sign stared back at me.

I was pregnant. I was shocked. Clearly, after thirteen months of trying and failing to get pregnant the year before, I knew how these things could happen, eventually. The first time I got pregnant, I wasn't breast-feeding like a dairy cow. After the brutal C-section, taking care of a new baby with so many medical needs, and going back to work, Jim and I weren't getting "marital" very often, so, I was shocked to be pregnant.

I hadn't gone back on the pill because I didn't want it to interfere with my milk production. We had decided we wanted another baby eventually, only we didn't think eventually would be so soon.

After work, I went home, pumped what I could, and decided how I would tell Jim. I went through a box and found Liam's pregnancy test and wrote his name on the back with a Sharpie. The tests were both the same purple and white sticks. Then, I brought one downstairs in each hand with one concealed behind my back.

Jim was on the floor playing with Liam, and I held out Liam's stick. "What do you think we should do with this?"

Jim smiled at our adorable little boy, who was barely six months old. "Oh, I thought you wanted to keep that. Aren't we going to keep it?"

"OK, well, what should I do with this one, then?" I held out the second stick.

It took him a second to realize that two sticks meant two babies. He stood up from the floor, then sat right back down on the arm of the chair. He tried to stand again, but went right back down. Jim was as shocked as I was. Thankfully, as the shock wore off, the happiness set in.

We were so excited for this brother or sister. We were excited to get a second chance at the fun pregnancy and expectations we'd lost halfway through the last time. Foolishly or optimistically, we didn't discuss the possibility of having another baby with a heart problem at first.

Congenital heart defects happen in 1 in 100 births. Six in one thousand are life-threatening at birth. Half of those are as complex as Liam's, meaning a little more than a quarter million Americans are living with half-hearts, and that's not counting the ones who didn't make it.

But, only one in a million babies has the exact kind of clusterfuck found inside my child's chest, so we took comfort in the obscurity of Liam's "last page in the freehand drawing book" status. In our denial of recurrence, we allowed ourselves stunned excitement. We decided, however, not to tell people right away, which was a challenge for a blurter like me.

It took a few weeks to get into the doctor. I didn't want to go back to the clinic where I'd seen the midwives. There were too many painful memories. There'd been too little follow up or reading of my chart, and they hadn't supported my choice to fight for Liam, or respected my fight.

The hands that had literally touched Liam's heart were the most gifted on the planet, and I was a certifiable doctor snob. A friend of mine who had survived ovarian cancer was in love with her OB/GYN for saving her life, so I decided that was where I would go.

When I called and told the receptionist I had a positive test, she scheduled me four weeks out. So I had my first OB appointment in early December after breaking the good news to family and friends at Thanksgiving. It was almost a year since devastation had flooded over our lives, and now we were full of hope.

At that first appointment, Dr. Cloyd pressed on my stomach, got out the Doppler, and said, "You are not eight weeks pregnant." He rolled in the ultrasound machine for a quick look. "You're at least ten weeks pregnant. I want you to go to the hospital for a full screening."

We were nervous and explained more about Liam, which he already knew about because he had actually read my chart. Imagine that! Dr. Cloyd explained there was now a one in ten chance our new baby would have a heart defect. We had to ask him to repeat that. We didn't realize that having a baby with a broken heart elevated the risk for subsequent babies, but it does.

He had plans in place for more detailed screenings in Denver at eighteen and twenty weeks, so he had our backs, and that felt good.

We were nervous when we went to the hospital for the ultrasound. The tech dated the baby's measurements at thirteen weeks, not the eight weeks I thought I was. So, back in October, I was pregnant. I have no idea what the three days of heavy bleeding were about, but I'm glad I didn't know because I would have freaked out.

I had pretty much missed my entire first trimester, most of it unaware I was even pregnant. Had I known, I wouldn't have drunk way too much Australian champagne at my sister-in-law's wedding and topped it off with a wonderful performance on the dance floor to the B52's "Love Shack." I remember being tired, but I suspected it was only because I was a new mom. Adding to that, I'd drunk obscene amounts of Diet Pepsi, and at the height of my pumping, I ate most of an entire package of Oreos and still was losing weight. I took prenatal vitamins because of all the pumping, but other than that, I hadn't taken care of myself at all. The guilt was immediate and substantial.

Our androgynous fetus quickly became he/she, and then we nicknamed it Sushi. Just like with Liam, I was desperate to know the gender because I wanted another boy. I wanted Liam to have a best friend who could stand up for him later in life. I also wanted to reuse all those adorable clothes in the same season. A boy just felt right. Another boy barely a year behind his brother, how perfect would that be?

But, Sushi wasn't giving up the goods. The first peek we got after that first ultrasound was the Level 2 ultraound at University Medical Center in Denver when Sushi was eighteen weeks along. The legs were up and the jig was not. The perinatologist told us how healthy our baby looked, and of course we had to go to cardiology at Children's for an echocardiogram to make sure the heart was as well-formed as it seemed. We would be doing that between weeks twenty and twenty-two.

Everything at the echo was perfect, and the likelihood of any abnormalities forming that late in the pregnancy was highly unlikely. The only disappointment this pregnancy would deliver was a prolonged but impermanent androgyny. Compared to the alternative, androgyny was entirely tolerable. Androgyny was beautiful.

Even though the kind tech in cardiology tried to get a look, he was only sixty percent certain Sushi might be a girl, and suggested refraining from buying anything yet.

Honestly, having been through what I'd experienced with Liam, I didn't care that much about the gender. I wanted to know because I'm snoopy. At the Children's Hospital, where the people treating us usually only see catastrophes like Liam's heart, this was probably a great day for them as much as it was for us. They got to see a perfect heart, and that perfect heart was inside my belly. I had no reason to be upset about not knowing Sushi's gender.

However, in the seven weeks that I knew I was pregnant with this child, all the time building up to a clean bill of heart health was riddled with fear. Now that I knew Sushi's heart was healthy, my own heart sank, not for the baby inside me, but for the baby beside me in the room. Liam wasn't even a year old, and he was sitting in his stroller next to the exam table.

When it was just Liam and us, there was no comparison. We had no healthy child in our home. Liam's delays were not quantified or qualified against anyone else. If a book caused me doubt, I shut it. A new child would be present and permanent, and I couldn't ignore the differences growing right in front of me. In the shadow of Sushi's health, Liam was going to be "our sick one," where before he was our only one. It seemed so much more real than it had before.

This healthy baby in my body now provided the glaring contrast of what could never be for Liam—what never was. He was never alive a day in his life that he didn't have to fight for, and I was conflicted. I felt guilty about feeling guilty. What about Sushi?

How was I going to be a parent to a normal healthy child when I was a Heart Mom? How was I going to be a good mom to both of my babies? How could I ever be fair when the world never was? Of course, *of course*, we were happy for Sushi, relieved for that healthy heart, but it was anticlimactic and painful in the light it cast on the reality of our lives and the uncertainty of our futures for all four of us. But the future came whether we were ready for it or not, and after all of that, we were approaching Liam's first birthday.

During Liam's first year, I saved months worth of empty baby food jars and went to Hobby Lobby to buy candle-fixin's. I spent two weekends melting wax over wicks to form party favors. Each meal Liam had eaten was a miracle and a blessing marked in his hard-fought life. I wanted him to have hundreds of birthday candles.

Liam's actual birthday was celebrated at Jim's parents' house, where Liam smeared green dragon frosting all over his beautiful pudgy face. The *big* party was the following weekend. We rented a picnic area in City Park on a warm and sunny day, and family came from three states to attend. We served a huge white cake with red frosting, and filled the pavilion with red heart-shaped balloons.

The seeds of my advocacy, sewn the previous August, were sprouting that spring when one hundred and thirty people came to celebrate the life that almost wasn't. Instead of bringing gifts, we asked Liam's guests to donate money to the Children's Hospital Heart Institute. People brought presents anyway, but we raised over $1,200 to help the hospital. We gave back in gratitude for what we'd received.

May 5th was a perfect day, exactly one year since we'd left PSL without a baby and were about to embark on this difficult adventure. It was a perfect day, being here with Liam and all of our friends, as if we'd never gone through hell to get there. It was cathartic for us to see people who'd followed Liam's story, to feel so much love and support, and to know that our hope was larger than the past seventeen months since that dark winter day when my life fell apart. That Saturday in the park was a high point, and every pinnacle can become a precipice from which to fall. The January before Sushi was born, Liam was still very stable. We went four full months between appointments. The longest we'd gone between appointments since Liam's birth was two months at a time, and that was just November to January.

On May 28, Liam, at age thirteen months, finally crawled. A few days before Liam crawled, Laurie, one of my Hypoplastic Right Hearts (HRH) support group friends, took her son Kolbey in for his Fontan (the last of the three surgeries we were expecting). Kolbey was two and a half when he had his Fontan, and Laurie had all the normal anxieties that accompany the entirely abnormal experience of handing your child over for a third open heart surgery in less than three years. The whole HRH group was on pins and needles while Kolbey was under the knife.

His surgery seemed to go well until everything went wrong. After a massive stroke, Laurie and her husband had to make a decision. It was May 28th, the same day Liam finally learned to crawl. That day in my townhouse, I was elated with my crawling baby, that night I was devastated by my friend's enormous loss. So it is with CHD, so it is with the company we keep.

Kolbey was still on my mind when Liam's cardiology reprieve was up and we went for an appointment. It turned out that Liam's Glenn failed to deliver the expected effect. It turned out that the rerouted pulmonary arteries designed to drain blood to his lungs didn't grow enough to supply sufficient oxygen to his body. His oxygen saturation was dropping.

Dr. Sondheimer's response was to schedule Liam for a heart catheterization in July to check his arteries more closely. Either Liam would have an angioplasty procedure to expand the artery to improve blood flow, or he would have to have his third surgery (the Fontan) much sooner than we hoped, or expected. While we waited between the May appointment and the July heart catheterization, I simply had to have another baby.

A few weeks after his May cardiology appointment, Liam was no longer an only child. The day Sushi got a real name was June 10,

2004, a day I chose because it was a Thursday. I'd get a day of rest while everyone was at work, before they'd swarm the hospital, or so I thought. They all showed up anyway!

That morning the first thing I noticed was the relaxed nature of checking me into my fancy room at the hospital. This was the room I thought I'd be in when giving birth to Liam the year before. The labor and delivery room was beautiful and full of warm woods, and it would have been wonderful to have used it. But it was only a pit stop before heading to the sterile OR for a C-section.

After the pain of the first C-section, I decided that with the likelihood of VBAC failing, it was better to skip the labor and go straight to the scalpel. So, I waddled to the OR carrying my Foley catheter bag like a purse—looking ever so glamorous. I got my spinal, which was similar but far more effective than the epidural. Then I grew nauseous from the opiates, and they pumped in several anti-nausea meds, upping it each time I burped.

Dr. Cloyd and Dr. King were there. They played relaxing music, which was surreal for me because there was no fear. Even Liam's pediatrician, Dr. O'Leary, happened to be the doctor on call that day. After the roller coaster of our last birthing experience, Jim and I couldn't tolerate the calm, and we began to wonder why it was taking so long.

Liam's C-section took less than five minutes. Literally, I was in my labor and delivery room at 7:00 P.M. and his birth in the OR was at 7:05 P.M. Why was this taking more than forty-five minutes? They laughed at us. This is how long they're supposed to take.

Dr. Cloyd casually mentioned that if I wanted a third child, I'd have to have a scheduled C-section at thirty-seven weeks because my uterine wall was too thin—it was the only time in my life any part of my body was deemed too thin. As it turned out, I was wise to trust my gut because going into labor could have killed me. And here I thought I had no intuition.

When Sushi's head was out, we asked if it was a boy or girl. The doctor's didn't answer, as they were busy pulling one human from another human. Once the whole baby was out, Dr. Cloyd's forearm blocked our view of all but its head. Jim shouted, "It's a boy, he looks JUST like Liam!"

Dr. Cloyd laughed.

Sushi was shi-she—and instantly became Moira Rose Adams. I cried at her voice as I had cried at her brother's birth. Shortly after my initial recovery, which happened much more quickly than the last time, Moira and I were reunited in a three-day slumber party.

When I wasn't holding Moira, she was in her little bassinet, like the one Liam never touched. I was in and out of bed far more easily than I imagined possible, attending to my precious little girl.

Us. Together. Me with Moira nested in my arms, watching Court TV all night. Me giving her back to the nurse for a couple of hours in the nursery so I could sleep. Moira back with me. We tried breast-feeding, it didn't go well. Even though I wasn't a new mother, I'd never been able to nurse Liam.

Everything else was so ridiculously normal. They took Moira's photo before we left the hospital. I ordered birth announcements. She came home from the hospital before her umbilical stump came off. She came home without oxygen. She'd never had oxygen.

Moira was normal.

I didn't recognize normal. Normal felt so foreign from what I knew. The hardest part of normal was the biological conditioning I developed with Liam. I negotiated phantom oxygen cords and IV lines when lifting Moira from her bed at the hospital and at home. These were never part of her life, but they were an integral part of my maternal training, along with supporting the neck.

Even now, years later if I pick up an infant, I am cognizant of historic tubes that I might catch on a rail or a chair if I'm not cautious. Something happened in my maternal imprinting that left me damaged by shadows of what was my own unique experience. I'm still trailing tubes and lines.

Moira was different from Liam. Liam was very tired and had a hospital at his disposal if he ever woke up. Moira cried all the time unless she was held, and because I was trying to nurse her, it was all on me.

She only fell asleep on her stomach, so I would sneak in and flip her on her back in due diligence against crib death. This meant a good fifteen to twenty minute wait after a feeding before I could sleep. It was hard because we didn't want her to wake up Liam and have two babies up in the middle of the night. It was hard because I was weary. It was harder than it needed to be because I didn't cut Moira any slack. She was healthy, so why was she making me suffer?

The first week of Moira's life, I was tired, constipated (thank you, spinal), frustrated, and angry at myself. She wouldn't latch on, she was jaundiced, and she screamed because she was starving. The only food she got was the milk I pumped. I finally gave up nursing and went back to the pump.

Those twenty-six months between Liam's birth and Moira's first birthday included three open-heart surgeries. I didn't have time to prioritize physical closeness or worry about regret. I was still on maternity leave when we were back at Children's Hospital with Liam.

Liam's cath was scheduled for July 9th. We didn't know exactly *what* would happen during the procedure, only that he needed it because his oxygen saturation was dropping too far too fast. The night of July 8th, we left Moira—not even a full month old—with my mom overnight so we could get up early and head to the hospital the next morning.

The three hardest parts about signing your one-year-old over for a heart cath are what goes on before the procedure: your child can't eat (and so if you're a halfway decent parent, neither do you—or at least not in front of your kid), signing the form that acknowledges risk of stroke, etc., and after the doctors are done and you've just absorbed whatever they've learned is going on inside your child. Then you have to convince your very small child to lay flat as a pancake and not so much as wiggle. If the child moves too much, the big puncture in the femoral artery that allowed the catheter into the body might "pop" its clot. Popping a clot can kill you as the blood rushes out of the artery. Flat. As. A. Pancake.

During the cath we worried. It was possible that if the angioplasty or coiling collateral (extra) veins didn't improve Liam's oxygen saturation, the huge Fontan surgery would come next. The doctors also brought the catheter into Liam's liver to check its health. Oh the liver, one more vital organ to fail if the heart falls into inefficiency, next come the kidneys, then . . . well, "then" is a bad place to visit. So we waited and we worried.

The cath procedure itself went well other than a leaky IV. Dr. Chan and Dr. Chang ended up killing off collateral venous growth. I asked if they used coils, and the calm doctors actually laughed. They said that the opening in the collateral growth was so large they had to use a platinum plug, there weren't coils enough to pinch that off.

Essentially, Liam's body didn't like what Dr. Starnes and Dr. Lacour-Gayet did to it, and decided to create its own re-plumbing project. This isn't uncommon, which is why I'd heard about it already. Without my HRH support group, though, it would have been foreign to me. So this cath bought us time by bringing Liam's oxygen sats back up closer to eighty percent.

To keep Liam docile after the cath, we found a tiny stuffed bear he'd brought and slid it down the inside of a curved vomit catcher over, and over, and over again—necessity is, indeed, the mother of invention.

Liam loved the idea of sliding. He'd prop the large throw pillows at home against the couch and slide down. Being barely one year old, Liam couldn't say "wee," so he said, "beeeee," and he said "beee" over and over again with his croaky extubated baby voice, though parched cracked lips, each time the bear took a slide down the vomit pan.

The nurses could not let him eat or drink, lest he throw up and need the bear's slide, and worse, pop the clot. So we stood there for nearly four hours in that dark, dim room sliding the bear in the barf bowl, singing "beee," and creating a beautiful memory from the shitty scraps of our lives. We built up our hope that things would get better, not worse.

Liam had to stay overnight because the IV had leaked and heparin (a blood thinner) had infiltrated his skin and muscle tissue. Fortunately, my mom had breast milk in her freezer and enough diapers to keep Moira for an extra day. We didn't know yet to always pack a toothbrush when heading to the cath lab because it's more common to stay over than go home.

The next morning, when I wondered down to the bleak cafeteria to get some food for Jim and myself, I was overcome by the date. It was July 10, and Moira was exactly one month old. I hadn't seen my newborn daughter for the better part of two days. It seemed the florescent lightening grew dimmer with my darkening mood. I missed my daughter who was an hour away, I worried for my son who was upstairs waiting for a plastic surgeon to verify he didn't have an internal chemical burn, and those were both the least of my worries. I was deflated and worn and the cafeteria tray seemed to weigh me down, but I bought bananas and a Diet Pepsi and trudged back to the elevator.

We saw Dr. Sondheimer again a few weeks later, who proclaimed that Liam was stable from the cath intervention. But by January, Liam's oxygen sats were down even farther again, and surgery was imminent. And this time it was big time. Beeeee!

15

What are You Waiting For? . . .
Living with Anticipatory Grief

After Liam was born, I routinely awoke in the middle of the night with back spasms. The chiropractor's x-ray showed my right hip was an inch and a half higher than my left. After one adjustment, I found out I was pregnant with Moira and discontinued my treatments. Following Moira's birth my back was even worse.

I was a mess, and Dr. Cross was my hero. At first I was in as often as twice a week, leaving work at 4:00 to head across town to her office. On these journeys I listened to a lot of NPR.

I remember a story about a couple whose young son went through hospice care. In the same bed where this little boy was conceived, he died in his parents' embrace. It hit way too close to home. That could have been us—it still could be us if things went badly. We escaped that fate, but Liam still faced more surgeries.

I drove across Fort Collins with tears streaming down my face. I parked the car, blew my nose into a fast food napkin, and did my best to get myself together before getting my back adjusted. I was in a perpetual state of adjustment.

On a different trip to the chiropractor, Michele Norris interviewed writer and Army wife, Kristin Henderson. Henderson wrote the book, *While They're Away*, which was about profiling military families suffering anticipatory grief. I'd never heard this term before, and was intrigued. She talked about how mothers, wives, children, and husbands of soldiers combated their own home front fears of loss, and I recognized this fear. I am not a military mom, but a Heart Mom faces similar fears in battling for her child's survival.

Anticipatory grief is a concept that comes from end of life psychology. But for military families and heart families, it's not the textbook case. Anticipatory grief for someone caring for a terminally ill Alzheimer's, AIDS, or cancer patient is the process of preparing for the ultimate separation. However, for those of us in the position where our loved one might or might not die, anticipatory grief is a false start to a terrifying, but uncertain, possibility.

That NPR story didn't leave me in tears, it left me in awe. Finally, there was a name for what we were enduring with Liam! The fears I bore, which everyone tried to assuage or minimize, were real and there was a label for my state. It was a revolutionary moment.

That was the first time I realized I was grieving not only for my lost expectations, which were clearly dead, but for the potential loss of my child. It was the first time I could stop and say, "No, this actually makes sense." I was angry and depressed for a reason. It wasn't all in my imagination. I wasn't crazy, I was just grieving.

Of course all those times when I was grieving and angry, I didn't rationalize or process it that way. I always felt crazy, but that one story on NPR and that wonderful Army wife gave me a priceless gift. There might be a way back to well-adjusted, and it started on my way to the chiropractor's office. Thank you, Kristin Henderson.

As the summer of 2004 faded away and the mornings were cooler and cooler, I found myself on the floor of Liam's new room in our new house putting his shorts and summer clothes into a box. The afternoons were still hot, and my legs sweated behind my bent knees, my shins sweated against the carpet, and the carpet left lumpy patterns in my skin.

I knew, by then, that another major heart surgery was forthcoming, and I thought it would be the Fontan. My sorrow for Kolbey assaulted me like the dying flies of autumn, and sweat ran down my face. As I picked up and folded each tiny pair of shorts, my motions brought me closer and closer to tears.

Finally, I cracked and started sobbing into that box of clothes. I wondered if I would ever get them out again. Unlike other mothers, I didn't wonder if my little boy might be too big to wear any of them in nine months, but if he would even be alive next year. I put all my hope for another summer with Liam in the box, and I put the box on the shelf at the top of his closet.

I also cried like that the Christmas of 2002, when I packed up all the "having a baby" ornaments, specifically the tiny harlequin patterned stocking with "Dad" embroidered in gold thread across the top that I'd prematurely bought for Jim. I wondered and worried if I'd see those ornaments in joy or in sorrow when another Christmas came.

So it was with many seasons, that I couldn't simply shift from one to the next without trepidation that this would be the last summer or fall or Christmas with Liam. I still can't take that Dad ornament out without remembering how I was drenched with fear when I first put it away. I wish I could say I'm over it, but I'm still afraid, not so much of losing Liam, but of expecting him to be here. I'm afraid if I get complacent, the cosmic forces that let me keep him will think I'm too full of myself and snatch him back. It's not a rational fear, like the fear I felt before surgery. It's just that once the first shoe dropped and the fight to save Liam was so brutal, it struck me as insanely wise to keep my expectations in check.

Here is the quintessential difference between hope and expectation. Unlike Heart Moms, regular parents have regular hopes and expectations. You might hope your child makes the basketball team, wins the prize at the piano recital, goes to Harvard, or doesn't make too many stupid choices in high school.

You might expect that your child will graduate high school at the very least. You expect your child will wake up every morning, or even from a nap, and will eventually be an adult who, if he/she is willing, will give you grandchildren. You expect your child will outlive you, and well you should.

If you're a Heart Mom, you don't expect a damned thing. You hope your child will wake up in the morning, will grow up and out-live you. You hope when your kid says he's tired and goes to take a nap that he's not going to die, because that's not an urban myth—it happens all the time.

The terrifying nap stories like, "Janie said she was tired, she took a nap and never woke up," are ubiquitous in the world of heart parents. Other parents are dying for their kids to take a nap, we're praying for ours to stay awake.

All that stuff like Harvard, sports, etc. would just be icing on the cake. When you're a Heart Mom you don't have the luxury of expectation. If you expect anything at all, it's only the worst, FBI style.

For a long time after Liam was born, I would hear "Tears in Heaven" on the radio and wonder if I would play that at Liam's funeral. My mind would wander, and I would wonder who would come to Liam's funeral, where we would have it, would it be sunny when he died?

It wasn't a sick fantasy. I felt tortured and haunted by these images of losing my son and it took years to shake them off. Even now they find me when I think they've lost my trail. I want so badly to drift off to sleep at night imagining Liam in high school, in college. I want to imagine him planning my funeral when we were both so old, it is a natural thing to do. That would be the normal thing to expect, but Heart Moms don't get great expectations, we just take what we can get. All we can do is get through to the next moment.

The weeks working up to the Fontan, and remembering Kolbey who died ten months before, I was so panicked and paralyzed. I was terrified and saw death everywhere. My paranoia, depression, and anger were all fighting to control me, and I was in a chaotic state of detachment for everything and everyone.

Then one day, about two weeks before the surgery, I walked into my bedroom and had an epiphany. Truly, a light washed over me, and a voice inside my head proclaimed, "You have done everything you can do. If Liam is going to die, you cannot stop it. There is nothing more to do but love him, and in this state, you can't even do that."

I knew at that moment it was time to let go. I wanted to be a whole person again.

Of course in the weeks, months, and years that followed, I still had the rational fear of losing my child to this disease. But I was never as paralyzed by it as I was for those two years. From first learning of Liam's broken heart and finally surrendering myself to the fact that as long as I was diligent in caring for him, I needed to take comfort in the fact there was nothing more I could do. Liam's ultimate survival was never up to me and it would never be. I simply had to keep marching.

That self-actualization was so liberating and healing. There was nothing more I could do, and by avoiding that truth, I was missing out on the good stuff. I was missing Liam every day because I was so terrified of losing him forever. And it wasn't just Liam—I was missing out on Moira's milestones, too. I was missing the very point of living because I was steeped in my fear of death.

Trapped and twisted up in that fear, "What if he died?" it never occurred to me before that day, "What if he lives?"

What if Liam didn't die, and I couldn't remember a single joyful moment from either of my kids' childhoods because all of my memories were tainted with ugly shadows of impenetrable fear? So, armed with my new freedom, I marched forward, because we had to, there was never any other way to go. That didn't mean it was easy, but I kept marching.

16
Informed Consent

Before Liam's third open-heart surgery, I was a wreck. I wrote sad angry poems. I was terrified. I demonstrated every extreme emotion rooted in a very rational fear for my child's life even as I smiled at my babies and tried to present a façade of strength to the people around me. I was a building shifting sand, appearing solid on the outside but crumbling inside. Even as I relinquished my illusions of control, the ground beneath me continued to move.

I was living the Fontan Fear, and I've yet to meet a mother who's had to sign her child over for that third colossal surgery who didn't feel it to very marrow of her bones. It's the ultimate expression of anticipatory grief, and the only way past it is straight through.

The Fontan.

It's an event no parent but a heart parent can imagine. By the time of the Fontan, about fifteen to twenty-five percent of kids like Liam are already dead. The statistics are always changing and the mortality rate depends on when in time you measure. Hope has a mortality rate, too, but if you make it to the Fontan, it's a last stand of sorts.

The Fontan is the make-or-break, do-or-die surgery. It's the event we've all been waiting for. The Fontan is the Promised Land where your blue baby will assume a pink pallor.

This is the third stage that necessitated the first two. The first two times they ripped your baby's chest open to reset the time bomb were dress rehearsals. This is the bomb squad trying to buy you years, maybe a decade, maybe three before you have to do this again.

Three stages.

This is the last hop on the lily pad to the rest of your life—all you have to do is give informed consent. Don't worry, there's only a five percent chance your child will die today by the combination of your hand on this pen and the surgeon's hand on his scalpel.

I call it Mount Fontan, and I have been counseled at the foot by a few wise mama Sherpas who surmounted it, only to come back down and prepare my successors. It's a mountain you start climbing the moment your child is diagnosed; it's the last hope, the final frontier, the land of milk and honey, the Garden of Eden that lies on the other side of Hell. For select Heart Moms and dads, it's the closest you will ever get to a normal life, if your child lived long enough to get here. Nearly a fourth of them don't.

Now that you've made that climb, these last few steps are a doozy. Hold on tight and try to keep your lungs from jumping out your throat and your heart from exploding from the pressure cooker of hope that everything is going to be OK, and the monumental fear that it's not.

We were told Liam would have his Fontan at age three, around thirty pounds. He was about twenty seven pounds, and not even two, but his heart was strained and under too much internal pressure. His arteries were constricted, and his future was bleak. We were cresting the peak.

In that haze of emotion, the surreal dream-like state of anticipatory grief for what might happen to turn my life into a nightmare, I was raw and I was, at times, uncharacteristically catatonic. When I did speak, I cried about how scared I was, and more than once people told me things like, "Any of us could be killed in a car accident on the way home."

Ah yes, the beer truck scenario—you could be struck by lightning, hit by a beer truck, die in a terrible accident. The Lightening Truck Accident, that's what I call it. All those threats have better odds against them than the five percent risk to my Liam's life, for which I must sign a form and accept the consequences. I'm glad it's down from twenty percent to five, but still it's not the same thing.

Yes, I might swim in the ocean and get bit by a shark, but I didn't offer the shark my leg to save the rest of my body. I had to put Liam through the torture of yet another open-heart surgery, risk his life again to save it again. We were still trying to save his life. . . and this time, oh this time he would be there, fully present.

Of course, he was there at two weeks old, at three months old, but now he talked. Now Liam called me, "Mommy." Now Liam walked and ran as much as his heart allowed. Now, he liked cars and trains and his Huggy Buggy books. He knew his colors and counted to ten. He had favorite toys, and his voice was more than the rebel yell of a newborn baby, it was the voice of my companion, my little buddy, my baby, my life, my very hope and love embodied in this little blond boy. Liam was my everything, and I had to hand him over and sign a form that said essentially, "I know that you might kill him trying to save him, but do it anyway." What other choice did I have?

Informed consent meant that Jim and I were going to let a team of strangers shove a tube down Liam's throat and silence that sweet voice that said "Mommy" and "Daddy." We were going to let these masked men and women place cuts in his jugular vein and carotid artery to run lines straight into his heart, pack his head and body in ice, cut through those crystalline scars on his little chest, saw the bone through, again, and unhinge his core.

We were signing over the right for them to hang Liam, our only son, down the deep well of death by a thin wire threaded through his body and connected to a heart-lung machine and slowly stop Liam's heart and slow his brain. Then, and only then, would this man we met only in this surreal place they call a hospital, cut into Liam's heart for a third time to remove the veins that God put there, the only ones He put in the right place, because everything else was so impossibly wrong.

Informed consent meant that not only were we going to let these people do these brutal things to our son's body, we were going to be god-damned grateful for it. God damn it . . . I'd rather be struck by lightning — it would hurt less and not last so long.

But this was my choice, in not signing a DNC form when I was pregnant or a DNR form when Liam was born, I was forced to sign form after form after form to arrive at the Mount Fontan and to let them try their best with this valiant act to save my child, yet again.

How could I complain, how dare I complain about the battle with so many lost along the way? I had to find my spine, but please, don't put this in the same class as a car accident. It's something else entirely; it's informed consent.

17

A Change of Plans

On February 2, 2005 I started Liam's CarePage, a medical blog for patients and families. Before the CarePage I'd sent blanket e-mails to family and friends about what was happening in our Liam-lives. Now I had a blog. On February 7th, we went in for another pre-op with Dr. Lacour-Gayet. This is what I wrote on Liam's CarePage:

"Well, we're officially freaked out. We just met with Dr. Lacour-Gayet, and it's a 50/50 shot that Liam will have a pulmonary artery repair and a Fontan or just a pulmonary artery repair tomorrow with the Fontan next year. He won't know until he gets in there.

"Liam has had every invasive and non-invasive pre-surgical diagnostic procedure done in the past ten days, and they still don't know exactly what's causing his left pulmonary artery to be half the size it needs to be. If it's viable, they'll correct it and proceed with the Fontan tomorrow. If it's not viable, they'll patch that critter up like no one's business and wait a year.

"So, there's a big chance that the Fontan might not be the best route tomorrow, which means four surgeries instead of one, but a failed Fontan means at least five surgeries—an extra one to take it down right away and another one to put it back when the pulmonary artery is stable. Aren't you glad you're not us right now?"

This time, Lacour-Gayet had reviewed the MRI of Liam's heart, Liam's cath results, and many echocardiograms. Liam's case went to surgical review with the cardiology staff twice. This wasn't going to be as simple or straightforward as the Glenn.

Lacour-Gayet told us plan A was to not perform the Fontan on Wednesday, but rather he would splice open Liam's faulty pulmonary arteries, add Gortex, and make them bigger. I didn't know this until I read Liam's medical records years later, but this had already been done during the Glenn surgery eighteen months before, and the arteries were still too narrow.

If something was simply pinching the artery that the doctors couldn't see from the views they had through the cath and cardiac MRI, Lacour-Gayet would opt for Plan B by correcting the crimp and going ahead with the Fontan. He wouldn't know for sure, and we wouldn't know his choice until he was inside our son.

Essentially, door number one (Plan A) promised at least one more open-heart-surgery, and door two (Plan B) was risky and might fail if conditions were not perfect. We already knew conditions weren't perfect with Liam's constricted arteries elevating the blood pressures, causing collateral veins to grow, and driving his oxygen saturations down, but just how imperfect his arteries were was yet to be seen.

I ended that post with, "Now, it's in God's hands. Put in a good word for us."

I always asked for prayers and good thoughts for Liam, for the people we met in the hospital, for our nurse whose mother was ill, and for anyone and everyone who needed it from people who were safely ensconced in their own lives and not on our path. I'm not a religious person, but I was raised on a steady stream of parables and scripture, and I know Jesus loves me, so I don't mind asking for a favor or two.

On February 9th, Liam entered the OR at 7:30 A.M. Shortly after, it was discovered that both the left and right pulmonary arteries were too small to do the Fontan procedure. Unfortunately, this meant that Liam would endure another surgery in the coming year, after the corrected artery was fully healed and more operational. The surgical team closed Liam's chest around 4:00 P.M., so we sat in the waiting room from 7:00 A.M. - 4:00 P.M. waiting for that to happen. Waiting, and waiting, and waiting for the clock to reset and life to come back from the brink.

The upside to delaying the Fontan was less risk of failure, more time for Liam to grow to a better size for success, and the doctors expected a shorter recovery period. So we didn't expect to be in the hospital as long as the three weeks that Dr. Sondheimer predicted for this surgery. The downside was that Dr. Lacour-Gayet essentially redid Liam's Glenn, and we would still need to do the Fontan. This was a $150,000 dress rehearsal. But it was more than that. Liam was so blue before this surgery that he was at risk for organ failure. It was necessary. We never consented to anything that wasn't entirely necessary.

This surgery was supposed to be Liam's final surgery. It was supposed to be the Fontan. It became known at home as the Glenn-Again, it was the Fon-tempt.

We were ready for Liam's inferior vena cava to catch up with his superior brother at the pulmonary branch. We had every expectation of finishing the third stage, but it was not meant to be. You would think I'd have learned about managing my expectations. Alas, this expectation was pinned on the advice of highly-qualified doctors.

So, I call it the Fon-tempt because it was a Fontan that was attempted but failed and became the Glenn-Again. The Glenn surgery was essentially redone to make way for the real Fontan of the future and keep Liam alive long enough to recover and grow strong enough to do it one more time. Disappointed is one word for how we felt.

When we first saw Liam after the surgery I felt like the wickedest woman on earth. After his DKS he was waxy and white and swollen, intubated, and entirely unconscious. After his Glenn he was bright purple, and swollen, intubated, and entirely unconscious. After the Fon-tempt, he was Liam, almost two, and wide-awake with an angry tube up his nose and down his throat.

Liam looked at me pleadingly with tears running down the side of his face and cracking through the pasty mask of dried skin. He mouthed, "Mommy" while reaching up through his Betadine cloud for a mother who could not hold him. His body shook with his weeping, and I saw his convulsing caused his newly bound sternum to quiver in pain. I felt faint and it took everything I had not to cry in front of Liam. His tears were enough for the three of us.

The nurses told us to leave so they could sedate him— it was no good for him to be like that so soon after surgery. Mercifully, the drugs separated us, and we each hid on our sides of the fence that survival had necessitated. God, I never wanted to hold my child as much as that moment he cried that silent Mommy.

Liam is the only child I know who had a Fon-tempt, and I know hundreds who've had the Fontan. I personally know four who didn't survive the Fontan, and dozens through the grapevine who've died, too. I guess you could call all those deaths failed Fon-tempts.

I've also known, through the same CHD grapevine, of kids whose Fontans failed and had to be "taken down." Basically, after the trauma of a third open-heart surgery, they are so un-recoverably sick that they have a fourth open-heart surgery to set things back to the way they were before just to keep them alive a little longer. They can't really survive with just the Glenn, but they'll die faster with the bad Fontan.

You never ever want a Fontan take-down. It means your last hope has failed catastrophically, and other options are slim to transplant. The Fon-tempt was better than death and better than a take-down. The Fon-tempt was disappointing, like a bronze medal is disappointing. It wasn't the best, but it was far from the worst thing we could have faced, and we were still in the game.

18

Visiting Hours

Like the two previous major surgeries, Liam's recovery was an ebb and flow, and eventually we worked our way through scary but manageable postoperative complications. Tragically, with every long hospital stay we've experienced the death of a neighbor. This time it was Audrey.

I ran into Audrey's parents in the dining room at the RMH while they were eating up their leftovers before hitting the road to plan their only child's funeral.

This shit always happened, and it is shit—horrible, terrible shit that stains peoples' lives forever. And it's always happening to someone. It could have happened to us. Always, there is a memorial service flier in the elevator of the RMH, or a grieving family in the conference room across from the CICU, or priests and chaplains at these miniature bedsides. Always, lives were ending just after they began. And here it was happening to our neighbors, and here we were hoping we got through the Fon-tempt so we could come back in a year to try again.

It always happens, but I never get used to it.

I went to Safeway and bought Audrey's mom Sudafed, to help her stop her breast milk production, and a card. They had about twelve cards for the inevitable death of a pet, but only one for the unimaginable death of a child. Only one card to mark eight months of a baby girl's life. The same card you'd give a ninety-year-old woman who lost her seventy-year-old son. It wouldn't matter if there were a million cards, there are no words for that loss.

That was one of those moments when I wished I could curl up and die without any thought to what that meant. I was trapped in a moment when reason left the room to time and emotion—this time that room was the Hallmark aisle at a Safeway store.

Audrey was eight months old, and so was Moira. Her mother and I were both trying to stop producing milk that week, for totally different reasons.

All that pain and disappointment happening in the hospital and RMH around Liam's stalled recovery and Audrey's death, and we only saw Moira every fourth day. When my mom finally brought Moira to see us, we were waiting for Dr. Sondheimer to rehash the transplant talk.

We all met in the hallway halfway between Liam's room, where I was dying of guilt for leaving him there. Jim and I visited with Moira on the floor in the waiting area where we eventually got to meet Dr. Sondheimer. When he arrived, we had to talk seriously.

Moira watched us walk toward the chairs, and she started to wail. My mom had to take her around the corner so she couldn't see us. I was heart-broken to lose sight of her again so soon. Pulled into yet another painful medical discussion full of brutal honesty.

Dr. Sondheimer explained that if Liam didn't pull himself out of this slump, transplant would be the next option. His heart wasn't strong and he wasn't recovering as they had hoped. Liam's oxygen started out at sixty-six and was now down to sixty-two after all that. Nothing seemed to be going our way.

As I sat there listening to this man who was always so disarmingly upbeat, kind, and funny tell us that Liam needed to get better—as if we could will him to do so—I heard my other child crying for me, just out of sight. I wanted to comfort her, and for her to comfort me, but I was trapped on the couch, hearing things I didn't want to hear in the dulcet tones of a fatherly doctor punctuated by the primal wails of my eight-month old daughter.

When Dr. Sondheimer left, we slowly rose to go back to Moira, but my mom was anxious to leave. She and Doyle were meeting his son Eric and daughter-in-law Anita for dinner, and they were already late because of the traffic and then having to wait for Dr. Sondheimer with us.

I asked my mom if she could just leave Moira with us and get her on her way out of town after dinner, and my mom said, "Eric and Anita want to see her too."

My cracked heart now shattered on the carpet. I wanted so badly to steal my own child back. I wanted to scream, "They want to see her, what about me? I'm her goddamned mother!"

This is one of a handful of memories that haunts my soul. Standing there, looking down the long hallway to the parking garage, my eyes welling with tears. I wanted to grab Moira and run like hell back to the Ronald McDonald House and hide in my room cuddling my little girl whom I missed in the most visceral way. I had visions of hiding in my room and thought, "They won't let my mom come in. She's not on the visitor list."

For a split second I thought I could keep Moira. Then cruel reason reared its ugly head, "What will you feed her? You don't have your breast pump or any bottles. You only have two diapers. When will you get to the store? Where will she sleep? You don't have a crib. What about Liam?"

I let go of my daughter because I wasn't prepared for the consequences of fighting, and I took the emotional beating that came with letting her go. I let someone "do me a favor" and it cost me a slice of my heart and piece of my soul.

I wouldn't see Moira for another four days, but by the end of those days despite the ups and downs of Liam's recovery, Dr. Sondheimer mercifully played his primary cardiologist card and discharged us, saying, "Let's send him home on the oxygen. If we keep him here people will start experimenting, and he will just be at higher risk for infection."

So, we were sent home with oxygen, hope, and a prayer to begin healing the entire family.

19

The House that Love Built

The McDonalds of my childhood is a vivid, happy place. It's where I ate lunch after a half-day at school with my Billy Goat Gruff paper sack puppet and where I got lost in the harlequin stained glass window that was unique to the 10th Street store in Greeley. McDonalds was for Happy Meals and ice cream cones.

Then one Halloween we stopped at McDonalds between cleaning the school and returning for the "Harvest Party." The Lutherans did an ix-ne on the Alloween-hay. That night, I stood out of the way with my sister while my mom ordered four Happy Meals and sandwiches for her and my dad.

I don't know why we went inside, maybe the drive-through was too busy, but I saw this little girl who, for all my overload of Biblical study, looked like she had leprosy. She practically shook in her red, blistered skin and simple cotton dress with a witch and broomstick print, every inch of her looking like pain personified. Her mother and sister flanked her. If she was burned in her flesh, her flesh was burned in my memory. I tried not to stare as they collectively shuffled aside to wait for their food.

Every night for years I prayed for that little girl. I'm saying a prayer for her and her mom and sister right now. Every single night, I prayed for that girl's pain. For those few moments when I laid eyes on her when I was only nine years old, I couldn't forget her if I tried.

Eventually my prayers included a little boy from my own school, Mark Alexander, who was diagnosed with leukemia. A nurse came to Greeley from the Children's Hospital. The nurse told us cancer wasn't contagious, and that we should treat Mark as we always had. But as his hair fell out and he grew painfully thin, no one treated him the same.

Mark was in my younger sister Megan's class and was two years behind me. Since, we were older, we all just ignored him before. Now, in a school with ninety students in nine grades, it was impossible to continue to ignore Mark as he became a bald fourth grader.

While Mark was so very sick, his family stayed at the original Ronald McDonald House. That was the first I'd heard of it and how wonderful it was for the family to have a place to sleep and shower and eat. I only heard of it, never saw it. Then I never saw Mark again.

The week Mark Alexander died, a headline on the front page of *The Greeley Tribune* quoted Mark, "In Heaven it will End." He was looking forward to the sweet release from his personal hell. Mark was ten years old when he found his release.

Years later, while working at McDonalds, after Jim and I shacked up, I opened a new box of tray liners and bounced to the front of the store. We were invited to a walk! The Ronald McDonald House in Denver was doing a fundraiser walk. I had a mission.

Later that summer, a legion from my little store descended on Denver with $762 in donations, a literal fortune to us minimum wage workers. Of course as fate and my terrible sense of direction would have it, Jim and I got lost and missed our team, but we showed up to watch them cross the finish line.

I never forgot Mark, and I never forgot his mom, Deb, who later lost her own battle to cancer. Deb beamed with gratitude for the kindness of the Ronald McDonald House at a time when she had so much more to lament than to appreciate. I never thought, with all my supportive good feelings, that I would ever see the inside of such a place, or that I would live there for weeks on end cumulating into months of my life.

Right after Liam's dramatic flight to Los Angeles, we arrived at CHLA and noticed there was a McDonalds restaurant in the basement. An irony made all the more amazing by the posters in the hospital about combating childhood obesity. Still, there it was, and there we were on our way across the street to our first Ronald McDonald House.

Our room at the LA Ronald McDonald House was sponsored by Travel Lodge, so there was a sleepwalking bear pattern on the pale blue bedspreads, drapes, upholstered chair and ottoman, and tiny child's chair. The only place I could escape "Sleepy" was to leave the room entirely. He was even on the shower curtain.

Occasionally, we found ants in our room because our roommates didn't all follow the rules about keeping food in the dining room. But décor and insects aside, it was a haven.

The RMH in Denver was even better. It was gorgeous and new. Almost twenty years, later they finally found the funds to build a big house to replace the little Victorian where Mark Alexander and Deb fought for his life. The magic of hope packed up and moved closer to the hospital. When the hospital moved, Denver needed a second RMH.

Our Denver Ronald McDonald House, the one that still serves PSL where Liam was born, houses dozens of very premature babies' parents still wandering in the purgatory of homelessness that is parenting over a hospital crib.

My kids love McDonalds' food, though they never had it until my mom took them there when Liam was three and Moira was two. I will say, for your money, and if you gotta have fast food, McDonalds are clean places with high standards (for the industry) that set me up for a solid work ethic.

So, every now and then I find myself inside a McDonalds with my kids, buying Happy Meals, looking around me for the specters of little girls with shredded skin and little boys with bald heads, and seeing only shining stainless steel. Say what you will about the nutritional value of McDonalds, as long as they keep that bucket outside the drive-through window to take my change, they can have my money. I'll never forget the months I found sanctuary at the houses that love built. Besides, McDonalds is where I met Jim, back where it all began.

20

Promises, Promises

Life between the Fon-tempt and the Fontan was good, for the most part. Liam came home with oxygen and was quite blue—a reality made painfully clear in a photo of Liam and Moira in the bath, side by side, little boy blue and our sweet pink girl. Life was Smurfy.

Liam made a slow but steady recovery, peaking with oxygen saturation levels in the mid eighties, only to start declining again. In the meantime, Liam turned two, and Moira turned one, and we managed to have a lovely Christmas. Santa brought Liam a Thomas the Tank Engine table and Moira a play kitchen.

Everything was good at home, but we'd lost friends in that year.

My friend Melinda's little girl Katie didn't survive her Fontan. She was the second Fontan fatality in my world. I've witnessed incalculable loss of children, but they don't all touch me in the same way. I didn't know everyone at the level I knew Melinda. I knew her love for Katie. Hers was no different than my love for my children. I literally got down on my knees in my home office and begged God to spare that little girl, and then Katie was gone.

Katie died in the fall of 2005. As Melinda was mourning her daughter, the nation was enduring the aftermath of Hurricane Katrina. From my view, the world seemed a mad and ugly place. Sorrow was everywhere around me, yet it was all on the outside. I felt stranded on an island of good fortune while the world around me drowned.

Even though Liam was growing progressively bluer, and his real Fontan was coming in the spring, and, I was never as afraid as I was before the Fon-tempt—even though Katie didn't survive the Fontan. I'd trained so hard for "the big one" the year before, and that dress rehearsal helped me through the next big performance. And what a performance it was.

First off, the Fontan is "supposed" to be the last surgery. That's what they sell parents of newborns when they decide to fight for their kids' lives. Three, three, three surgeries. That's the plan. And they never *ever* tell you that it's a fix. The Fontan is not a repair, it's a palliation.

Palliative is a word that comes from hospice or end-of-life care, and the very fact they use that same word in relation to the violence exacted on my child's body to keep him alive is too ironic for my brain to digest. Palliation means crutch, palliative means the best the surgeon can do with what the children don't have. A halfhearted child, unlike Liam's cousin, Trace, and his omphalocele, can never be fixed.

Here's a dirty little secret — it's not always three surgeries.

Nope, Liam already endured three open-heart surgeries, and they were no cakewalk for any of us. Then came four; the Fontan was finally happening. The "final" step in the palliation. That inferior vena cava was coming off the heart and heading for the lungs, and the fallout would be messy.

Imagine taking your garden hose off a big sprinkler head and then screwing it to a tiny nozzle. Now the lungs are filling up with all that fast moving blood without the moderation of a beating heart. It's a human lung flood. Top it off with a heart that just had its most major vein lopped off and the arteries connected to the lungs were splayed open and reconstructed with artificial material. Liam's body had been sliced and diced, and the recovery was appropriately rough.

So, there we were on April 5th, 2006, and the operation, despite the scar tissue and enormous complexity, went extraordinarily well. It couldn't have gone better. Liam seemed headed for a slow but steady recovery, so maybe it would only be one or two weeks instead of the three Dr. Sondheimer prescribed. But then nothing is ever as it seems.

The Saturday before Liam's Fontan, my mom got remarried. I tried my best to care, but my mind was constantly in battle mode for the surgery on Wednesday, just four days away. I was paranoid about having Liam around all those people and getting sick. I was bracing myself because I was on a collision course with informed consent. I knew kids died during the Fontan, and I hoped it wouldn't be my child. I knew there was a small but significant degree of probability that Liam would not be alive in four days, so it's no wonder I was a bit of a Debbie Downer for my mom's wedding.

By Tuesday, April 4, we were back in the hospital for pre-op. Liam already had a cath, his fourth, the month before. Dr. Chan and Dr. Chang didn't coil those pesky invasive collateral veins that time, expecting them to be clamped off in the operating room the following day.

We did the things that were far too familiar. Liam played in the room full of toys, the room kids get to play in before they are put under. The photo that Jim took of us was typical—Liam was wearing his hospital pajamas, and I was wearing a look of dread.

Back in the pre-op station, I held Liam on my lap while the nurses swarmed and swirled around us taking his temperature, blood pressure, documenting all the vitals. We met one of the many—too many—cardiac anesthesiologists we've met along the way. This one told us what they all tell us, that we're signing our child over to twilight. Only now, after having Liam put under for four caths, three open hearts, and a cardiac MRI, we both knew what we were actually consenting to.

The knowledge is its own sedative, and Jim and I both began to shut down. Remaining cognizant of what is about to happen, even as we sign our consent, is not an option. To consent to this, we must pretend everything we just acknowledged might happen to Liam could not possibly happen, even as we undersign the very threat of it. Otherwise, we couldn't let them take our child.

We know what we're doing, but we ignore reality and instead climb a ladder of hope to higher ground before we're washed away by the fear of what we've just done. We have set our child out to sea in a basket with little more than a prayer that he will come back with the changing tide. We can't go with him, so we all fade out of reality for a few hours.

Then, just like that, like always, the nurse carried Liam off to his operating room as if he might not die in the next few hours. Jim and I left and performed our ritual weeping alone at the far end of the hallway before being enfolded into our surgery waiting area entourage. We were so numb that the next few hours felt like they belonged to other people. We lived outside of the story of our own lives, even as it was being written.

The ten days that followed Liam out of the operating room were a roller coaster. Moira got so sick on Friday night that I ended up taking her to the ER. Liam had his fifth death-defying surgery a week out when his bone was so infected it came apart inside the surgical wires, and when Esther discovered it, Liam was rushed to surgery. Then just two days after the night we nearly lost Liam, my grandpa went to the hospital for his own heart cath, and never came home again. He died on Easter Sunday, my mother's birthday, and I was at the hospital with Liam when the rest of my family was at another hospital with my grandparents.

Sunday, April 23, was my thirty-second birthday. Liam was supposed to go home that day and I was over the moon. I left the hospital pack up our clothes at the RMH, while Jim kept his vigil with Liam. I was eager to get home and back to work because our eighteen days at the hospital had wiped out my remaining vacation. I arrived at the hospital to get Jim and Liam only to find out Liam wouldn't be discharged because he wasn't stable enough to go home. Moira and I ate dinner alone after we left Jim and Liam at the hospital.

By Friday, April 27, Liam was stable enough and finally discharged. We scheduled his oxygen and vancomyacin (the antibiotic used to combat flesh eating bacteria) deliveries to treat Liam's bone-eating infection, and the home nurse to come train us.

Before we were released with our first born for the seventh time, we learned how to flush an IV in our child's arm. This was just too weird, but we were so glad to be going home.

We came home on a Friday evening and Jim bought groceries because the cupboards were bare. The next day was Liam's third birthday, and we served nonfat angel food cake. Liam was restricted to one gram of fat per meal, slowly increasing to three until July because of the tear in the pleural lining from the trauma of the last surgery. Liam blew out his candles while wearing oxygen. Our three year old was living dangerously.

On Sunday, our second day home, we watched the *Chicken Little* DVD Liam got for his birthday while we snuggled on the couch. We battled the oxygen tether all day and slept in our own beds under the same roof. I prayed little gasps of thanksgiving, but it wasn't to last. The next morning, we went to the North Denver outpatient office for a follow up appointment. Liam's chest x-ray showed cloudy wet lungs, and Dr. Sondheimer admitted us directly to the hospital, do not stop by home, do not collect your toothbrush.

Liam knew his bed so well he walked right into 3N and tried to get in, but someone was sleeping in his bed. Now Liam's bed was by the door. This was the same physical space he'd occupied after his Glenn, the same location where I encountered Click-Clack two years before. Liam was barely four months old then, and this time, he was barely three years old. I turned and walked out the door, leaving Jim and Liam at the hospital to get Moira and pack a bag for Liam and Jim. As I walked down that long hall past the familiar painting of the black dog on the beach, I had the sinking feeling that we were going nowhere.

21

Gallows Humor at the Tower of Bablefish

While Liam was enduring his Fontan lot in Denver, across the country a baby named Jillian was in Manhattan, surviving open-heart surgery and a stroke. Her mother, Vicki, lamented how when she parked her minivan, half of it was ripped away by a hit and run driver. Before that, it was broken into several times until there was nothing left to steal.

Didn't these people know that the driver's baby was in the hospital fighting for her life, that the vacant car seat in the car they vandalized symbolized humanities greatest hopes and fears? No, I suppose they just wanted the stereo. We all lived in such a vacuum where our realities did not mesh with the world beyond a hospital.

In the face of the absurdities of her life, Vicki would crack an occasional joke on her Carepage, which some of her fans failed to appreciate. One day, Vicki posted a contrite statement that still had an undercurrent of defiance. Didn't these people know that if we don't laugh, we will certainly cry? Didn't they know that we don't have the luxury of breaking down at our children's bedside. . . that we can never let our kids see us cry. If they see us cry, they are going to want to know why we're crying. How do you tell your child you're crying because you're afraid he will die?

So we laugh. Laughter should need no explanation, but people outside the hospital often can't find the humor. It's not so much funny as it is essential.

Laughter is one medicine, camaraderie is another. As my grandfather died fifty miles away, I took a mental reprieve at one hospital thinking about my family at another hospital. I worried about my grandma waiting for her husband to die. I was back in the same place where I'd had conversations with parents and children during Liam's Glenn recovery. As the world fell away around me, I felt so stranded and lost.

While I sat there with my computer on April 16, a Hispanic woman came in the parents' lounge. She pointed at the TV and said, "'s ok?" and tried to turn the TV channel. She was too short. So was I.

I made a joke about height, but she no habla Englase and I no habla Espanol, so I pulled up Bablefish on my laptop and initiated a conversation *madre a servir de madre.*

She lived in Greeley, the town I where I grew up, the town where my grandfather lay dying. Her husband came from Germany, and she came from Mexico. The beautiful blonde children I'd seen her pulling in the red wagon came from her womb.

Oh, yes, I thought she was a nanny or family helper when I saw her with her sandy-haired white husband, and no, I am not proud of myself. I presumed her place in her own family by the color of her skin and the texture of her hair. I am a fool.

I own being an insulated and ignorant white person, though I don't consider myself willfully racist. I'm not even willfully ignorant. I do not dodge my ignorance. I am not hateful. If I were, I wouldn't have motioned for this stranger to sit next to me on the small couch and initiated a conversation mediated by technology.

No, I am ignorant, but I'm kind, and I am always eager to learn and grow. In my limited world I am often crowded by own ignorance. I appreciate each person who chips away at that wall, even as I'm embarrassed that it exists. I won't deny it exists, if I did I could never see it well enough to tear it down.

I want to be free of the burden of my ill-formed and false assumptions. That freedom has a price of shame each time the foolishness fades and the growing pains of owning my own ugliness. It's not always comfortable to outgrow my skin, but it's necessary. I want to shed my skin and be more human, and opportunities for sloughing come in the strangest places, such as a cave-like hole in the wall in a hospital.

According to Babelfish, my new friend met her German husband in Mexico, they both immigrated to the US legally, but he was out of work. Their youngest son was diagnosed with a rampant liver tumor that forced removing half the organ. Her son was living with half a liver as Liam was living with half a heart.

All of this knowledge and experience we shared through the magic of my laptop passed back and forth across on a worn love seat. This woman, whose name I can't remember because I'm excellent with dates and terrible with names, taught me again the life-long lesson of not judging a book by its cover. But she taught me something else. During our computer mediated conversation, I lamented that I was having a bad day.

She read the translation and responded with something like, "There are no bad days, as long as we're blessed with life and love and memories, every day is a gift." She was right.

I have hard days, challenging days, but I have never since meeting my friend written any day off as categorically bad. On the last day of one of the hardest days of my life that concluded one of the hardest weeks I've ever known, I was given an enormous gift by a woman whose language I could not speak. I've not had a bad day since.

She and I were in a foxhole fighting for our son's lives, willing their survival, hoping for more than a half-life with their half organs. We were both suffering the isolation in that marginal sound between home and a funeral home. We took small comfort in each other, and she saved a piece of my soul that day by showing me the light of perception. I wish I weren't so bad with names, she deserves my endless gratitude. She deserves for the whole world to know her name.

22
The Heartland

In high school, during my suicidal phase, I left the cafeteria line the wrong way and disappeared halfway up the library stairs to sit alone with my tray on the landing where the cinder blocks jutted out to form a window seat of sorts. I was frequently joined by uninvited lonely girls whose very presence usurped my self-image of an outcast. I embraced my lack of popularity as a strange sort of martyrdom. I was a very a successful victim in 1989, and I've no intention of returning to that state of mind.

By the time I liked myself enough to not care about popularity, I had plenty of friends. Funny how that works. In the space between depressed teenager and Heart Mom, my life was rounded out with comfortable friendships.

When I became a Heart Mom, all those friendships fractured because the earthquake in my life left so much destruction. I could make the argument it wasn't my fault my world changed, and I changed with it. .

Surely, not everyone fled, but there was a distance that I put between myself and others. Of the friends who wriggled away from the wreckage of my life because I was too angry, too whiny, too difficult to endure with all the drama in my life, I am forgiving. I can't expect anyone else to understand how life was for me. I didn't understand it myself, and it took all my energy to get through those first few years. I won't say it was the right thing to do, but I didn't have the strength to work on being a good friend. I also owned my own share of weakness in the face of my friends' challenges. It happens, things happen, and people change, they fail, and they grow apart.

For every friend that drifted away, a hundred more washed up on the shores of what I call the Heartland. The Heartland exists on the Internet in chat rooms, forums, Carepages, and Facebook. It exists in Pediatric Cardiac Intensive Care Units, Ronald McDonald House dining halls, and cardiology outpatient offices. The Heartland is a state of mind, and the residents are the people who were not my friends until my life changed. Now they are a huge part of my life. Now they are my family.

For me the pilgrims of the Heartland were those first few people I found on iVillage message boards when I was pregnant with Liam. They were colonists and pioneers connecting in the still-early days of the Internet.

A glutton for information and knowledge, I have a do-it-myself character flaw. From the beginning when Liam was first diagnosed, I e-mailed and called anyone anytime for more information about my child's prognosis. I started this behavioral pattern when Liam was still in my womb. I called a hospital in Michigan that did a stem cell transplant into a boy's heart. I called, I asked questions, I did cord blood banking. I was insatiable.

I have another character flaw that has fed my resentment for the lameness of my wedding reception, and other minor disappointments in life. But it serves me well as an advocate. "Never good enough" is great for getting answers to help parents be more informed about their kids' surgical options. When channeled effectively, my personal perpetual dissatisfaction is quite powerful. What began as a way to find other mothers whose kids were like Liam, developed into a serious mission to empower parents to ask hard questions and demand honest answers.

Once we established that we were indeed not alone, we HRH parents needed more current and more robust information. It wasn't on the Internet until we put it there through conversations and comparing notes. We learned from each other and changed the way we parented.

In 2005, I filed the paperwork to incorporate Hypoplastic Right Hearts as a 501 C 3 nonprofit. I couldn't have done it without Tommy, Kim, Dorothy, Tammy, Jan, Valerie and the others who later joined our board of directors. They were our start and our future.

Then in 2008, something we only dreamed about finally happened. We climbed out of our computers and came together in Bloomington, MN for Hearts United.

I went from a devastated young woman to an unexpected leader all because I loved Liam too much to buy into "wait and see," or "love him while you've got him." We had twenty families at that first conference.

Not long after I founded Hypoplastic Right Hearts, I heard about a National Institutes of Health (NIH) study on the Fontan, and I called Boston Children's Hospital to learn more. After several calls and emails, I was able to secure Dr. Roger Breitbart to speak about this study at Heart United. He was impressed by how sharp my heart families were. We aren't sitting on our hands waiting for the shoe to drop. We're standing at the neighbor's door with a shoetree to collect knowledge and sense of power over the things we fear, one shoe at a time. We are motivated and in it for the long haul.

Those were the people that impressed Dr. Breitbart, who was a researcher from Harvard University. Men advanced in their fields were blown away by our bright mamas. These women continue to impress, and I knew them when they were brokenhearted with their baby bumps and a horrible diagnosis. Those are my people, and I'm so proud every time one of them makes a transcript of their conversations with a cardiothoracic surgeon, or gets a second opinion about a high-risk procedure, or raises a dollar to advance research, advocacy, or support programs. I'm endlessly proud of them.

As amazing as it was for me to be surrounded by couples who had kids like Liam, and as awesome as it was to know that one little thing I did in desperation created all this love and support, it got even better. The best part by far was the fact that Liam, at age five, could see real kids with special hearts his age all around him. Moira, age four, made friends with other little girls whose older brothers got "special treatment," and one little girl with a special heart. Both of my children made friends for life with kids from families who knew that "for life" doesn't quite mean what we used to believe. Now, we believe in each other.

The last night of Hearts United, we had six little boys ages three through seven peel off their summer t-shirts and flex their muscles while showing their scars.

We are badass parents, and I am proud that I brought us together. HRH is my third child. While I'm not the president anymore, I gave that up to start a chapter of the Children's Heart Foundation here in Colorado, I'm still involved and still proud of my people, my Heart Family that never backs down.

When I founded Hypoplastic Right Hearts, with my little ragtag A team of three moms that quickly became eight and never slowed down, I never imagined that years later our membership would edge toward nine hundred moms, dads, and adult survivors. At our rate of growth, by our tenth year HRH will have over 1,000 members in our little Heartland settlement in cyberspace.

Deaths aside, the saddest stories I know from the Heartland are the childhood memories of those rare adults like Leslie, Steve, and others who recounted how alone they were with their CHD in adolescence. Before the Internet took hold, before I was a Heart Mom, the Heartland didn't exist. Back then, kids like Liam thought they were the only ones and often they were. They lay in bed listening to their malformed hearts, fearing sleep, lest they never awake.

I cannot prevent that basic fear for Liam or the other kids, but I have done something with my life to make it so that they aren't afraid to talk about it. I opened a door and ushered in a community of families and kids who could talk and laugh and cry and live together. In doing so, we have quashed isolation. None of us is alone.

No, I didn't create the Heartland, but I am definitely one of its pioneers. Every time a woman with a four-year-old reaches back to me and tells me that I made a difference for her when she was pregnant, I know I've done something that matters. People have told me they were lost until they found HRH. I know that even if I died tomorrow and never accomplished anything else, I did an act of merit that gave value to my life. But I'm not done.

The Heartland is bigger than HRH. This year we donated money to help a non HRH girl in Uganda get heart surgery in India, and I counseled a friend of a family in Iraq who was desperate to get their HRH baby on the bus to India for heart surgery. I also started the Colorado chapter of the Children's Heart Foundation. At least one in one thousand American kids has only half a heart. One in one hundred has a heart defect ranging from a hole to HLHS, the most life-threatening CHD. Every year forty thousand babies are born with CHD, half of them will need heart surgery in the first year, eight thousand of them won't see a full year of life. This is so much bigger than me.

I had to start HRH when I did because the information and the hope weren't there for me. I found the hope, the information, and the friendship to create an organization that educates and inspires. Now it's time to take that wider. Now that I know what I know, there are more people I can help and there is more work to be done.

Still, it's hard to be an advocate. It's totally natural to do it for Liam, but it's exhausting to do it for thousands of people who aren't represented. When I host an event and get tons of community support, and no one shows up, it shakes my faith, but it doesn't break it. If Liam isn't at the event, I go home to the source of my passion and the reason I'm never satisfied with the status quo. Liam deserves better than the way things are. The way things *are* is not good enough for my son.

The way things are is this: I know four adults who "shouldn't have survived," and because the HRH mortality rate was one hundred percent when they were born, the social security administration didn't recognize their condition because it was excluded from the SSI checklist. These people with half a heart and fifty percent oxygen saturation in their blood who can't stand for more than fifteen minute stretches, are on O2, and experiencing liver failure, were sent to appeals again and again. Until recently when the laws changed, some CHD patients died before their Medicaid kicked in.

I don't accept that. I don't accept it for them, and I don't accept it for Liam. I don't accept that I have no part in that discussion. I didn't accept the responsibility of raising this child to be a contributing adult only to abandon him to the capriciousness of a world that questions his very existence. But things have changed thanks the Children's Heart Foundation and the Adult Congenital Heart Association. It changed because my fellow Heartland fighters went to Capitol Hill. There are enough downsides to being a miracle, and being able to see a doctor without going bankrupt shouldn't be one of them. But there is more work to do.

So I spend hours at this. I have plans and visions, and I use my blurting about Liam to speak the truth for thousands. Change needs to happen, and I am part of that change.

I learned so much medical and institutional information the hard way and hold an inordinate amount of information that can be helpful to thousands of parents. It is my obligation to put that information to good use. It is my responsibility to represent the Heartland to the "normal" world.

I am a little David in the face of that Goliath, and I've got more rocks than I need for my lone sling shot. I can, should, and will share my rocks. That's my role in the Heartland, a messenger, scout, and foot soldier with a little extra ammo that can help the person next to me in her own battle for her baby's life.

In the Heartland I have not a nation of followers or fans, but a nation of family. We are all brothers and sisters in arms fighting for our kids and taking comfort in each other. That is the beauty of the Heartland and its very reason for being. In the Heartland, none of us is alone.

23

Little Losses

I knew early on that breastfeeding, the real Le Leche type bond-with-your-baby-for-life type breast-feeding, was probably not in my cards. That much was pretty clear after our tour of the PSL NICU, and I could see that the preemies who were on vents or oxygen weren't very "hold-able." I knew if Liam were anything like that, my bond-with-your-baby-for-life type breast-feeding time would be limited at best.

So I resigned myself to pumping even before he was born. I figured that with everything else I'd lost so far, that so help me God, I would make milk!

Everyone on the heart defect message boards said it was hard to pump. Some women couldn't make milk under the strain of hospitalization. Encouragement abounded.

"Don't give up!"

"You're not a failure,"

"You can do this!"

But lo and behold, in a former life I must have been a sacred dairy cow, because I was udderly brilliant at milk making. My approach consisted of a healthy fear of failing, and I pumped every three hours from the minute my milk came in. EVERY THREE HOURS—even waking up for it. The only times I missed a pumping was traveling on an airplane, or I was unable to get a room. And at that, I made up for it. I pumped like it was liquid gold.

Then, not more than ten days into Liam's life, the nurses stopped feeding him. But they told me to continue pumping because Liam would need it when he got better. In a way, pumping sustained my hope that he would get better.

Once, in the parent room across from the CTICU, I accidentally tipped the bottle over and spilled the milk all over an empty desk. It was sticky and warm, and there were no sinks in the room in which to clean up my mess, so I limped back and forth, back and forth, hoping I got most of it. It seemed incredible that tiny three-ounce bottle could hold so much milk. I was so sad to waste it, so sad about the mess, and so sad that I was wasting time when I should be with Liam. All that time away, and I had nothing to show for it. And I would do it again in three hours.

Still, I pumped and pumped, and filled the tiny cubical freezer space we were allotted at the RMH. I filled my eighth of a shelf in the CTICU fridge to the point where there was nowhere left for my milk to go. So one night, knowing I had absolutely nowhere to put it, I cried as I dumped my milk down the drain and into the Los Angeles sewer through our bathroom sink at the Ronald McDonald House.

I could see myself in the mirror, face wet with tears, as I emptied the last bottle. I wept because I worked so hard for that milk, and at times it brought me great pain in my breasts; too full, too clogged, too much. Now, here I was rinsing it into the stinky sink.

I quit the meticulous process of washing my pump parts once I started pouring it down the sink. I used to pump, clean myself up, take my milk down to the RMH kitchen to store in the freezer, and then spend fifteen minutes thoroughly sterilizing my pump parts with boiling water and soap so that I could keep everything as sterile and pristine as I could for Liam and his health. My hands bled from all the heat and constant hand washing in the hospital. When I bled on the parts, I had to start all over again.

Once I started dumping my milk, I didn't care much about sanitation. Since there was no milk to take downstairs to the freezer, why bother going? And that attitude gained me an extra forty minutes of sleep at night.

A selfish truth is that a benefit of pumping every three hours at first, eventually stretching it to four, was that I got some quiet time — away from the doctors, the nurses, Liam, and Jim — for twenty minutes a few times a day. With the sleep deprivation, it was my only rest. I never slept in the pump room, but I did relax a little, and the chairs were more comfortable there than in the CTICU. As all that milk left my body, my spirit could decompress in a small amount of solitude.

I kept it up when I got home and eventually made so much milk that I was able to bring a huge cooler of it back to PSL to donate to the preemie babies in the milk bank program. I loved giving it away to those in need. But when the milk I brought to LAX for our return trip thawed out too soon, I cringed as threw it in the trash. Pumping was the only symbol of my motherhood I could hold during all those weeks while Liam was in a hospital bed and I could not hold him. It was proof of our bond, even if he never took it straight from my breast.

Producing breast milk was my big success. Liam ate it, he grew, and he didn't have the much-feared feeding issues common to many children with severe heart defects. Even though Liam was tethered to his oxygen tank, forcing me to cradle him very carefully because his sternum had been so recently severed, and even though he looked so terribly fragile, as long as I was making milk and Liam was eating it, I felt like I was really his mom.

It was different with Moira. When she was born, we were at the breastfeeding clinic every day to get her weight, then to the lab for heel sticks. Moira was going back to the hospital if she wouldn't eat. The Breastfeeding Nazis pressured me to try all kinds of trick and tools, and I finally got to the point of being literally full of my own shit from my post spinal block constipation that I couldn't take theirs, too.

I'd pumped for Liam, I would pump for Moira, and I did. Moira had breast milk every day until she was eleven months old, and today she's a healthy gorgeous little girl. So suck on that.

I joke, but I do regret not nursing my two kids, even though I was at least able to feed them with my own milk. I think I accepted the loss of that closeness so readily with Liam because his situation was so dire. By the time Moira was a few days old, I had to give in, I was literally sick and stressed beyond comprehension. In less than three weeks I knew Liam would be back in the hospital. Less than nine months before he'd been a tiny baby having his second open-heart surgery. It was so much and too much, and in the chaos of it I missed out on a very important part of motherhood not just for one of my children, but for both of them and for myself

There are genuinely valid and good reasons why some Heart Moms cannot breastfeed, and those reasons were part of my life. But there are some heart babies who can. If you're a Heart Mom, it never hurts to ask and keep asking if breastfeeding is an option for you. I can attest that it can hurt if you let the opportunity pass you by because you're afraid. The end result is that you'll miss the chance at that closeness with your child. If it's not to be, then so be it, but don't let one more thing be stolen from you if you're capable of reclaiming it.

24
Never Better, or It's Complicated

In the first Harry Potter film, Hermoine emphatically states that she was "Never better," to reassure her friends of her state of being. It's a common phrase, so common it rarely occurs to us that it can mean something else entirely.

For a while, our Children's Hospital had a tag line of "All Better," which was ironic because it only applied to the part of the population they treat who can truly get "all better." Similarly, the American Heart Association had "Learn, Live" and now, "You're the Cure."

All these clichés are Lilliputian spears dragging me ever downward. I've educated myself to the point where I know more about CHD than many pedestrian medical professionals, but my knowledge doesn't sustain Liam's life. It just makes me a better advocate. It also has cruelly informed me that "all better" is not something we can even aspire to, and never better. . . well, there's the rub. Liam will *never* be better.

Ask any parent of a hypoplastic heart child (left or right) what one question burns them up, gets under their skin more than any other, and it's, "So, now that she's had all of her surgeries, is she all better?" No, no, no, and *hell no!*

They are never better. These kids are just hanging by a rope. Transplant is an even stickier situation—you're just jumping from one frayed rope hanging over a cliff to a new one, one that is entirely likely to wear out in ten years and carries it's own splinters.

Let me make this as clear as humanly possible, THERE IS NO CURE FOR CONGENITAL HEART DISEASE. A heart born broken is always intrinsically broken. Even if it's "repaired" to something like normal function, it is still scarred and fragile. Think of a coffee mug that is dropped on a tile floor and shatters. You glue it back together. It looks like a jigsaw puzzle. Do you put liquid in it again? Do you ever expect to use it, but ever so gingerly?

And HRHS/HLHS kids are a whole other shattered mug. There is no handle—there never was a handle. It's supposed to be a mug, but a piece was always missing. That heart is all busted up, and no matter how all the king's horses and all the king's men try, they just ain't putting that thing back together again. It's mother-fucking-broken, and we're just trying to get it to stumble along well enough for these kids to not die.

So, sometimes when people ask if Liam's all better, I want to say, "He's not dead."

Now, I know I shouldn't get angry at the innocent curiosity or naïve but genuine concern of those who inquire after my child's health. My gut reaction, which I share with many Heart Moms and Dads, belies a deeper frustration with trying to advocate for a child whose very anatomy is beyond the comprehension of most human beings. It certainly has taken me every day of the past seven years and eleven months to gather the expertise required to be an effective parent and guardian for Liam. When people ask such innocent questions, it's like being sucked back through a wormhole to where it all began. Eighty to zero in one second flat, and it's a painful whiplash.

The truth is that all the convoluted surgeries for which we are infinitely grateful are just a very expensive and sophisticated MacGyver move toward not dying . . . for now. When we are asked if it's over, we are forced to remember how hard fought and temporary our good fortune truly is.

To top that off, most moms of hypoplasts get a generous three-course meal of open-heart surgery with a chaser of at least one other health complication. Whether it's gastroenterology issues that necessitate any range of feeding tubes, neurology issues from strokes or seizures, or learning disabilities, many of us extend with our medical marathon beyond just our children's hearts. This isn't really that unusual when you think about it. Why wouldn't there be other birth defects? With surgeries this intense, there will be some who suffer from long-term complications as well.

Liam's complications outside of the CICU are orthopedic. I first noticed his left leg was bigger than his right after his Glenn. We were referred to an orthopedist who x-rayed Liam's legs and pelvis, and found a spinal malformation at the top of the picture.

Liam has an extra lumbar vertebrae in his spine, which would be absolutely no big deal if it were shaped like the other large bones vertebrae in his spine. It's not, it's lopsided, and so is Liam. He also has a birth defect that causes his entire right side (including his heart) to be smaller than his left side. So his left foot is two full shoe sizes bigger. His left ribcage is bigger than his right, so he's asymmetrical to his bones.

Liam was a very late crawler and a very late walker. He didn't jump until he got special braces on his feet at age three, and he still falls a lot. Sports aren't part of our lives, and I'm constantly on the lookout for Pilates or yoga classes for him, but they're hard to find for his age group in our price range.

Liam's extra helpings are relatively minor in the realm of possibility, but they are likely, in time, to have more impact on his quality of life than not. That worries me. When we're off to our annual ortho appointment, I'm always nervous for that he'll need surgery on his spine or his legs. I'm nervous for limitations, and I'm nervous that there are orthopedic shoes waiting to drop on our heads. Mostly, I'm worried for Liam. He's had enough pain in his seven years. He's full, and we'd like to skip dessert.

So, even if a Heart Mom is fortunate enough to *only* be dealing with heart defects, the next painful, but slightly more enlightened question we all hear, "Does he need more surgeries?"

Oh, what a loaded question. The most accurate answer in most half-hearted kids' cases is, "Probably." In Liam's case the answer is, "Absolutely, yes." I know that Liam will get a pace maker before he gets a driver's license. I know he's going to go back to the cath lab before he starts middle school. I know that is all coming. Some parents don't know it for sure, but it's all on the table in this crap buffet of unpleasant possibilities.

The best we can hope for is to ride this peak where they look good and are not having complications. Just beneath the painful reality that these children's hearts are permanently broken, lays the deepest darkest secret. The reason we Heart Moms get so bitchy about that "all better" question and the kernel of truth under all that emotional baggage, is that we will never be better, either. We are still broken, we are still damaged, we are still and always, forever afraid. Not only are our children never better, this is never over, and we'll never be "over it."

Heart Moms don't get annoyed because the inquisitor is cruel or stupid. We get annoyed because the truth hurts. No, dear friend, this child I love more than life itself cannot be fixed. I put him through hell to keep him from heaven, and I will do it again and again until he tells me to stop or until there is no more that can be done. It only ends when one of us dies; and it will never be better than it is right now. That is the answer to your question; and that it why the question gives us trouble. Please forgive us, we Heart Moms, if we take or give offense, but it's a hard place to go to understand why that question hurts so much, and the knowledge is salt in the wound.

25

Apples to Oranges, Cuts to Bruises

Once upon a time I wondered if it was OK for me to write this book. Had I suffered enough? Liam didn't die. He's still here. I have happiness, I have joy, I have hope. I haven't suffered as much as Laurie and an endless heart wrenching list of mothers I know whose children died. My greatest tragedy was the death of expectation, but I still have hope.

Only occasionally do I meet a family whose child has had more open-heart surgeries than Liam and still survived. Usually the "child" is an adult by the time they've racked up comparable mileage in the OR. On the other hand, I know families whose marathon hospital stays with their child on the ventilator for months ended well, and I know those whose ended tragically. I know people who've consented to fewer surgeries but logged more hospital time. It's all apples to oranges.

Is our story less compelling because Liam didn't die? Does it have enough meaning to commit to the page if he's only spent five months of his life in the hospital instead of twelve? These are the questions that shouldn't even be asked.

I compare all things, including that which is incomparable and incomprehensible. Like, is it worse for a Heart Mom to lose her only child and her identity as a parent than for Laurie to lose Kolbey and still be a mother because she has two living children? Or is it worse for Laurie because then she must manage her surviving children's grief on top of her own? These are all ridiculous questions formed in my confused mind. These are just as absurd as people telling any mother, "Well at least you still have a child." As if any mother could choose one child she could live without.

Such terrible statements are the brain and the mouth acting in concert to attempt to make sense of a reality that defies all reason or logic. These questions of comparison have no place in the realm of pure emotion where so nuanced and extraordinary is each woman's grief that it defies human comprehension. Only the angels can interpret the language of grief. We humans are at a loss to appraise loss.

When we think about the questions of grief and suffering and pain, and try to find the impossible and nonexistent answer to the riddle of absolute loss, we will learn the landscape of a broken heart. I ask these absurd questions only to myself. In comparing what is worse, I've learned that the dimensions to human suffering are limitless. By asking the question and finding no logical answer, the journey through absurdity tempered me. It taught me that all suffering can teach, even my own.

A dear friend of mine, Melissa French, taught me the most valuable lesson. Her daughter Maddy was post-shunt and post-Glenn when we met for a picnic at a park. Her son, Myles, is the same age as Liam and providence has made us near-neighbors living in bordering towns. As we walked down a hill one sunny summer afternoon, Melissa asked me if I'd read the one CHD book on the market. I owned it, but I was dismissive of it because there were no kids like Liam in the book.

"Yeah," she said, "but don't you think we can learn something from the pain and fear that each family has faced? I liked to see that people came away from this with a lesson about life."

I had foolishly diminished the experiences of others because they didn't match my own. Any parent forced to give informed consent, regardless of the number of times or the degree of risk deserves compassion and recognition that this is not the norm. Every cut needs attention, every bruise needs relief. Grief has no quota, pain has no limits and so empathy and compassion must be similarly boundless.

Being dismissive and comparing experiences made me closed minded. It doesn't matter if a child has one open-heart surgery or eight, the fear of his parents is enormous. The realization of mortality is the same for all of us. We are all veterans of this war for our children's lives, regardless of the numbers of tours we've taken.

Just because some of us are wiser and more weathered doesn't make us less fearful. We should help each other. We should make goodness from the ugliness. Like burning cow patties to warm your house, there has to be a use for this misery.

I haven't lost Liam, but I've seen so much, lost so much, and gained so much, that I have something to say. I don't *know* half as much as I have *felt*, but those feelings own a truth that defies, yet deserves words. I have learned to stop—stop comparing apples to oranges and cuts to bruises. Instead, I have learned to study the curve of the apple, the texture of the orange, the promise of hope, and the compassion required to digest this bitter fruit.

26

A Mortal Coil

When Liam was four, he figured out reincarnation all on his own. He asked me out of the blue, "When people die, do they get to be a baby again and be born again?"

I told him a lot of people believe that's how it works and asked if he thought so. He did, so I let it drop. I have my own little Siddhartha.

When he was five and a half, Liam sat at our kitchen table and asked, "Is Evan going to die?" I nearly fell out of my chair.

Evan is a little boy from Texas with HRH whom we met at Hearts United. Liam just fell in love with him and has a framed picture of the two of them together on his wall. I asked Liam, in a very gentle way, why he would ask that. He said, "Well, your daddy died and Daddy's doggy died," then he paused and got that blinking, teary look he gets when he's trying to be brave and not cry, and said, "Sometimes babies and kids die. Then they are gone and you can't ever see them again."

I was speechless and my heart hurt. We progressed through a painful conversation about how my dad died eleven years before. We talked about how Grandpa Alan smoked and chewed tobacco and didn't eat healthy foods and didn't exercise. I had to stress that my dad was a good person even though these bad habits hurt him. I also explained that some people who get cancer do get better, and some don't. Ironically, a few months later Jim's mom Karen was diagnosed with breast cancer. She recovered, but it was a rough year. Everything grew more present as we went through a having a parent with cancer again.

I never expected to have this mortality conversation with a five year old, especially not my five year old who has almost died twice and shared the same physical space and time with children who died around him. There were times we were sent out of the CICU while children were dying, but Liam was left there alone in the room with a dying child.

When Audrey died two beds over from Liam, he wasn't even two. I can't imagine he remembers that, but who knows what he's heard or seen that I haven't realized, or what I may have even said not knowing he heard me?

That first time, I expected him to mention something about Evan having a special heart. I figured he asked about Evan because he was transferring questions about himself through someone familiar. I know kids do that a lot—hell adults do that.

Of course Moira was there, and she piped up, "I'm not going to die!"

So I said, "Neither of you are going to die until you are very, very old."

"Like one hundred?" asked Liam.

"Yeah, like one hundred, Liam." I took the first escape because I didn't like this conversation. Couldn't they ask about sex?

Then we ate dinner and talked about enjoying mint chocolate chip ice cream afterward. Yes, it was awkward and difficult, but I'm lucky that as Liam has had more questions, he asked me. Not that I have the answers, but a young child shouldn't be left to ponder these things on his own, even if his mother isn't too helpful.

I worry that I caused Liam extra fears, but I never want to be dishonest with him or Moira, either. I do try not to talk about the bad and scary parts of Liam's heart disease around him. I wasn't as careful when he was much younger, but I wonder how much he remembers from two or three years ago, not just what I said, but what he saw in the hospital. I know he remembers more than I ever expected he would. Since then, I've monitored myself even more closely, but I've also welcomed questions if he brings them. And they keep coming.

Right before his seventh birthday, Liam said, "Mommy, how old will I be when you're one hundred?"

I knew where this was going because I kept deflecting him by telling him we all will live to be one hundred. He keeps poking holes in my lie with facts like my dad was only forty-eight when he died. I told him, "You will be sixty-nine, Liam."

Of course, he got a little weepy and said, "Then I will miss you when I'm sixty-nine."

That would be fine with me to live to see Liam be sixty-nine. But a few hours later this ended up on the floor of my bedroom with lots of hugs and tears as he asked questions like, "How will my toys get to heaven, and what if they fall through the clouds?"

And, I made it all up as I went along. I am a liar. I lie when I tell Liam we're going to live to one hundred, and I lie when I tell him that heaven is whatever it wants to be. Maybe those things will happen, but I don't know it for certain, so I'm a liar. I lie and lie and lie because I don't have the answers he needs, and I don't trust anyone else's answers any better than my own.

I believe in God, but I don't believe that He would send billions of innocent children and genuinely good people to Hell for being on the wrong dogmatic track, according to whomever's track they're not on. Bin Laden, Hitler, McVeigh, Bundy—oh yes, Hell is for them. My Hindi friend whose baby died at one month old, well I don't believe her baby is burning in Hell with Joseph Goebbels, and no one is going to convince me otherwise.

In the meantime, I'm trying my best to stumble through helping my child with his questions about mortality when he should be asking me why the sky is blue. That one I've got covered.

27

Jenny McCarthy is Not the Anti-Christ and Oprah is not Our Fairy Godmother

In the past few years, I've read more than a hundred memoirs. It was bound to happen as I planned to write a memoir about raising a special needs child that I would run across Jenny McCarthy's books. I was jealous of Jenny McCarthy because one April her face was all over the "Autism Awareness Month" end cap at Barnes & Nobel. I want an end cap or a "Think Pink" October, or something like that. Not with my face or even my book on the display, I just want an end cap for CHD. I want the invisibility to end.

Even in February, which is heart month, we have no end caps or special displays for CHD. There aren't any books in the whole store about CHD. There are tons about preventing adult onset heart disease, but nothing about the world's most common and fatal birth defect. Yet, once I went to a book signing in that very same store for an author of young adult books whose baby died from CHD. I knew about her baby before I ever knew she was a writer. Dr. Sondheimer connected us.

The Heartland is everywhere, and yet we are so painfully invisible, hiding in plain sight just like our scarred children hide inside their clothes. It's not fair to blame Jenny McCarthy or her son, or any of the advocates for autistic children for the absence of attention for CHD, but it's easy to do it. It's easy to look at any other movement that has an extraordinarily wealthy and well-connected sponsors and advocates making progress and say, "Where's ours?"

Kids and adults born with CHD get the same amazing financial devastation, mortality rates, and endless supply of fear that comes with those other killer diseases, but for CHD the resources and research are far less. Ironically, the CHD population is larger and subsequently the death toll is far higher than any other childhood illness, but no one sees us outside of the Heartland.

I wish Liam didn't have CHD, wish he didn't nearly die twice, and I wish he didn't need twelve heart surgeries with no end in sight. But I'm glad Liam doesn't have cancer. I'm glad Liam's not autistic. And, I'm glad that if Liam had those diseases that there are people like Marlo Thomas and Jenny McCarthy standing up to make the world better for him.

As much as I might I wish someone famous and powerful like say, Oprah, would stand up with me for Liam and all the kids like him, that's not our reality. Our reality is that every year without fail since at least January of 2006, probably earlier, a congenital heart group (it's never the same one) starts a "let's deluge Oprah" campaign. It's usually around CHD awareness and heart month in February, but it's always a complete disaster. Oprah's producers ignore CHD, February ends, and we all go back to being the invisible parents of invisible children with an invisible but lethal disease.

The sad fact is even if we were on Oprah (when there still was an Oprah show) it wouldn't matter. Oprah can't save our kids, and after fifteen minutes of making the audience cry for us, we'd be as obscure as we are right now. Oprah has not cured AIDS or cancer. Oprah has not stopped domestic violence or saved the world. My friend Steve said that Oprah would never have a CHD show because there are no quick tips to prevent or treat it. CHD is bigger than Oprah. All Oprah can do is open a dialog. As advantageous as that would be, it is not a solution to our larger problems.

The true problem isn't that we couldn't get on Oprah, but that we *wanted* to get on Oprah more than we want to work together. Our problem is that we see Oprah's show as a destination, our promised land that will make everything better. Oprah and the celebrity culture and media influence she represents is not the Mount Everest that we need to climb to reach our destination.

Rather than pinning our hopes on celebrities, we must rally our friends, our family, our coworkers, and the world at large to understand Congenital Heart Disease. CHD is deadly, prevalent, and silent, and that is our real problem. When Oprah is long gone, we'll still be here with the same problems we've always had.

Understanding CHD, understanding our challenges, and working together is our real Mount Everest. We are our own biggest challenge, and getting over ourselves to get to work is our destination.

28

How to Change the World in
Six Excruciatingly Difficult Steps

What can the Heartland do to make the world a better place for those with broken hearts? First and foremost, accept that it's not the public's fault that they don't know what they don't know. Who knew about blood diamonds in Africa, the Dafur violence, or famine in North Korea without diligent reporting by people who care? People die from indifference and hatred all over the world every day. It's not a competition to have the saddest story. Everyone loses that race.

I know it is disheartening to hear that we have to work even harder. Wasn't this hard enough? Isn't this hard enough? Yes it is, and that's part of the reason it's so hard to find people who want to work even harder to make a difference. We are between the rock and the hard place, and the only way out is up.

Welcome to the guided tour to making the world a better place for those born with CHD and to honor those who've died. This is a six-step process, and it's going to take a lot of work. Shall we begin?

Part One: Get Your Head Out of the Sand

Congenital Heart Disease has no cure. It doesn't matter if it's an Atrial Septal Defect (one of the most treatable heart defects) or Hypoplastic Left Heart Syndrome (the most lethal heart defect), both are treated, but neither is ever "cured."

For example, a kid is born with a hole in her heart, an ASD. The doctors catch it when she's seven. They avoid open-heart surgery by putting an occluder (plug) in the ASD (hole) and voilà she's fixed! Not so fast, buster. Her heart has been working overtime to make up for its inefficiencies for years. It started out damaged, and it's still damaged. It needs to be monitored.

At the very least we have the ever-present risk of endocarditis (an infection of the heart). See, not fixed. I liken this to a guy who shatters his femur and has it reset with pins. It's "repaired," but let's not pretend it is as good as new.

So it is with any CHD, and that's why those CHD families, who got off relatively easy compared to the HLHS cases of the world, need to stay in the game. No one guarantees your luck won't run out. If a kid with a "fixed" valve or hole doesn't get routine follow up care as an adult, he could be competing with Liam for a heart transplant in twenty years. That's avoidable, and that's a shame.

The parents of all CHD kids need to be diligent about long-term care, and we need their help. I know that families want to buy into that "good as new" lie, and why wouldn't they? If there were even a tiny possibility that we could pretend Liam was all better, I'd jump on that train. But we can't, and the families of "repaired" and less complex heart defects shouldn't either. We need them advocating with us, because they are part of the two million North American families facing CHD.

Part Two: Get Out of the Closet – What Are You Ashamed Of?

I once read an adult hypoplast's (person with half a heart) blog criticizing parents for taking pictures of their kids in the hospital because it was demeaning. Keep in mind we're talking about newborns who might not survive and these might be the only photos the parents ever have. This person also took exception with revealing small children's scars to the world because they might be bullied eight to ten years down the road.

To that I ask why anyone should be allowed to bully anyone else, ever?

The idea that this scar is a source of shame or weakness makes it so ridiculously hard to get public awareness that will drive better research funding for kids and adults with CHD. I do not understand this attitude. Good people who didn't do anything wrong should feel no guilt or shame.

If CHD kids and adults want to feel badly about their fears, their anger, their frustrations, that's fine. Those are valid, nasty things we all have to work through as we grieve. But feeling shame and guilt over the surgeries that saved their lives? That just does not compute for me. More importantly it undermines the cause.

Part Three: Get Over Yourself, It's Not All About You

When Liam was a baby we used his first birthday celebration as a reason to raise money for The Children's Hospital Heart Institute. Over the years Liam's been the "poster child" for several CHD events and TV appearances.

We've cut back recently for two reasons. The first and most important reason is that Liam is more than his CHD, and constantly putting him in the spotlight messes with the family dynamics now that both kids are old enough to notice.

The second reason we've scaled back Liam's presence onstage is that other people need to heal. I also have receded. Instead of sharing Liam's story, I'll introduce another family who will share their CHD story. Storytelling heals as it empowers each parent and child to decide what part of their story matters most to them.

We all have a story, and over two million people in the USA and Canada have CHD. Over eighty million CHD hearts beat on this planet. There are far more stories than Liam's and mine. By monopolizing the discussion, we distract from the enormity of the mission. Yes, I am aware of the irony that this statement is buried in a book about our story, but someone had to start the discussion.

Still, each compelling story needs to be told, so tell yours, write a blog, keep a diary for your child, express yourself so you can heal a bit, and then step aside and listen. We have so much to learn from each other. We can help each other so much more when we show compassion and concern beyond our own pain.

Part Four: Team Up and Play Nice

Like I said before, there is no cure for CHD. So, even while we're trying to recruit the more "treatable" cases to our team and common cause, all you folks out there who've played in the big leagues with the huge nasty heart defects need to let them in.

Yes, that means coming to terms with your sense that it's not fair that their kid only had one open heart surgery or even got by with just going to the cath lab. I know you think that because after signing my kid over for general anesthesia thirteen times in five years I've certainly thought it. It's still wrong.

It's not fair for any person to be born with a heart defect, and while it does suck to have a bigger helping of shit on your plate, everyone in this club has to go through the crap buffet. When we're too busy comparing scars to respect that we're all in pain, the research dollars we need to help all our kids disappear.

All that resentment we have for the "normal" world, and "healthy" kids, and even the heart kids who are doing so much better than ours needs to first be owned. I'm not saying it's right, but it's OK that you felt it as a gut reaction. Now throw it up before you choke on it. Everyone hurts, let's put the hurt to good use as fuel to make a difference.

Part Five: Find Your Strengths and Celebrate Your Successes

I've hosted CHD awareness events where one person showed up and where hundreds of people showed up, events that were rained out, events that were sad, and events that lost money — those hurt the most — but I keep trying, and I've raised far more than I've spent or lost.

Maybe events aren't your thing. Maybe asking for money isn't your thing. That's fine; find your thing, whatever it is. Everyone has a passion. Find yours and see if your passion and talent can be harnessed creatively to help the cause. How?

Take your pain and put it to work. I've often wondered if sharing Liam's story might make me seem like I'm exploiting him.

But I believe I'm helping him, and others like him, by normalizing what we've gone through so that other Heart Families know it's OK and so people can start to see the Heartland and join us. If you're intensely private and can't bear to bare your soul, then sign up to walk at the Congenital Heart Walk, make a donation, bring dinner to the Ronald McDonald House, be a supporter of the Heartland and become a Heart Warrior in a way that works for you.

If I didn't hit your passion, your option, your next step in the territory of The Heartland, then what should you do? I don't know, that's your homework. I can't do everything, and that's the point. We need each other.

Part Six: Don't You Dare Give Up

I crumple those days I feel the most alone as I stand against so much. I know I'm not alone, but it's often too quiet here in the Heartland. Not all the Whos in Whooville are shouting yet. How can we make them shout?

It's easy to get mad at people who don't support our cause. Yes, anger and blame are easy, but they're wrong. It's not right to resent advocates for other causes. It is right to listen and learn from them and to support them because we have far more in common than not. Still, the question stands, what about CHD. . .what about my son?

It all comes down to choosing your label in life: Victim or Advocate. Every time I have disappointing results with my advocacy efforts, I try to remember that we've overcome so much more. I remember what I'm fighting for, and I don't give up. Team CHD, my friends of the Heartland, that's our theme – we never give up.

29

Death in the Family

Not long ago, my friend Steve Catoe wrote the most amazing narrative nonfiction piece about the first-ever Blalock–Taussig (BT) Shunt (open heart surgery) performed on a child. He published it to his Funky Heart blog the eve of the sixtieth anniversary of that surgery. I got an alert after he published it, and I read it straight away, knowing he was working so hard at it over the month of November.

Sometime that night between pushing the "publish" button for his blog and when I checked my email the next morning, Steve died. He was forty-four years old. If born today he would have been one of the better-case scenarios for half hearted tricuspid atresia patients. However, in 1966, just like the little girl who was the subject of Steve's narrative and died fifteen years before he was born, Steve Catoe was one of a kind.

When Steve died, it brought the Heartland to its knees. He was so bright, so energetic, and so committed to the cause of CHD advocacy that his following could not believe he was gone. He was the greatest hope for so many families facing down surgery after surgery and asking where it would end. If it ended with a life like Steve's, full of inspiration, passion, and kindness, that was encouraging. But then Steve's life abruptly ended.

Steve Catoe was one of the oldest hypoplasts I ever knew. He came to Hearts ReUnited, he spoke, he inspired, he rode around in our rental car. Now he's gone. I'm still not sure where to put that knowledge because my heart hasn't unclenched enough for me to file it away.

We haven't told Liam that Steve died. They made fast friends. Liam always makes friends with those who have "special hearts." He's drawn to them. But this is the first time one of Liam's own friends died. I guess we won't tell Liam until he asks. I don't know if there is a right way to do this. I don't know what mistakes I'm making. The Heartland is full of frontiers.

Still, as hard as it was to lose Steve, we've lost so many before, and I know it's not over. There are always losses. My friend Joanie, age twenty-six, died after her pioneering Fontan was redone. Joanie was too long in the care of a cardiologist who was not knowledgeable in CHD. She was in multiple organ failure. A Fontan redo was her only chance, but we lost her anyway.

I've known dozens upon dozens of mothers whose children were born like Liam who didn't make it one month. I know fewer whose children made it a full year, and I know fewer still whose children didn't make it through the Fontan. Then there is a small scattering of parents whose children survived the Fontan and died unexpectedly later. Each one, every single loss is insurmountable.

My greatest truth is that the only thing worse than fighting for Liam's life would be losing that battle. I celebrate every day that I get to fight, exhausting as it is, because the alternative is desolation.

For me, on the periphery of their grief, the bereft mothers I've known longer and better are harder on my heart. I have a deeper connection to those families and their children. But they all hurt. The tiny baby boy who died last week after two weeks fighting for his life broke my heart again. Even after hundreds have died on my watch as an advocate for my own family and families like mine, my heart still breaks.

Every death is hard. The worst part about befriending another Heart Mom is that the very thing we have in common might, one day, tear us apart. It's cruel and self-destructive for certain bereft moms to stay in contact with the Heart Moms who are still fighting and hoping. We're not in the same fight anymore, and they need to find their new role. We keep pulling them back, and that's not fair.

The incongruity of experience, the divergence into grief, and actualized loss of life draws a veil between us. We're closer to understanding it than most people, but there can be nothing more isolating than a loss that deep. It is a cruel world where a woman envies my enormous fears because she no longer has a reason to hope.

When my friend Lori's son David died, I wept at work. I read it on his CarePage. My friends at work couldn't understand how I could feel so deeply for Lori and Bill, or how I could mourn so wholly for David's death because I'd never met them in person. We were online friends, but it's so much deeper and stronger than that. We were Heart family, and each loss diminishes us as a whole. It's not just sad when a heart child loses this monumental fight—it's tragic. A loss in the Heartland is a death in the family.

Long ago I stopped transferring myself into the shoes of the bereft mothers. Early on, I couldn't help it. I imagined how I would feel if it was Liam. It wasn't studied or planned; it was instinctual. I lost that instinct as Liam aged and could no longer be *that* baby, *that* toddler, or *that* preschooler who died. We got past those stages, we didn't lose Liam, but we lost friends in the carnage that took their children. We mourn the death of the hope that bonded us and we mourn the death of their beloved children.

Outsiders don't understand the grief because they think we should have expected it. Even people in our own flesh and blood families think we shouldn't be attached to our own kids who might die—kids like Liam. Close family on both sides told me, "I didn't want to get too attached to Liam in case he didn't make it."

They had no idea how deeply that cut me. No, we don't expect them to live, but the gaping hole left by our hope when it dies with a child is bigger than most people can ever imagine. I worked at a Fortune Twelve company for the last decade, and I witnessed wave after wave of layoffs. In the first part of my career, I was hit with a lot of survivor's guilt. At the end of my time there, doing the work of five people with no relief in sight, I no longer felt guilty. I felt frustrated.

Having watched countless children lose their battles with CHD, I have never once felt guilty that Liam has survived. It doesn't diminish my grief for my friends, but I refuse to feel any regret for my child's survival. I refuse to begrudge my son his life because another parent lost her child.

In much the same way I would never in a million years wish CHD on any family, I don't wish to know the surreal pain of losing Liam. I don't wish it on anyone including myself. I see it so often that I cannot pretend that we are safe. I cannot pretend, even as fewer and fewer children die as they age, that it won't happen to Liam. So I keep moving forward, seeking joy while watching my back for the death we've cheated along the way. I know it's stalking us. I know we're never truly safe.

Yet, as much as I fear losing my child, I fear more life without him. I hate the thought of surviving Liam, that's even how they phrase it in an obit . . ."survived by his mother." Surviving your child means physical pain and aching for the life your own body created. It means people saying the stupidest shit to you and being so wounded you can't even respond. It means people like me trying to understand what is entirely incomprehensible.

Surviving your child means moving ever forward away from the time when the person you loved more than you thought you were capable of loving was real and living in this world, and watching that vivid light fade to a darkness that leaves you permanently cold. It means seeking that light into your own grave, just waiting and aching.

I don't want to know this. I don't want this lesson for myself. Yet my friends have taught me, and how can I turn away when I know they suffer even more deeply than I can understand from where I stand, still in the fight? I can't, and I won't.

I fear that the veil of death will not only separate me from my child, whom I love so ceaselessly, but the shadow that casts over me will separate me from the living, and all that unrequited love will warp and wear my heart away. I fear being left bitter and barren to joy, and I fear the anger I've worked so hard to overcome. I know I would survive losing, but I fear who I would become without him. Yet there is one thing I fear more than that.

My greatest and most unspeakable fear, the one I can't look you in the eye and talk about without crying is not that Liam will die but that I will have to choose when and how he will die. I do not want to make that choice. I do not want to be in that place, next to his bed signing away my very last informed consent. I don't ever want to be forced to surrender what I've fought so hard to preserve. As Liam's mother, I gave him life, and I never want to be the one to take it away.

I knew this even before I knew of Liam's heart. I knew this from Ruth, by best friend Mary's mother, who had to let her go by signing consent to remove her ventilator tube.

I knew this the moment I heard an arrogant preacher say that letting a loved one go was taking the easy way out.

I knew that the worst situation a person could face was making *that* choice. I made the choice before when I chose not to abort and chose not to seek hospice care. Each time the choice was before me, I always chose to fight. Because there was always reason to hope, we fought.

I fear that after all I've made Liam suffer for my love, I will face that choice again and there will be no fight left in either of us, and one day I will have to let him go. I can't bear the thought of that making that choice. Ironically, the only elixir for the fear of losing my hope is hope itself. Liam is the only real thing in this centrifuge of extreme emotion, and I hold fast.

I hold fast.

30
Not My Life to Take

I never debated whether or not I would keep Liam. It wasn't something that required much thought because the compulsion to fight for him was so strong. However, I also never stopped to think about what his life might be like.

I have a good friend who once told me that her husband and she debated over dinner whether or not I did the right thing by allowing Liam to go through all he has instead of giving up and letting him die either by termination or hospice. Their verdict was that I had done the right thing. I didn't tell her at the time that I was exasperated that they saw fit to assess my decisions having never faced that on their own. I did say, "If God gave him to me, I felt it was my duty to give him every chance at life."

My exasperation faded. It was a valid question. With so many children born dying of congenital heart disease, is it right to make them suffer to survive? My answer is yes. Even now, as Liam asks me if he is going to die from his special heart, I cling to the belief that I made the right decision. Even as life will become increasingly harder for my son as his awareness grows and his body declines, I believe in his life and his right to forge his own path. No one has an easy life, so why should the difficulty of Liam's make it less worth living?

At first I thought I was choosing between life and death, but I never saw far enough ahead to see how challenging Liam's life might be. Even so, knowing what I know, I believe Jim and I did the right thing, not simply because of the quintessential value of life, but because of my faith in Liam to make the most of his life and find his own happiness.

I am a spiritual person but not a religious one. Dogma and absolutes bother me in a world where no one plays by the same rules or on a level playing field. I am no pro-lifer who would bomb a clinic, or shove those terrible pictures in someone's face. I know that horrible things happen and abortions are sometimes necessary. I've rolled my share of snake eyes in life, and it's not for me to play John Roberts. I simply I will not judge that decision any more than people can judge me for fighting for Liam.

Still, it bothers me that so many people seem to think of abortion as birth control. It's an exit strategy that should be a last resort, not plan A. If you live in the woods with bears and you leave your door open, the bear will get in and eat all your goodies. Lock your damned doors! Refusing to use effective birth control when it's so easily available and then destroying the life that miraculously finds its light in one's body seems capricious and cruel, vain and stupid. Sure, birth control occasionally fails when used correctly, but that's the exception, not the norm.

I look at my friends and family who struggled so fiercely and painfully with infertility for years on end, and it is hard for me to defend the right to choose to end the possibility a pregnancy holds. I don't understand it, but I know that I don't understand it. I know that I walk only in my own shoes and see things from my own vantage point. I've also swallowed enough of my own fear in life to know its flavor, and everyone must fight or flight as she sees fit.

I will not judge a stranger anymore than accept a stranger's judgment for my own actions. We play with the cards we're dealt, and both the consequences and rewards are ours alone to bear, whatever they may be.

I decided to carry Liam to term, and once we got there I let him suffer to live. The consequences were mine to bear, but they are also his inheritances. I put my child through a literal hell on earth to prevent him from returning to heaven, and now he is trapped in a purgatory of life-long chronic health issues and an ambiguous future. This is what I made of the hand I was dealt, and now these are Liam's cards to play. I hope by the time he leaves my nest, I've prepared him to fly above his challenges and live fully. That's what I owe him, the chance to forge his own path unencumbered by his mother's fears.

I don't think anyone should judge me, but they certainly will ask if I did the right thing. Ultimately, only Liam can answer that definitively, but for inquiring minds, you should have known Leslie McCall.

I first met Leslie in the waiting room at Denver Children's during Liam's Fon-tempt, in the hour or two before we knew it would not be a Fontan. Liam's surgical nurse, Esther, brought Leslie to meet us, and the entire room lit up.

Leslie was born in 1980 with tricupsid atresia and weird septal defects that allowed her to live long enough to have one of the first Fontans ever done in the state of Colorado. In high school Leslie had a heart transplant, and a massive stroke. Formerly a straight A student, she had to relearn potty training and tying her shoes. It took her years, but she would not be deterred.

If you didn't know that, you would have thought her slightly crooked smile was simply God's way of making her beautiful face not exactly perfect. A minor flaw that makes a beautiful woman all the more compelling, like Lauren Hutton's tooth gap.

Leslie was beautiful from the inside out and brimming with joy. She sat with us the whole day except for brief interludes to be interviewed downstairs. She was at the hospital most of that week helping with the annual Children's Miracle Telethon, answering phones periodically, and bearing witness to the importance of the hospital in saving and changing lives.

A few days after Liam's surgery, he developed a terrible pneumothorax (his lung collapsed) and he was writhing in pain. Liam was so stressed that he ground his teeth every night in his sleep. I would reach over him to put his pacifier in his mouth so he would stop grinding.

Liam grew terrified of the nurses and x-ray techs. He just whimpered when they came for his blood in the mornings. All we could do was hold his hand and rub his head. We couldn't hold him in our arms because of the drainage tubes, even though he would reach out for us to pick him up. Every time he'd reach for me I would tell him, "Mommy is so, so sorry. I want to hold you but I can't. I am so, so sorry." Then I would get as close as I could for an almost-hug and turn my face to the next bed where the curtain was mercifully closed so no one would see my tears. I had to pretend I wasn't the most useless mother on the planet.

When Liam met Leslie, even though he was terrified by all strangers that approached his bed because of the painful new chest tube, Liam turned to her and gave her his hand. They stared into each other's eyes and held hands silently. They spoke without words, a language of the broken-hearted that I understood only by proxy.

Leslie, unlike any of us, understood Liam's pain and fear, and most importantly, his strength. Leslie was a native speaker. In that moment, reflected by that young woman, I saw just how strong and wise my little boy was, even though he was only twenty-one months old.

Leslie knew what Liam endured because she had been inside that hospital bed, not just beside it. Leslie could speak for Liam. She explained how much the tubes hurt, how important it was not to lift him under his arms. We knew about the lifting from the doctors, but the doctors couldn't tell us how much it actually hurt, like being squeezed like a nut by a serrated cracker that sends hot stabbing waves through your lungs, and pins and needles in your sternum. It was like being folded into oneself, cracked in half and left bruised and bent. Leslie knew it. Leslie lived it, and imparted her knowledge to help us be better parents to Liam.

We kept in touch by email, but Leslie grew ill. Her body rejected her donor's heart, and she had to go to San Francisco for a second transplant. Leslie's unique complications made the distant clinic her best hope, and she held out for months.

When Leslie died, I was shocked.

You might think, "Amanda, you dolt! Even I could tell Leslie wasn't going to make it."

But to know Leslie, to see her sparkle, her fight, her misaligned smile, her amazing spirit, anyone would be surprised that she didn't beat Death back yet again, charm Him into letting her stay at life's party just a little longer. She radiated a life force unlike any I'd seen before, or since. I guess God just got tired of waiting for Leslie. She was too good for this earth, and we were lucky to have her at all.

Leslie's life taught me something I didn't understand before. I didn't learn it with my best friend, Mary, who had died when we were twenty-five, or Joanie when she was twenty-six, or my dad who died at forty-eight, but in Leslie, who only lived twenty-six full years, I finally learned it wholly. Any life, no matter how short, is a full life. We don't get to choose when it ends, whether it's three days, three weeks, seven, seventeen, twenty-six, or forty-eight years, it's not up to us. We get called home when we get called, so we better live it up while we're here. I miss her constantly, but hers was a life without waste or regret.

Leslie filled up the bookends of her twenty-six years. She lived a far bigger and more meaningful life than so many people I know who are twice her age and older. She lived better and bigger than many Heart Kids who aren't nearly as sick, and many healthy people who've never known true physical pain.

In looking at Leslie, I don't see all that my dad, or Mary, or Joanie lost with the ends of their lives, but all that they enjoyed, all that they were when they were here. Looking at Leslie I can believe that even if I lose Liam in my own lifetime, he will have a complete life while he is here. That is one of the most precious gifts I've ever received, and I'll be grateful to Leslie all of my own life for giving it to me. Life really is what you make of it, and it's my job to give Liam the best tools to build his own life, to make it what he will. That's all I can do, the rest is up to him.

I will always fear losing Liam, fear being the decision maker. More so, I deeply fear the strength I know I have and never, ever want to use. Yet, I believe in Liam's life and his right to live it. Liam has brought us far more joy than the fear of losing him has brought us pain. Beyond what he has given us, he has felt his own joy. He has laughed so deeply, smiled so broadly, felt so completely in only seven years.

Liam has already lived a lifetime, and I greedily and lustfully want more. More years, more joy, more life for my son. I just want more of what I have and I have contentment in how much Liam has lived already. I agree with my friends, Jim and I made the right choice.

31

William (Liam) James Adams,
You've Got A Lot of Names

When Liam was three and we nearly lost him, I sent away to a nonprofit called Songs of Love. It's an awesome organization that writes original songs for critically ill children to celebrate their lives and make them happy. When I filled out the form, I put Liam's legal name on it with the (Liam) in parentheses. The songwriter made a joke out of it, and the title and refrain of Liam's song is "William Liam James Adams, You've Got a Lot of Names."

Who is Liam? Liam is laughter. He laughs like Jim but deeper, with a reverberation like a million tiny bells peeling from deep within his soul. I believe all heart kids are a little more of whatever they would have been with healthy hearts. They are enhanced by the experience of cheating death. Some kids are quieter, sadder, angrier, happier, or even sweeter.

Liam is more joyful. He laughs with a joy so profound and pure, it alights my soul. So much that, as much as it breaks my heart to imagine letting Liam go, his laughter, like his first cry, bespeak a grace that I know will see him safely wherever he goes. That might seem a foolish faith to atheists and extremists both, but it is my faith. My faith is in Liam.

Liam is also a true believer and Heartland patriot. While we were planning the first Congenital Heart Walk in Colorado, Liam would walk up to anyone and everyone he met—in line for a Happy Meal, on the street, anywhere—and thrust out his small still-dimpled hand, and say, "Hi, I'm Liam James Adams, do you have a special heart like me?"

Once he met a woman whose son also had heart surgery. Once he met a woman whose husband had heart surgery. Most of the time he just tells random strangers that he's had twelve heart surgeries and that they should come to the Heart Walk with us, ". . .because it's going to be a lot of fun. We have balloons!"

Yep, my son is following my example, and as long as he's not jaded or compromised I'm not going to stop him. Who better to tell the story than the man who lived it, even if he's just a little man who hasn't lost any baby teeth yet?

Aside from his championing of the cause, Liam is pretty typical. He loves Marvel Comic Book characters, Transformers, Ben Ten Alien Force, oh and the Power Puff Girls and Rainbow Magic Fairies. I don't know why my son loves the Rainbow Fairies, but they make him happy so I love them too.

Everyone loves Liam Last year at the end of school, I opened his desk and pulled out love letters from four different girls. There were only five girls in his class. The teachers love Liam because he has great manners, the boys love Liam because he tells fart jokes, and the girls love Liam because, well, he's pretty damned cute.

I worry because I'm too smart not too. I know too much, and I love him so much that I'm never going to stop worrying about him. Never has a night gone by with us under the same roof when I've not gone into his room and kissed him goodnight after he's long since fallen asleep. I do the same for Moira, but I never fear she won't wake up in the morning.

I have admitted my greatest fear is losing hope and giving up on Liam's life. My greatest hope, however, is not that Liam will outlive me. Of course I hope for that, but even more than his longevity I hope that Liam is happy for his entire life. I hope he never resents the life we've forced on him. My greatest hope is that the joy Liam demonstrates so effortlessly now will never leave him so long as he lives, no matter how long that may be. He didn't have a normal start, but I still hope he has a normal life.

I worry about what he's going to come up against as he faces his own mortality. Considering what that reality has done to me, I fear for him. But Liam is so strong, and I believe he can handle it if for no other reason than he doesn't know differently. Jim and I will do our best to get him through that harsh realization about the real threat inside his physical body. But if Liam can one day get back to where he is right now, back to his true self, full of joy and laughter, he will be just fine.

I don't worry too much about him fitting in and being a productive and responsible adult if he remains true to himself. Wherever life takes him, his heart, no matter its physical condition, has always been in the right place. That will see him through this world better than many people with completely healthy bodies. If nothing else, I take comfort in the fact that Liam is at home and loved where ever he goes, and that is an enormous blessing for us all. I just pray we'll get through his day of reckoning and the fallout without the blind and angry mistakes I've already made. I pray for the gift of grace for my son on his path, even as I have stumbled on my own journey. Still, Liam is entitled to define his life and face his challenges on his own terms, and all I can do is support him. As long as I can do that right, nothing else matters.

32
We're All In This Together

Growing up Jim was responsible for his younger brother and sister after school. Karen, their mother, is the neat and tidy type. A couple of years ago, one of our nieces broke a barometer at Bill and Karen's house. I cleaned up the blue dye, and I swear to the patron saint of cleanliness, whoever she is, not a single speck of dirt came up from the floor along the baseboards. That floor was spotless, but for the dye. Jim's not as clean as his mother, but he's close.

Jim is also the king of exaggeration. For example, I check the mail, and I put the things I need to deal with later in a small pile on the edge of the counter top. Jim proceeds to make dinner, and upon encountering the mail, "Why has this stuff been sitting in my kitchen for five days?" On occasion, I will show him the postmark to disprove his proclamations, but I digress. Jim is neat and he exaggerates, and that's the worst I can say about my husband because otherwise he is better than good and the salt of the earth.

I've heard my husband described as, "the one who is always smiling." I've heard some variation of that theme for most of the eighteen years Jim and I have been together. Always smiling . . . that bright temperament makes it difficult to handle a great darkness, like the threat of your newborn son's mortality, that shadows your life. So living with Sunny Jim who was prone to exaggeration the first few years of our son's life, I refused to burden him with my fears.

At night, in those three years of surgery after surgery, my mind would race and wonder to horrible places – places without Liam. I would lie in our bed and sob silently, enormous tears collecting in my ears, running down my neck. Jim slept. Jim can sleep anywhere, any time. I would cry and cry and cry until I had to blow my nose, and I would sneak out of bed. I snuck off to the bathroom, and I slid the pocket door closed behind me as softly as I could. Still, I cried silently. A million sobs have broken and fallen in my throat, never making contact with the air. Silent trees falling unheard in the forest of my thorax. In Liam's life I remember only three or four times of ever sobbing aloud, of ever letting the grief or fear break through and be heard. The rest of the time I cried silently, and it was a true effort.

I believed I was sparing Jim the burden my fear and pain, but also I didn't want to release my emotion into his echo chamber of exaggeration. If I let Jim hear me cry, he would know I was worried about Liam dying, and he would say things like, "It doesn't matter he's going to die anyway." Or so I thought.

When Jim read the first draft of this book he said, "I never realized you were as scared as I was." Maybe I have a career in acting ahead of me. Looking back from this place in our relationship, I regret that I didn't cry in front of Jim. Those times he released those frustrated utterances about the futility of hope may have been in response to the inaccessibility of my own hope. Maybe he wanted to find my cracks, wanted to relate. The more I held back and held tight to my stalwart hope, the more alone we both were with our unspoken fears. In protecting Jim I hurt him and myself. The unintended consequences of our best intentions always come back to bite us.

Still, we made it through all that. We had moments, deep into the seemingly endless weeks in the hospital where we rubbed each other's raw nerves and one of us would storm off for a walk, but we each came back. We came back to Liam, but we also came back to our second half.

Five and half years ago, when Moira was eleven months old, Jim quit his job become a full-time father. It was the right for a variety of personal and financial reasons. It was also the right choice because as much as I love my children I do not like playing with them.

Jim, by contrast is quite playful. When it came down to temperament, Daddy was the right choice to stay home. But that decision like all choices had a cost. In the years Jim was home sharpening his parenting skills, his identity and confidence took a bruising. Any stay-at-home mom will probably shout "Amen," to this assertion, but for a man there is another dimension and more isolation because there are so few full-time at home dads.

Jim rounds me out. All his lightness counterbalances my darkness. Jim is bright and loving, and I am routinely accused of being deep. Being deep means going to dark places, and Jim pulls me back to a world of light and love and laughter, always laughter. But being light-hearted can sometimes make the burden of fear all the heavier.

Men and women are different and each person is unique. Where I ran as fast as I could from becoming depressed and latched on to anger in my grief over Liam's broken heart, Jim sank into depression and was only occasionally angry. Neither of us spent much time in denial, but we each found our most comfortable groove in grief and eventually helped the other out of it.

I've heard varying statistics over the years about parents of children with health crises or parents of children who die. The national divorce rate for any US couple is 50%, for couples with sick kids it might be as high as 85%. I can understand how it happens. The strain, the pain, the constant worry and the social isolation of an ongoing medical crisis is hard enough, but when a couple can't meet each other's needs, things just crumble. I've seen it again and again in my circle of friends. Some seek counseling, and if that fails they seek lawyers.

We all seek solace when our children are so sick, but some couples can't find it in their marriages. It's heartbreaking to see two people already so broken-hearted unable to keep what they thought they wanted in life. Maybe they wouldn't have made it anyway even without a medical crisis. We'll never know though because "what might have been" is the most dangerous place for people who are just trying to get through the day.

Even when marriages survive and even if they thrive, a heart family is often more than a marriage plus one desperately ill child. Often there are healthy children who are equal shareholders in the fortunes of the family despite being the most powerless members.

I've stumbled and fallen in this journey. The facts of my motherhood include evidence of my anger, coldness, lapses in grace and tact, moments of reactionary foolishness, and plainly being a difficult person. I accept that, and I make apologies or amends where necessary. But one thing I will not abide is the hint or notion that I love one of my children more or better than the other, and the mere implication of it sends me into a rage, not because it's true but because from the moment I knew I was pregnant with Moira I made a commitment to do my best by both of my children.

Moira is as much a part of our family, our life, as Liam or Jim or me. She's the fourth corner in our square, and we're incomplete without her. But, Moira hasn't nearly died. Moira has no visible scars. Moira is healthy, and so life with Moira, while plenty full of all the dramas of life with any six-year old girl is not quite so dramatic as Liam's life has been. That doesn't mean we don't love her.

Let me tell you about my girl. Moira will fight to the death about being right. She growls, screams, cries her protestations. For the full first half of first grade she argued with Jim that the teacher's lounge was the "teacher's lunch," because they ate lunch in there. When the girl thinks she's right, she is a firm believer.

Moira's world is fairly black and white, but despite her independence and stubbornness, Moira is the single most generous human being I know. She told me recently, "Mommy, I want a gumball machine for Christmas, so people can put money in it."

"You want people to buy your gum?" I asked.

"No, they can have their money back, I just want them to have fun buying gumballs. Everyone likes gum."

Moira is always making little presents for us and her teachers. Tonight she drew me a picture of Rudolf the Red Nose Reindeer and spent twenty minutes coloring two sides of a sheet of paper so she could wrap up the gift. She lives to give. When I grow up I want to be more like my six-year-old daughter.

I suppose she gets that from Jim who doesn't think twice about giving me the biggest slice of cake. Not me, I take the big one for myself. I've always been that way, and I'm astounded by my husband and my daughter. Liam is more like me, and I feel badly for him. It is better to give than receive, but that truth is hard-learned. Moira is ahead of the game.

We're lucky Moira doesn't know any different. She was born second and born into a heart family. I worry for my friends whose healthy children come first and are displaced by the trauma of a sick sibling. I worry for my friend whose teenage son was depressed to watch his parents' marriage break up, his little brother go through three open-heart surgeries, and his mother struggle to make ends meet. I worry about her oldest son who, as a teenage boy, shouldn't bear these burdens when, really, isn't it hard enough to just be a teenage boy?

I have two amazing and beautiful children, but only one healthy child. For that healthy child, I know what it means to own the hopes and expectations that are intact and, therefore, too powerful. I love my healthy child, but when I see her face, she can seem like a stranger. I've spent a million lifetimes willing Liam to survive, holding him in a hospital, staring endlessly at his beautiful face. His face is more familiar to me than my own.

With Moira, I have never willed time to stop so that she would not die. I have never held her tiny body in an embrace and begged her to stay with me. I've never cried with a primal fear for her life. I missed almost as much of her first year as I spent in the hospital with Liam during his. Even though Moira is six, I've never had the hours to memorize her face. Just when I think I've got it down it changes.

Moira is so beautiful, and even though it feels like Liam is on loan, he is more mine because of the imprinting than Moira can be. I wish I could have absorbed her face, but the cost was too steep. The price of my familiarity with Liam was the imminent threat of his death. The cost of Moira's good health is a natural distance that seems so foreign because it's completely normal.

I feel, always, like I'm trying to consume my daughter, take her in before she's gone forward into time away from me, floating into her amazing limitless future. I know what it is to have a healthy child, but even that is different in the shadows of my fears.

At our worst moments battling for Liam's life, Moira was a distant dream, a missing piece of the puzzle. She was separated from us by necessity, and her absence intensified the pain. At the best of times Moira is a totem of reality, a symbol we cling to reassure us that we belong in the peaceful wake, that she and stability and normalcy are really ours to keep.

As strong and fast and healthy as Moira is, the coarse worries that tether my heart make raising her different than another healthy child in non-heart/non-special needs families. My first worry isn't a worry anymore but it consumed me for the first three years of Moira's life.

When Kolbey died and left Kynleigh, his one year old sister behind, it made me so sad this little girl would have no memory of her brother that was her own. Kynleigh was a baby. Kolbey was gone. She would only ever see him through their parents' eyes.

This all happened just weeks before Moira was born, and I carried my sorrow for Kynleigh as worry into Moira's life. Even today, I see pictures of Kynleigh and her oldest brother Kyle on Facebook, and I see the shadow of Kolbey, the middle brother. My memories fill the space between his siblings and my love for their mother and pain for her grief wounds me in Kolbey's pronounced absence. My grief for my friend is constant.

However, my worry for Moira's memory is now gone. It expired with Moira's advent toward the age of reason. Yet it has been replaced with a new worry that Moira will suffer greatly if Liam dies. That hit me hardest the night before Liam's sixth heart cath, the summer before he started kindergarten.

Moira turned four the month before, and I hadn't realized just how much Liam was a part of *her* life. Sending Moira off to stay with my sister and looking in her empty room left me breathless and weak.

There was a possibility, slim yes, but possible, that her brother might die the next day and the next time she came home, she would come back an only child. Until that moment, I hadn't appreciated the impact of losing Liam would have on Moira. I'd been preoccupied with the grief that Liam's loss would bring to me, to Jim, and whether our marriage would endure the strain.. When I realized how much pain Moira would suffer if Liam died, my burden of anticipatory grief instantly doubled to include my worry for the child I would *not* lose. I was overwhelmed by it.

That worry intensified that summer because the first cath wasn't enough and we went back in August for another. The fear for Moira eased, but once it settled in my heart it never left. I don't have to seek or invent these worries, they are real because they have manifested themselves like weeds in the lives of my friends. There but for the grace of God, go I. These worries add to the things I have to confront and overcome to keep an even keel, and I know I am not alone.

One of my worries affects all parents of more than one child, but to different degrees, it is worry that I be fair. I can't be even, I can't be exactly equal, but I try to be fair. Moira has had moments, like when Liam had a kidney ultrasound, where she wanted one too. She wants the attention that Liam gets for having a "special heart," but at age six, she can't begin to comprehend the price of that attention.

However, this concern about Moira's confusion over the fairness of Liam receiving this attention, like the fear that Moira wouldn't remember Liam, will fade when Moira realizes what having a special heart truly means, and then my final worry will become a reality. It's inevitable. I've seen it again and again in families like mine. I have a friend whose daughter lamented how she could not ever be angry at her older brother because she knew he was sick and knew he might die. This is what I worry about for Moira.

When Moira comes to understand—what Liam is coming to understand—that a special heart is not a golden apple, but a ticking time bomb, she will be devastated. I've seen this devastation in heart sisters and brothers the world over when they realize, "Oh shit, my brother/sister might die."

Imagine that. Imagine being ten years old and discovering that your best playmate, your worst enemy, both in one person is so vulnerable and his place in your life is tentative at best. Imagine that all the love you feel for that person overwhelming you and the guilt you bear for the most mundane sibling rivalry and natural spirit of competition. Imagine comforting your child when she realizes your greatest fears and owns them for herself.

Imagine the guilt our heart-healthy children feel for wanting to be recognized and for questioning that the world hasn't been fair to them when it's been so much crueler to the person they love. I know the poison that will infect Moira's heart because she loves her brother so much. All I can do is wait for it to take hold and help her through it.

What is there for us Heart Moms though? I have reached out to therapists and experts in the field. Their studies, when they touch on CHD, are always about moms and kids in acute care situations in the hospitals, not on the home front. I've heard of one study that shows siblings of sick children have more empathy than their peers, but I've not seen any studies about how to keep a Heart Family whole and healthy. I've asked the experts about the mental health of our Heart Kids, of our healthy kids, of the stability of marriage, but like all things CHD, this is still on the frontiers of medicine.

How many moms have to go through what we endure? If there are, like the CDC implies, over 36 million American families raising a child with a special medical need, how many of us struggle with a family dynamic that includes anticipatory grief? I'm still trying to figure out how I will rise to that challenge, but I know I will rise because I get up every morning and face it. I love Moira, Liam, and Jim too much to fail them.

33
Fighting An Invisible Disease

Having a child with severe CHD means that most of the time I can hide Liam's disability with a turtleneck sweater. True, there has been oxygen to contend with, and the cyanosis is visible to the trained eye. Yet, I cannot count the number of times people tell me, "If you didn't know Liam had a heart condition, you'd never know he was sick," or "To look at him, you'd never know what he's been through."

That's a blessing and a curse. Unless you pull up Liam's shirt and observe twenty-one different puncture wounds from twenty-one different chest tubes, Frankenstein stitching on his sternum from the six times the skin has been sliced open, or the numerous cut down marks littering his neck, arms, and groin, you'd never know this child has survived twelve different invasive surgical procedures just to keep him alive—all before kindergarten.

Once, when Liam was still very small, we took him to the zoo. He was on Jim's shoulders with a balloon tied around his wrist. A well-meaning older woman came up to us and told us his hand was blue and that the balloon must be tied too tightly. I calmly explained that I made sure my two fingers would fit under the string when I tied it, and she said maybe it worked itself tighter.

So, I showed her Liam's other blue but balloon-free hand and explained his heart condition. She sheepishly apologized and said she just was worried. I tried to help her feel better, but I probably made her feel worse. Believing you've stumbled into another person's living nightmare brings dissonance to one's life. She could never imagine—so few people can. That is the phrase I've heard more than any other in Liam's life, "I can't even imagine," or its companion phrase, "I can *only* imagine."

She thought our lives were awful. Our lives are wonderful, but it's hard to get past the scary parts. It was hard for us for years, why shouldn't it be hard for strangers for minutes?

I don't hide Liam's heart defect, and I'm certainly not ashamed of it. Aside from my status as a chronic blurter and my involvement with charities and speaking out, I frankly don't care if I make the public occasionally uncomfortable with our everyday truth.

Quite the contrary, I prefer the discomfort of others to any shame for us. It's either strangers or Liam who has to be uncomfortable, and for them it's temporary. For Liam it's cumulative. Better we all face down CHD to make it less scary, so Liam and every kid like him can be more comfortable in their own scarred skin. Why should Liam be the boogey man? Why can't we tell the truth?

Some kids face down death, but they're still kids who have to live in this world. Most parents know the challenge of raising a child to be a healthy, well-adjusted, respectful human being, and a contributing adult. What they can't imagine is doing it when the whole time you don't know if the finish line is going to vaporize and whether the ground will fall away beneath you. When you can't see the disease, you can't imagine the burden.

I want what all parents want, but I have to get over myself to get there. People see me do this dance and tell me I'm strong, they tell me I'm doing a great job, but they don't know what this is really like. Liam's heart is not my real problem. My real problem is my *own* heart, my *own* fears, real and imagined and the isolation is an echo chamber for the fear. That's why speaking out is important. That's why the Heartland matters so much. We need a place to voice and vent our fears and feel less invisible. Just because Liam seems OK to the untrained eye, doesn't mean the Boogey Man is thwarted.

There are days when I walk by Liam's room and a flash of fear sends me into a nightmare of packing his things away because he's gone. With absolutely no prompting, those funeral songs pop back into my head and I wonder who would come for us, for Liam, if it all ended. It never goes away; I've just gotten better at fighting it off. This will always be part of my life. I still have nights, far rarer than in the beginning, when a mantra of pleading, "Please don't take him, please don't take him, please don't take him," rattles through my head and leaves me breathless and sobbing.

My burden is my own baggage and it makes my load unwittingly and unintentionally heavier. But it's there, and it's my own, and its essence has almost nothing to do with Liam as a person, but how I define myself as his mother. There's no room for my drama in his life; that would defeat the purpose of his survival.

My challenge worsens for me when I worry that Liam will be so physically frail in adulthood that he will be disillusioned and broken along with his dreams, or worse, that he'll never make it that far. I ground that fear in the handful of post Fontan adults I've met. But it's not a fair comparison. Liam is an artifact of his own time, not theirs. The surgeries change month-by-month and patient-by-patient. I truly don't know what the future holds for my son— one way or the other. It's wrong for me to let me fear impact his future because it really may be limitless. That takes a leap of faith that is difficult for me, but that faith is just as valid as my fear.

Things are great now, but the truth is that they were great before and during Liam's surgeries too. I just never saw how great they were at the beginning because I was overcome by the fear and the pain of bearing it. Even then, in public, I stayed positive on every front because I couldn't and I can't let the fear win, but damn if it isn't still there.

I often feel that because I've been given a miracle, I'm not allowed to feel the normal pains or complaints of motherhood— neither by the cosmic forces who may be listening, nor by the people around me who always have to interrupt with their "but don't you think?" As if I'm being ungracious for feeling what I feel.

For instance, should I lament how fast Liam is growing up and how sad I feel to say goodbye to the baby days, the toddler days, the preschool days as they all slip away and he becomes incredibly independent? People will say, "But aren't you so glad he's come this far?"

Well, duh! Of course I am, and it came at great cost to him. Can't you just let me lament the joy that is fading for a moment before the next sun rises to warm our days?

Maybe they think, "If that were me, I would just be so grateful." I don't know how grateful people are that they are *not* me. Maybe if I felt others were grateful for having what I don't have, then I would feel allowed to feel my grief.

Still, I am my own worst enemy with the judgment and the censoring of feelings. I do myself more harm than any of the people who are trying to help.

We have endured ugly tantrums in the store. Liam + any kind of shopping experience/level of tiredness and or boredom = mega meltdown. Liam is a good-natured child almost anywhere but a store. Then he becomes a whiny, irritating, bored tyrant. I love him to no end, but if forced to choose between taking Liam shopping or having a tooth pulled, I might head to the dentist. Still, when Liam throws a tantrum, and I'm humiliated, I feel my own shame at being angry at him.

It's like I'm cosmically prohibited from wanting to push my child into a clothing rack to get him to shut up. I never would, but that doesn't mean I haven't wanted to do it. And I feel guilty for being mad, which makes me madder.

It's so strange that I never get as angry at Moira as I do at Liam, yet I don't think I would feel as guilty about being angry at her. Maybe he's just better at pushing my buttons, or maybe my attempts to temper my anger to prevent karmic retribution make it worse.

I just know that I never feel free to be justifiably angry at my son, even though he's done everything to earn it. Don't get me wrong, the child gets punished. No TV or an iPad ban is the best defense against Liam's offensive behavior, and he's even been spanked two or three times. Liam stands in the corner on occasion, and he doesn't get away with much. He's not a spoiled brat, but it's hard for me to manage my feelings when I worry that if I get too angry, fate is going to say, "Oh, well, I guess I'll just take him back then."

This is how it is for me: I didn't cry the day Liam started kindergarten because I was still numb from the week before we had been in the hospital where Dr. Chang put a stent in Liam's pulmonary artery. At the hospital overnight the monitors went crazy because Liam's heart gets funky when he sleeps. This is how it is for my son: he ran into his kindergarten class room, jumped into circle time, shooed us out the door, and got on with his life. This is how it should be.

This is how it is. When Liam saw the elves at the Woodward Governor Christmas display and said, "Man they are working hard for the kids," I did cry in the front seat of my car because that moment was priceless. He still believes in Santa and Elves, and he doesn't know he might die before he ever grows up. Liam doesn't know right now, and I know that "now" is fleeting, so I cried for how much I love this moment right now. This is how it is to be me on the other side of where my motherhood began. Liam is normal, I am not. I was changed, not all for the better and not all for the worse, but I was changed by this life.

The other day, seemingly at random, Jim asked me, "What would we be like if Liam had been born healthy?" I paused to consider, and the words formed in my mouth before my brain was even finished with the thought. Without irony or humor came the answer, "I can't even imagine."

The truth is that this disease that is part of my son's biology has become so much a part of my identity that I cannot imagine my life without the passion I have for this fight. I don't know who I would be without this battle, and while that scares me a little, it also makes me more entrenched in the cause. I'm sure I would have latched onto something, but this is my passion. It's not so much that CHD defines me as I want to redefine this invisible disease.

I'm a Taurus, and while my sign implies stubbornness, I generally think I'm fairly open-minded. However, I am willful and tenacious and I never give up. I started graduate school with the best intentions in 2000. It took me five years of stops and starts after Liam was born, but, eventually, I started my thesis over and made some traction. No sooner had I made progress in school than that same summer Liam went back to the hospital twice. It just felt like I was never going to finish. At one point I had lunch with my thesis adviser, and she said, "Amanda, there is no shame in quitting, you don't have to graduate. Nobody is going to think less of you if you don't finish."

Oh, but I did have to finish, not because of what anyone else thought of me, but what I thought of myself. I had to finish not just so I could put the M.S. on my resume or claim my hard-earned high GPA—and not just because I really am an academic nerd. I had to finish for the same reason I had to take that proof book back the day of Liam's diagnosis; quitting was not an option. I had to finish the things I started before my life changed, and this was the last big thing from my life before the landslide.

Yet that was not all of it. All those things came into play, yes, but mostly I had to finish and graduate because I could never, ever let Liam's illness be an excuse to quit. By failing to finish, I was afraid I'd be saying to Liam, and Moira, and to myself that it's OK to quit. Leslie McCall fighting for her second heart transplant taught me different. I owed it Leslie and Liam, and every person who has to battle their own illness, to suck it up and get 'er done.

I graduated on May 14, 2010. Exactly seven years before graduation day, Jim and I walked down Sunset Blvd. after being shooed out by Liam's nurses at CHLA. Now I walked with my regalia to get my degree. I never imagined, back when I got that first failed thesis proposal together or when I took that last final exam right before Liam's diagnosis, how far I would walk to claim my degree. How much I would stumble, stop, and start, and stop and start. I never knew how hard it would be to get through that last mile.

Finishing grad school and actually graduating was doing for myself what I've done all along for Liam and other Heart Families. I was finally following my own example in my tenacious and dogged work as an advocate. For years, aside from Liam's surgeries and my second pregnancy, I devoted all of my free time to Hypoplastic Right Hearts and later to the Children's Heart Foundation. This is part of the reason it took me so long to graduate.

But CHD wouldn't wait. So I hosted an enormous garage sale, I did several Heart Walks, I raised tens of thousands of dollars for research, support, and education. I was fueled by my self-righteous anger over Liam's illness, but I was also fueled by my own independent spirit. I never wanted to be helpless.

Over the years my rationale for advocacy has matured. I no longer feel indignant when people don't want to donate money to CHD. We all have our own causes and concerns. I no longer expect massive crowds, and the lower I've set my expectations, the more pleasantly I've been surprised.

It took a lot of effort to get to the point where I understood what it meant to advocate. Now I have a valuable perspective, and people seek me out for advice because I've mellowed without burning out. I still carry the CHD Flag, but I hold it steady instead of waving it wildly. I've grown more approachable, but no less passionate.

I was recently at a Heart Event, as an organizer and I made connections I wouldn't have been able to make five, or even three years ago. I've assumed a leadership role in the CHD community not because I'm angry or impatient or even stubborn, but because I owe it to my son and all the kids and adults like him to do my best as a steward for their futures. I do it, not because other people won't, but because I can. I do this because I care.

I've been asked to mentor other heart moms as they grow into advocates, and that's the greatest honor I've ever had. I occasionally help mothers and friends of mothers in foreign countries find contact information for US Hospitals. Sometimes I help connect moms in the US with leading doctors in the areas where they need help. I frequently connect with expecting moms and dads and grandparents and give them tips about how to ask the right questions to help them learn from their doctors about their children. While I never give medical advice, I do coach expectant parents on the best way to get the best advice and most appropriate information from their medical experts. All of these parents are on their way to becoming Heart Warriors. They are growing past their pain and using their emotions to fuel change. Someday, perhaps they will pay it forward and do more than I could ever imagine. Being in their company blesses and humbles me, and I'm honored to have been there to help them at the beginning of their journey.

My friend Steve coined the term Heart Warrior, but he meant it for himself and other adults with CHD. He considered Liam and other minors to be Cardiac Kids, children too young to be their own advocates. He considered Heart Parents advocates, but reserved the Warrior term for those who fought the disease in their own bodies. Not being a heart parent himself, I don't know if he realized that there is a difference between Heart Parents who are paralyzed by their fear, or burn bright with the desire for change, only to burn out when their grief changes stages. Those parents are not lasting advocates, but they are human beings in a state of grieving and healing.

A true advocate, a true Heart Warrior doesn't care whose child has CHD, but fights for them all.

Steve was a true Heart Warrior, and Liam is already becoming a Heart Warrior, even though he's just a little boy. By Steve's core definition, I'm just a Heart Mom, but I aspire to be a Heart Warrior, too.

My definition of a Heart Warrior is broader. A Heart Mom is anyone raising, or who has lost, a child with CHD. A Heart Warrior doesn't stop fighting at the crib, she fights for research dollars, political improvements, and quality of life—not just survival. All Heart Moms fight for their children's survival, but Heart Warriors don't leave the fight as the scars heal, and they never pretend it's all better, or that the war is over.

Even if my own heart was not malformed, as long as I live, my heart will remain broken for what I could not give my son in this life. No matter how much I accept reality, I will always mourn for Liam's broken heart. I don't feel guilty or responsible for Liam's heart defects, but I do feel responsible to make his life longer and the quality of his life better than it would be if I sat on my couch and cried for eighteen years.

I also feel that I have the power and the skill to advocate for parents and kids who lack that power and who need my help. I feel that I have a responsibility for every mother who has six kids instead of two and can't find the time to do what I can do. I feel the responsibility for every heart kid whose parents are in the middle of a divorce and can't raise money for the research that might save his life. I don't feel Noblesse Oblige because, after all, I grew up in a trailer park and am hardly noble. But I feel I've been blessed with a voice and some access, and I have a responsibility to put both to good use. I'm a bull in a china shop, so I might as well make my way through the place and shake things up. I will see this through.

A Heart Warrior never gives up. The Heartland is full of Heart Moms, Heart Dads, Cardiac Kids, and Adult Survivors, but true Heart Warriors are rarer. Heart Warriors want to make a difference and will work with as many different people as they can to improve the lives of those facing CHD.

Heart warriors aren't zealots, rather they're soldiers in it for the long haul. Heart Warriors aren't angry, but they're ambitious. Heart Warriors don't in-fight about whose charity is better or more worthy, but they work with all the relevant charities to find a strategy that benefits everyone. Heart Warriors realize that there are many faces and fronts in the war against Congenital Heart Disease, and only by camaraderie, purpose, and hard work will anything come of that. Heart Warriors see beyond their own homes and their own battles to a larger purpose and calling.

Heart Warriors aren't generals or admirals; they're in the trenches at Congenital Heart Walks and Medical Advisory Boards and Cardiac ICUs. Heart Warriors are on the front lines on Capitol Hill and petitioning for pulse-ox screenings on all newborns. Heart Warriors are fighting to get a CHD registry so medical records aren't lost and meaningful patient data can be viewed over time in order to keep an eye on indicating trends and treatments. Heart Warriors will ask for second opinions, demand that institutions work together to help more children, and focus on outcomes to prevent health declines not just respond to them after the fact.

Mostly, the biggest difference between a Heart Mom, a Survivor, and a Heart Warrior is that the first two fight the acute disease on an individual basis, the third fights for the larger cause. Yes, it is enough to fight the disease one heart at a time. But for true change in the world, we need Heart Warriors. We need Heart Heroes like Steve, and we need to keep them alive for longer than forty-four years.

34

All the World is a Stage, but Grief Has Five

It's been my experience that the stages of grief are neither even, nor sequential. Some professionals in the field of grief don't believe in the stages. I'm not a grief professional. I'm not even a grief expert in general terms. I'm My Own Personal grief expert. I know what I've been through, and I know what it's meant to me. I also know that hundreds of other moms and dads like me have gone through the same thing because I routinely hear comments about how what I wrote on a blog, forum post, or newsletter, or said in person has "put into words exactly what I felt." I know I'm not far off the mark or I wouldn't have written this book.

I also have had email conversations with a leading psychiatrist who also studies cardiology. I've asked my questions to him, to counselors and therapists, to social workers, nurses, and physicians, and the truth is that there is no ready-made home in clinical circles for Heart Families. It's pretty intuitive that we're grieving a prolonged sense of loss for the stability we expected for our children and their health, and the anticipatory grief issue is also fairly obvious, but no one has really studied us outside of the hospital. Nobody is publishing books to help us help ourselves. So I'm what you've got today, and here's my take on the stages of grief.

Denial: I really spent no time here at the beginning. My denial manifested when I was reluctant to admit Liam really qualified for a Make A Wish Trip, but I got over it when he nearly died. I was also in denial Liam's first year of school. I didn't want to get him a medical care plan at school. I didn't want him to be labeled "disabled," but he is disabled—as disabled as a child with one lung or one hand. He has limitations, and while I readily jumped to accepting his crucial health issues, I've been in denial at times with his chronic challenges.

I've seen other families in dangerous denial; one or both parents believe that their child is cured, healthy, all better. That's not reality and it's not safe. It also allows the child to go through life on their parents' cloud of denial only to crash to earth in a painful reckoning when the heart needs attention later in life. Even worse, by being inattentive and avoiding medical care, minor issues can become big problems. Denial can be a bad place to get stuck, but it's not been my problem area.

Bargaining: I don't know if it was the enormity of the situation or the need for drastic action, but I was never in sufficient denial to think I could bargain. I knew from the start that Liam's case was incredibly serious, and that knowledge only deepened over time. Because the hope we have for Liam is not futile and seems to build itself up with each new medical innovation, I don't think my advocacy efforts are really bargaining.

Perhaps my refusal to act out, my fear of seeming ungrateful to God or the Fates is symptomatic of bargaining. Maybe subconsciously I overcompensate as an expression of bargaining. However, in the truest sense I've never been deluded enough to think I could get us out of this situation, only through it.

I've seen families at the bargaining stage, and I am ever so cautious when I share information with them about other heart families. For instance, there is a great revolution happening in cardiac catheterization where in some fetuses and some newborns can receive intervention that lessens or cures their hypoplastic ventricles. The problem is that it is only a select few children who have the perfect storm of treatable defects. Liam would never have qualified, maybe someday they'll get there, but it's not today.

That knowledge I hold from my work as an advocate must be dispatched with compassion and caution. I always make sure to explain to the newly diagnosed families that these procedures aren't for everyone, and debrief them on the types of defects that *can* be treated so they can use that knowledge to ask the right questions. But I never, ever want to keep them in the bargaining phase of their grief with false hopes.

Anger: This is my grief rut. I fell into it when my dad died, and I festered with it when Liam was diagnosed. I didn't recognize it as anger because in its truest form it feels so justified. I was so self-righteous for so long that it really took writing this book to get enough perspective to see it for what it was. I've spent enough time on the topic to give testimony to anger's effects and the dangers of playing too long on that stage, but I confess my guilt unequivocally.

I've been one angry mother.

I don't know if I've seen many other Heart Moms as angry as I was. I've seen some, and I recognize myself in their venom, and it's not flattering. In its expression, anger does not help our cause. However, more than denial, bargaining, or depression, anger's ability to mobilize us as advocates is very potent. The problem is that if you're fueled only by anger, you burn hot and burn out. It's a good ignition, but it can't sustain anything constructive.

I hope the rest of this book gives sufficient insights in how to work through anger and move forward to empathy. But there's still that big dip of depression to cover still. Buckle up, we're going down.

Depression: For me this came after acceptance. My depression was kept at bay for years by my willful refusal to go there, and my insane anger-fueled ride of ceaseless activity. I wouldn't allow myself to move out of anger into depression because I'd been depressed before. I'd been scary looking-for-pills-to-end-it-all depressed, and it scared me too much to let myself get anywhere near that place again. I don't know if I stayed angry because it felt safer, or because it felt righteous, or both, but I never really got depressed until I stopped being angry.

When the anger dissipated, I was exhausted. I'd run so far, so fast, and for so long, fueled by my indignation and resentments that when I let them go and stopped running, I fell flat on my face. The depression wasn't crippling or lasting, but I was sad. In a sick way I kind of missed the anger because I'd held it so long. It was like taking roller skates off and in walking again. I was wobbly. That was my depression, the wobbly bits while I found my footing.

That was my experience. I've seen Heart Moms and Dads fall far and fall fast. As fast as I was running in anger, they are falling into a deep depression. If you find yourself there, get help, and get it fast. Take the good pills, see the therapist, *and get help.* New moms have hormones and sleep deprivations to contend with, and that's the tip of the iceberg. Depression is a dangerous thing, and even if you don't want to hurt yourself, not wanting to help yourself is just killing yourself slowly.

Jim dealt with his own depression. That's his story, but he dealt with it. I helped him, and he helped himself. He also helped me with my anger, as did the Heartland. If you feel so alone that you can't even talk to your spouse, talk to your child's cardiologist and make them find someone who can help you. You can't parent and advocate or rise to the challenge if you're so far under.

Depression is not your fault. It's a stage of grief so cluttered with baggage that you can't exit. I wasn't so depressed about Liam's illness, but I was in that black place once, and I will never forget how it felt. Let yourself be helped, and take your ovation.

Acceptance: Sorry, we're just visiting. Yes, my anticipatory grief-stricken friends. When you do the chronic-illness dance, you change partners often enough that you don't get to stay in Acceptance all the time. That said, the better you get at the dance, the more stealth and speed you have to work your way back there. I hit acceptance of the facts very fast, but acceptance of my identity, acceptance of my powerlessness, and acceptance of the permanence of that powerlessness and the impermanent nature of anything around me took much, much longer to attain.

I have seen people who achieved their acceptance far faster than it took me. Usually, they're the uber-faithful. They are devout Christians and Jews who relinquish control to the higher power with ease, and that helps them through the angry phase. I didn't do that, so anger was my Purgatory. Some depressed people turn to God to help them out, and that works for them too. I'm not proselytizing because I will never be dogmatic. Dogma doesn't agree with me, but it works for some.

Grief: Grief is unique to each of us. Whichever stage you're in is going to be shaped by your previous experiences in life, your temperament, your support network, and your ability to process and compartmentalize information and new experiences. There is no right way to do it, but I think we all need to recognize that we're in the thick of it to make any sense of it at all. The first step is admitting you have a problem, right? We have real problems, we have to find solutions, but we don't have to do it alone.

35
We Don't Know What We Don't Know

When Liam was born in Denver and we were routed to Los Angeles, I had no idea that the Boston option we passed on was our best bet. I also had no idea when we stayed in Denver for the Glenn, the Fon-tempt, and the Fontan, that there were even better hospitals, including CHLA, we could have gone to instead.

I have very few regrets and the ones I carry have nothing to do with the hospitals that have saved Liam's life. Denver and CHLA both did right by Liam, and he's here and doing well because of these amazing hospitals. It's kind of like comparing epic sports heroes where a marginal difference is a deciding factor, but you win either way. Still, I didn't know what I didn't know. Now I do.

If your child has some weird complication, something the doctors call out as unusual, anything that they've not seen before, then get a second opinion. I don't regret how things turned out, but I wish I had gotten a second opinion on Liam's hypoplastic pulmonary branch arteries. It may have made no difference, and we may have gone on exactly the same path, but I will never know. I didn't have the knowledge or confidence to ask for alternatives when the condition was so rare and unusual that I barely understood it.

I don't wish that I had asked because I expected a better outcome. I just wish I had asked because if Liam has problems with these cutting-edge Gortex grafts in his future, it could mean that I missed the boat on seeking alternatives in the past. I didn't necessarily step up and advocate for him like I might have if I hadn't been so scared and shell-shocked.

The one huge regret I do have was not fighting Liam on his Chloral Hydrate sedative before the two heart caths he had in July and August of 2008. The second one was just days before he started kindergarten. Liam doesn't like liquid medicines. He gags on them and feels more in control with a pill. They don't have a pediatric dose of the sedative in pill form at the Children's Hospital, just liquid.

Liam is so laid-back and calm. To prove my point, just a year earlier he amused the entire staff in pre-op when he raced down the all to the OR to have his sternal wires removed. He's always been positive and pleasant in the hospital. So the day of the first cath, I declined the sedative. Later I asked how he did, and they said he was "a little upset," but he did fine.

That first cath was more than seven hours long. Parents came and went in the waiting room finishing up open-heart surgeries in the time Liam was still in the cath lab. His collateral (extra and bad) veins were too numerous to treat fully. So we went back a month later for more, including positioning a stent in his left pulmonary artery which was not staying open despite the angioplasty.

That August, I passed on the chloral again, but Liam wanted us to go to the lab with him. For the first time ever, he wanted us to go with him. So we went, and he tried to negotiate. He asked if he could have an echo instead (he saw the echocardiogram machine in the corner of the room) and asked for the "cold ketchup" the lubricant in the bottle that they squirt on his chest. He offered to take a poke instead. I didn't understand until he was being held down on the table and screamed in terror when the gas mask came down over his face that he was scared of the mask itself. He was scared of being smothered into a sleep that I feared as much as he did.

After he stopped fighting and was unconscious, he made a horrible noise like a barking dog. The anesthesiologist told us it was just Liam's vocal chords, wet from the spit and effort of his fight. That gave me no comfort. I've never had to hold him down like that before or since. I never saw my child so afraid, and it was the worst I'd felt since he woke up after the Fon-tempt calling to me through his ventilator tube and drug induced fog . . . "Mommy." I am Mommy, and this is what I must do. I regret I didn't fight him in the pre-op room over the liquid medicine and had to hold him down until he drowned in the nitrous oxide. I regret I didn't know how to pick my battle.

Though I have this regret, I don't judge myself for what I didn't know. I forgive myself and take the pain and scars of those moments and lessons with me into the future. I share them with you so you might not trip where I tripped. And I bear no tolerance for anyone else's judgment for how I got through each morning that I surrendered my son to surgery, the weeks in the hospital at the mercy of the Fates, or any part of my motherhood for that matter. Just like old Blue Eyes, "I did it my way." It was the only way through the fire.

36

Me and the Virgin Mary on a Tightrope

I spent the first nine years of my education at Trinity Lutheran Day School. I went to church and Sunday school every weekend and was at the church school in the basement five days a week. That's a whole lot of Bible. I was about six when we studied Mary and Elizabeth both being told by angels about the babies they carried, and the line about how Mary kept these things in her heart and pondered them always stayed with me.

She pondered that her son would be the savior of creation and would die for it. Even as a small child I thought that was a sorrowful proclamation to bear in your heart. After the angels of ultrasound informed me of Liam's fate, I felt a kinship with Mary that was a new revelation in my soul.

Liam has a multi-million dollar designer heart, and there is no money-back guarantee. We get what we get, and we have no idea what that will be. The oldest child I knew of who was the most similar to Liam was a little boy named Michael Hall. One morning a year ago, he kissed his mom Jennifer goodbye, told her he loved her, and went off to school.

He left school in an ambulance, and Jennifer never saw him alive again. He was nine years old. I don't know exactly what took Michael's life, whether it was his heart, lungs, or brain that failed so suddenly. I'm not his mother, and I don't have the right to know. What I do know is how she misses her boy, how she keens to hear his name, and how she doesn't want Michael to be forgotten. I know that, and I remember him almost every day for Michael, for Jen, for Liam and for myself. I remember Michael and pray for the persistence and generosity of grace in my life and the grace of comfort and healing in Jen's.

I really don't know if Liam didn't come home one day if I would push for more postmortem study to learn more about my own child or not. As an advocate, I say I would, but I don't really know. I might want a study, but because each of these kids are so different, it probably wouldn't matter anyway. Besides, I would likely melt into mourning and devastation. One never knows how she will truly react when her world ends. That's the gist of it, the end of an identity, the end of the world as it was and the beginning of a new world order where everything one was has now become "other." It's the ultimate casting out with the greatest dose of pain.

My reality is this: I'm lucky my child is alive today. That's what I've got, and that's all I get, but that also hurts. I won't allow myself to let down my guard. The thing that alleviates the tension and pain is hope. The knowledge that Liam's heart slows down to twenty-nine beats or less per minute when he sleeps, that his rhythm is suspect, that humans were not meant to live with only one half of a heart that sometimes barely beats, and the knowledge of the these amazingly terrible things the surgeons did inside of my child are wholly unnatural is so much bigger than me that I lose my footing.

When I'm swayed in one direction by fear, I pull myself the other way with hope. It's a tight rope, and the only way to stay on is to balance the fear and the hope.

Falling into the fear will ruin my life and undermine Liam's self worth. Yet, sticking my head in the sand pretending nothing is wrong could kill my child. There is a healthy dose of fear that keeps my feet on the rope and moving forward, but it's a hard job figuring out what that dose is. . . it's truly a balancing act.

Hope is my balancing bar as I walk this tightrope between Liam's birth and the other side where one of us dies. I hope when I get to the end of the tightrope it's me that dies first, and that I die old - very, very old. I don't understand grouchy old people, my dad made it forty-eight years, Michael Hall was nine. How unbelievably lucky are you to be eighty-nine? I know I need to work on my empathy with the aged. But wow, to have such an opportunity for a full life,

I'm not wasting a minute of it. I'll meet my maker with all my faults and failures but with confidence that I made the most of what I was given.

In spite of all that parochial school, I still believe in God. One of my favorite parables is about the Pharisee who was a zealot and performed his prayers for the masses. Jesus called our attention to the man in the closet who kept his prayers to God private. I always liked that and, growing up, I felt that God was listening to me, even though He never spoke back. I'm no longer the little girl with that ferocious, fearful faith. I still have a faith, but my faith is personal, it fills the quiet space I share with God.

Some people believe that refusal to condemn non-Christians, gays, etc. is the same as picking and choosing from the Bible. To that I say, "See the Samaritan, and cast the first stone."

I choose to focus on the love in the Bible because it's far more impressive than the hate or fear. I've had enough of fear in my daily life. Hate is cheap and easy. Grace and love will give your soul a good workout.

Some people don't believe in any God or god. That's cool. If you're right, it's unfortunate that you'll never get the satisfaction of gloating over the rest of us in the void of nothingness. Then again, if you're right, all things will end and that is that. Then what will it matter?

Truthfully, I'm more of an agnostic with Christian training and tendencies. I don't believe in a divinity because I'm some lost creature who needs dogma to get through the day, nor do I feel superior to others because of my beliefs. I believe because it comforts me to seek order in the chaos of life.

I choose to believe because I've seen the miracles of children who've survived against all odds and the grace of mothers who've lost their children. It's ethereal and sublime that anyone can raise her head after her heart is crushed and drained dry like grapes for the bitterest wine. That is a miracle that makes me believe humans are more than the void from which we came.

No, I've seen too much to believe we're alone. I love too much to believe God is as vengeful as he's been portrayed by film and fundamentalists. I see things my way, and it's simply my way. I'm no evangelical. I don't expect or want anyone else to see the world the way I do. No one else has seen exactly what I've seen to shape that view, and I'm not so vain as to prescribe my faith to others.

The first day I learned about Liam's heart, that day the old me died, I asked, "Why me?" for about twenty minutes. Then, maybe it was God, or maybe it was just good sense, but the answer came. *Why not you? Why anyone? What makes you so special that this shouldn't happen to you?*

With that, I chose to be chosen. Not Moses and the burning bush chosen, just chosen. I decided to believe that Liam was going to be born as he was regardless of who gave birth to him. His affliction was his lot, not mine, and I was blessed to be his steward in a challenging life. I imagine God said, "Oh, you want a baby so bad, have I got the kid for you!"

For the year that I couldn't get pregnant, my worldview was angry and bitter and self-destructive. I thought, "God doesn't think I'd make a good mother. He doesn't want me to have a baby at all."

I now believe that God (fate or whatever benevolent force you choose) thinks very highly of Heart Moms. It's not everyone who can handle the pain, the fear, and the anticipatory grief that comes with this job description. A Heart Mom is a different kind of creature, and while I don't relish the pain of watching my son struggle, I'm paradoxically humbled and honored to be of this breed.

I believe, and you can call me delusional, that God gave me Liam because He/She knew I had more in me than I ever imagined. Because I believe that I was chosen for this amazing responsibility and blessed with the honor of being Liam's mom, I reach farther and try harder to make a difference for other kids and other families. I don't think I would have the passion for the Heartland if I didn't feel it was my destiny to be there. I don't think I became a Heart Mom because I was *special*, but I think being blessed with Liam made me strive to be a better person on his behalf. Was that was God's intention or just a side effect of circumstances? Moreover, who cares?

If I ask, "Why me?" then I answer, "Because I *can* make a difference, because I *will* make a difference, because I *have* made a difference."

Why not me? I'm the perfect 'Manda for this job, and I pray to God constantly for the grace to help me do it right. Why anyone? Why should any child suffer what my child has suffered? I have no canned answer for that question. No one else can ever tell my why it happened, so I've decided to write my own answer.

People might think I'm narcissistic to form that view, arrogant to think that God thinks highly of Heart Moms. What's my alternative? I can believe it doesn't matter at all, that this life and these struggles are completely meaningless and I have nothing to learn and nothing to teach. This journey has been too painful for me to believe it holds no value.

The other alternative is the core belief that being Liam's mother is a punishment for something I did, or for something I failed to do. I reject the idea of punishment outright because implicit therein is the idea that I resent Liam. That idea devalues my son and the merit of his life, and that I will not accept.

Liam is not a punishment, nor do I believe he is being punished. We are both challenged. Liam is not a burden, but he has the burden of managing his own broken heart. I would never add to Liam's burden with a layer of guilt for my own suffering. I chose to be his mother, chose Liam for the months it took me to get pregnant, chose Liam when I was offered termination, and chose Liam the morning after his birth when I chose to fight for his life instead of taking him home to die in my bed.

I am an honest being. I look inside myself and I see remnants of my anger, my misplaced resentments on those who haven't walked in my shoes, my jealously for what I've lost, and I know they're part of me. I am not perfect, and I am always seeking grace. But I say with all truth that never, not once, have I ever resented Liam. I chose to walk this path. Though I am weary, I never regret that I brought my son into this world and have done what I could to keep him here.

So, if not meaningless, and if not a punishment, then how else can I see the role set down before me as Liam's mother than as a blessing? I started this walk quite wobbly with high winds challenging me, now I'm doing cute tricks, even laughing and telling jokes as I defy gravity and good sense as I pirouette through my life. I'm still on the tight rope, and I have to be careful about embracing expectations or letting my hope slip, but I've turned out to be quite the acrobat. I think I can hear Mother Mary applauding me right now.

37
Psychiatry, 5 Cents

When I reflect on the past eight years, I wonder how I made it without a steady dose of therapy and drugs. Yet, here I am, footloose and Zoloft-free after all these years.

Writing, talking, never shutting up . . . that explains a lot. I have epiphanies and breakthrough moments all over town. The poor employees of Ross and Party America are my therapists when I rail about why I won't buy a $1 heart for the American Heart Association during Heart Month as long as only one penny will go to Congenital Heart Disease initiatives.

Moira's therapist was my therapist when I explained the context of her separation anxiety — our separation anxiety. But, I've only once sought professional help. Jim and I saw a counselor before Liam's Fon-tempt. He was very nice, but was clearly overwhelmed by our story, and didn't know how to help us with our anticipatory grief. He suggested date night.

We never went back.

The world is my therapist, listening passively as I work through this shit on my own terms in my own time. Thank you to a thousand strangers for being my therapist. Many people think going to therapy or taking drugs will solve all their problems. People think that about church, too. I am sure both things help, but real solutions are self-sought. You have to be an active participant in your own salvation. No one else can fix our problems for us. A sounding board and a support system surely helps, but it takes strenuous internal work to change the way we see the world.

The world does not yield to you or to me. The only thing we can change is the way we see it. I've had a random pattern of revelations that have allowed adjustments in my perspective. The first huge one was when I stopped fighting my fear that Liam would die. I just let go, let it wash over me, and acknowledged that it's not up to me. Ironically, the fact that I fought my feelings for so long is why it took me so long to get through them.

Relinquishing any false sense of control was the first step to taking my life back. I do have limited control, such as which doctor we see, which hospital we choose, what questions to ask, what activities my kids do, and the example I set for them. But the biggest things—the "is he going to die and when?" question—is entirely beyond my control.

What will be will be, and once I embraced the fact that I did everything I could in preparation for a hurricane that may or may not come, I could go back into my life and start enjoying the rain on the roof and the flowers it brought.

So as I lick my wounds and gaze into my scars, I guess I'm glad I skidded through these chapters of my life on my own chemical balance. I don't recommend avoiding help. It's there for a reason. If you need it by all means seek it and accept it. There's no reason to make life any harder on you than it has to be—it's hard enough!

Still, I got through this, and now I know I can get through anything. Knowing that scares the hell out of me. No one wants to be that strong. No one wants to ever need that strength. Being strong enough to get through hell means putting heaven on hold and earth at the bottom of your priority list. Strength can be as alienating as it is admirable.

More than once I was at work when the conversations of my friends centered on shopping or vacations, and I zoned out. I was so broke from medical bills, the only place I could afford to shop was the two clearance racks at Kohl's. I had no money for a vacation, and I'd spent all of my vacation time at the hospital or taking Liam to doctor visits. I only took six weeks medical leave for Moira's birth because I knew I needed my vacation time for Liam's next surgery.

I had to devalue vacation, make it meaningless, so that *not* having one couldn't hurt me.

All that banter and excitement made me ill tempered. I wrote angry poems, I excused myself from conversations where I had no input. When I had input, I felt like Debbie Downer. To be sure, my friends tolerated my sad sack comments about the deaths of children whose mothers were my other friends. My real-world friends tolerated my references to my Heartland family.

My Heartland family never talked about shopping or vacations, they talked about medical expenses and Make A Wish applications. Heart family conversations were war stories about our children's PTSD. Ironically, our own PTSD remained taboo. For us, owning our own suffering was to undermine our children's pain. Logical? No, but under these circumstances logic need not apply.

I related better to the Heart Moms because we were more intuitively aligned. I didn't want to be in the place where I resented my old friends, but I couldn't help myself, especially those first three years building up to the final Fontan.

I wasn't full of self-pity because I was too hardened for that. But I was blunt. I did a lot of fundraising to help me feel empowered, and I was honest about what I was going through. Some people can't handle that honesty and don't want to hear there are people who have it worse than they have it. Many people can't stand the radiating pain that is so hot and angry that it makes everyone uncomfortable. We are all so human.

It's taken me a long time to get away from the place where someone told me her dog died and think, "That's nothing, you should know what happened to my friend Melinda."

Of course I never said that out loud. Instead, I tried to remember my grief when my dog Murphy died. I tried to dig deep to find the empathy, but too often it was missing. For a long time I was disgusted with all levels of pain or grief that didn't necessitate informed consent of the degree I knew—or worse, the losses my Heart Family endured.

People freaking out about their kids' sports performance or SAT scores annoyed me to no end. Stress over a wedding or a party seemed self-indulgent, and I didn't want to hear about it. At work, my policy became, "Is someone going to die over this? No. Well, then maybe you're over-reacting."

Inwardly, I had zero tolerance for the drama of the masses; but outwardly I held it together most of the time. Inwardly, I devalued everything I had been before to make losing myself and my old identity seem like less of a loss. I was coping by demeaning everything I was and everything I'd lost. When that devaluation came out, it was off-putting to others who still valued all the things I undermined. It caused conflict, but for me to appreciate the things I couldn't have—the shopping, the vacations, the easy expectations that tomorrow was coming and wouldn't bring more shattering loss—would be to calculate how much I had already lost.

As strong as I was, I couldn't bear to add up my losses. I threw them overboard to keep afloat. I dismissed my longings for normalcy because I coveted so much and the pain of it distracted me from just getting through the challenges of accepting Liam's mortality. I had so much to grieve and I had to prioritize. In my zeal to throw things overboard, I was hitting people in the head with my ugly truths.

I don't think I was entirely wrong to feel that way because it was how I coped. I was surviving while the people around me were simply living their lives. A person can only handle so much. But the way I handled or mishandled reintegrating with the "normal" world where CHD wasn't anyone's priority or problem but mine stunted me and kept me in a separate universe.

It was like when I was a little girl and my friends would twirl the big jump rope. When it was my turn to jump in, I was always so afraid of being hit by the swinging beads that I never could join the fun. My timing was always off. Early on after Liam's diagnosis, I felt displaced from the world outside of my grief. By refusing to care about "lesser" problems of ordinary people, I relegated myself in the refugee state.

I know people stopped inviting and including me in things because all I ever talked about was congenital heart disease or what was happening with Liam. People didn't want to deal with my shit, and it's OK, I had a lot of shit to deal with, and it stunk.

Complicating my life was the fact that I never named my grief, never counted my losses. I just tried to pretend that what was lost wasn't worth mourning. I was wrong.

To escape the spin cycle of running from my loss, I had to find my way to a new kind of normal, where I could participate in the world around me. I had to find my way back to being a whole person, even if I would never be the same again. I kept trying and eventually, after much trial and error, I chipped away at my shell of bitterness until I could find my soft center that can be more human than soldier mother.

I did harden myself early on to get through the fire, but the time came to shed that burnt skin and emerge as a kinder person. What I've learned with that painful sloughing process is that it's better to fully feel whatever I am experiencing, good or bad.

A woman who grieves for her cat is capable of a great love, and to lose the object of her affection is a tearing away of something deep inside of her. It's always going to hurt to love someone or something. Everyone who loves gets pain, and by dismissing the pain of my real-world friends, I was undermining their love and basic humanity. I wasn't better than them for my suffering; I was broken by it.

It wasn't that their concerns were vapid or pointless so much as it was that I was hardened and angry. I was in a hard chrysalis of grief and everything on the outside lost all meaning. I couldn't understand why anything else mattered. For a very long time, I simply could not connect.

It took a lot of time and healing for me to understand that any human in pain deserves empathy. If you cut off a fingertip, a knuckle, a hand, a forearm, or a shoulder, the long-term disability caused by each injury will vary, but the pain of any of those losses is extraordinary regardless of the injury. It doesn't help to tell a man whose thumb was just dismembered how lucky he was it wasn't his whole arm. He still hurts.

I've learned this lesson more completely through Moira. She is so sensitive and will cry about almost anything. Rather than ridicule her, I comfort her, even if it seems silly to me. I never wanted to get Liam through the hell we've endured so far only to become frozen in a hard shell—inaccessible and demeaning. If I can't comfort my small children over small potatoes, will they ever come to me when the stakes are higher?

I had to get my kindness back, my empathy intact, or else this situation would have stolen my humanity along with my expectations. I had to get past the denial and anger of my grief. I never felt I had permission to grieve. I felt that grief was a luxury afforded only to those with the greatest and absolute losses. Since I denied it to myself, I would be damned if I would permit it for others. I caused much of my deepest pain by limiting my right to feel it and let it go.

I still have recessive moments, when I find a school fundraiser silly compared to initiatives to fund CHD research. Then I step back and think about how much I love my kids' school. Jim works there now, and I want to contribute to its success. It's just that my gut reaction is not always one of support. I still have healing to do.

But I've come a long way too. Once a friend said to me, "I know it's nothing compared to what you've been through with Liam, but I just hate taking my son for shots."

I said, "No, you're completely right. Shots are still hard for me, with both of my kids."

Shots suck, you hate to force your child to be poked. Is it as hard as signing your child over for twelve different heart surgeries? No, it's not that hard, but that doesn't mean it's easy.

And that's the point. Yes the darkest hours of my life were spent in a cardiac intensive care unit waiting for my son to turn the corner back to survival, but even the happiest moments at home were not always easy. There were, and are, a lot of hard moments for all people, and I had to unlock my damaged mind to remember that, and to remember that surviving a depression that almost killed me at fourteen, losing my father at twenty-two, then losing my best friend three years after that, were all terrible things that hurt me deeply. I'd never willingly relive those moments. But those experiences also left me strong enough to get through what came after. Sometimes we run so fast from our pain that we don't relish the fact that it's the pain that fueled the flight until we've reached the destination.

Lucky are the people who don't know how lucky they are to have the problems they have. Luckier still are those who know things could always be worse and don't invite trouble. Luckiest of all are those who can look past their own troubles and give comfort to those around them, and that's where I want to go. I'm still working on it, but I think I'm on the right path.

Empathy works two ways. It's not all about understanding another person's pain and sorrow. Sometimes, it's about sharing joy, about not minimizing what makes another person happy. I used to be revolted by those ugly enormous butterflies that old people (particularly in my Grandparents' trailer park) stick on their homes. I thought there could be nothing in the world so tacky.

Now, guess who adores butterflies? My daughter. If Moira could be a butterfly, her life would be complete. So, now, when I see a tacky butterfly, I see my beautiful daughter. It warms my heart that it doesn't matter to Moira whether they are gossamer or plastic, butterflies—it makes her smile.

I can extend that warmth to the old woman whose middle-aged son nailed that butterfly on the last home she'll ever own. I wasn't in that place before I got pregnant with Liam, and I certainly wasn't in that place for the first few years after he was born. But I'm there now, and I'm happy my heart has healed enough to feel that.

Similarly, my old snarkier self hated heart shaped jewelry. I thought it was tacky and saccharine. Now I have learned so many mysteries of the heart—its depths, its channels, its capacity—and I'm still discovering every day. I realize that wearing a heart is not kitchy if you know what it means. So I wear a heart-shaped necklace charm proudly, like I might wear my heart on my sleeve. It means something now, something bigger than my persnickety fashion sense.

Finding my way back to empathy has taken me a step further toward my new normalcy, and now I can share in simple joys where before I couldn't see past the plastic. It was a priceless and painful journey and maybe it would have been easier if I'd asked for help, but here I am. I'm not better than the suicidal teenager, the comfortable entitled young woman, or the shattered new Heart Mom that I have been, but I'm wiser for having worn and shed those skins, and I'm sure I'll outgrow this one someday too.

Life is so painfully short and there is too much risk to stand still or be stuck in a single stage of grief, be it depression or anger, constant bargaining or denial. We have to keep moving, growing, reaching for more satisfaction and meaning in the lives we have. We move forward toward peace and sanity. We keep moving to set the right example for our kids. We have to keep changing to rise to the challenges we don't even know we're going to face down the road. To paraphrase Gandhi, we change on the inside to be the change we wish to see beyond ourselves in the greater world. It's the only way to make peace with our pain and fear, and it's the only way to be a whole person instead of a broken shell. Metamorphosis is painful, but the stagnant alternative is crippling.

38
A Man on a Mission

Liam loves babies. No, that is an understatement; Liam is obsessed with babies. He acts like an aging woman with grandma-envy every time he sees a baby. Fortunately, we reel him in just after Liam flatters the subject's mother with his emphatic approval of her child, but before he has the chance to genuinely creep out the parents with too much interest.

Liam could spend an entire day with a baby and never get bored or annoyed. In fact, he has every intention of having his own baby some day.

This is his take on his future:

Liam: "I'm going to have a baby named Tom. I'm going to take him to work with me."

Me: "Where are you going to work?"

Liam: "I'm going to be a chef like Daddy, and drive a skid steer loader."

Me: "Where will Tom be when you're working?"

Liam: "In his car seat."

Me: "In the skid steer loader?"

Liam: "Yeah, and then he can sit in the high chair when I'm a chef."

I've not initiated these discussions with Liam about what he wants to be when he grows up, he initiates them. "I want to be just like Daddy when I grow up," he routinely announces.

This summer, when we were visiting our Heartland friends in Houston, and Liam was very blessed to drive a skid steer loader with our friend Toby, who is also a Heart Dad to Justin. Despite the day being 103 degrees with 100% humidity, Liam wasn't deterred from his passion for construction vehicles. He also drove a digger and a forklift.

Liam doesn't fear that his future won't come, he just lives and looks forward. He doesn't know any better, and I wish he never had to know what I know. I wish the truth weren't pressing down on us with each new day.

Moira likes babies too, but she's not obsessed with them. She is certain she will have two little girls and proclaims that she will bring her babies to school with her when she's a teacher. Both of my kids have big plans.

I see Moira's future effortlessly. I see more of our fun shopping trips escalating to prom dresses and a wedding gown and baby clothes for those two little girls. I see Moira's graduation, wedding, and children. I can close my eyes and see my daughter's life spread out like a beautiful marriage quilt built on texture and substance. I can practically touch it because it's so real to me.

It's too easy, and it's the ease of seeing Moira's future that hurts because looking forward with Liam is like looking through a bottle of milk. I want to be free to imagine Liam's future too. I want to see him going to culinary school, but instead I see him getting exhausted or going back on oxygen. I want to see him getting married and having a baby, but I see specters of complications, sudden death, a return to the heart donor waiting list. I'm still too scared to look too far down the road.

But, even if Liam's best imaginable future includes struggle, it also includes opportunity. I need to get over my fears of Liam suffering to support his pursuits and opportunities. I need to get over myself and my fears, even the justifiable ones, and just let Liam just live.

I don't want to see bad things for my son or put my own baggage before his dreams. I want to carry my hope beyond today. But to do that skirts dangerously near the edge of expectation. I walk a fine line but I must take more risk on the side of hope, lest I steal Liam's own expectations for himself. While my own expectations were dashed, I have no right to steal Liam's.

I've seen so many parents steal their children's hope before they even knew they had reason to fear. I've met kids so emotionally crippled by their parents' own fear that they can't function as adults. I've heard other adult survivors call their peers "cardiac cripples." They weren't crippled by their CHD, they were crippled by their parents' fear of it.

Those parents clung so tightly that they malformed their children's spirits worse than their already-misshapen hearts. I've met adult CHD patients who have no idea what is wrong with their hearts either because their parents *wouldn't* tell them, or *couldn't* tell them because the parents were too afraid to learn what their kids would need to know as they grew older.

I don't really blame these parents, not all of them. The oldest of the bunch were told not to save or college or weddings, but to set money aside for a funeral. They were told, "Take her home and love her," and given to expect nothing more than a short life for their children. It might surprise you, but the family mental health and counseling needs for families like ours are still inadequate. But that's not really an excuse to put our issues on our kids and make their lives even harder.

I know teen and adult CHD'ers who believe they won't grow up. I know one mom whose daughter is almost a teenager and she still doesn't believe she'll live to be an adult. But sadly, she never believed she'd live to be ten, and now she's almost thirteen.

If the parents hold no hope, how can their children find it? It's a nagging question, and while I do my best not to judge, I can't help but believe some of these families are so paralyzed by their grief and fear that they've ceased to function. Now, the future they refused to have faith in is now on top of them. How do these kids face their future when their parents refused to believe it would come?

Liam sees an infinite future for himself, and well he should. Liam has amazed doctors and nurses with his stamina and attitude, and I won't limit his vision or cast my own shadows on his horizons. I've no right or reason to sell my son short; what kind of mother would that make me?

Liam holds the compass to his own path, and if we follow him he won't steer us wrong. He's the only native in the Heartland, and we must let the little chef be our guide. He's indigenous to his own heart, and his heart is not the catastrophe to him that it was to us. Liam's heart is simply a challenge he faces in life. As the burden of decision-making shifts completely from me to him in the coming decade, I have to let his view be the one that shapes how our family treats his condition. It is after all about the person, not the disease. It's all about Liam, the whole person who just happens to have half a heart.

As much as I fear my own dangerous expectations and as much as I fear for Liam's own awakening, I take comfort in a single vision. I hold tight to the flash of an image that blessed my brain when I was pregnant with Liam. After the diagnosis I foolishly read *Angela's Ashes*. After Angela lost her second and third child, I tossed the book on Jim's pillow and rolled to my left side to weep into the corner of my purple bedroom.

Lying there with my eyes wide open, I saw a vision in my head. A young man stood atop a rocky cliff, clearly in our Colorado Mountains. He looked like Jim but with very blond hair and a longer face, his features influenced by me, my high forehead and cheekbones. This boy had a huge smile and was all dressed up for hiking in boots and utility shorts. He was beaming, he was happy, and he was fit. I knew it wasn't Jim, and I realized, that boy who visited me from the future was my son. The star of this waking dream was Liam, and he was gone as quickly as he appeared.

After that, I went out to REI to buy a carabineer—a relic on which to hang my hope. Maybe that young man is the same child who just argued with me about doing his homework. Maybe he will step out of my dream one day, cook me a meal, and run off to meet the girl who will give him a baby named Tom. Maybe not, but I can always hope. All of us in the Heartland, we must never lose hope, it's the only thing we can really give our children.

39
Paling around with Pandora

At the beginning of this adventure, I was Pandora. I intruded where I wasn't meant to be in the private realm of my developing child. Already a meddling mother, I opened the box to find broken hearts all around, Liam's, mine, Jim's, and so many people who love Liam. Beyond my own womb and my own home, I found heartbreak all the way around the globe, endless, terrifying heartbreak and heart-stopping fear.

Yet, just like Pandora, at the bottom of the box, smaller than all the ills, the fears, or the anger I found a tiny spark of Hope. I found it in my bathtub on diagnosis night. I found it in Dr. Porreco's reassuring words and warm embrace, in Dr. Badran's protectiveness, in Nurse Mark LeGaoult's encouragement, in Dr. Bushman's kind patience. I found hope in the boundless skill and courage of Dr. Starnes and Lacour-Gayet and all the Ilbawis, Mees, Frasers, Norwoods and others of their caliber who harness hope and stoke it into a flaming life.

I find hope in the cadre of medical professionals who have never given up on Liam or kids like him, from the sardonic Dr. Sondheimer to the bemused Dr. Chang. I find hope in the banter, battles, and affection Moira and Liam exchange daily. I find hope in my husband's tears at a wedding when we watch the groom dance with his mother, and we keep on hoping we'll get there too. I find hope wherever it can be found.

I find hope every day in every Heart Family I've met. I found hope in Leslie and in Steve, and it didn't die with them. Hope is in the love I see between Jim and Liam as Jim rediscovers and shares the treasures of his childhood with his son. Hope radiates off both of my children when they are affectionate and sweet and when they fight as though everything is normal. Because it is normal, Liam and Moira are just brother and sister in a world where fighting is what all brothers and sisters do. I find hope in the fabric of every moment of my life with Liam even forcing him to clean his room or when he has a tantrum in Target. Bringing him his birthday lunch in the cafeteria and his enthusiasm for Christmas lights have brought me profound moments of joy. I never forget how close I came to missing those moments or how tenuous they are. Mostly though, Liam himself is the embodiment of hope and love.

It is Liam who doesn't care that his heart is special except that it's a platform for making friends. He's the one who hops up and down from exam table to exam table like it's no big deal. Liam's astounding ability to take what shattered my understanding of the word, "normal," call it his life, and make it a good life – that is what gives me the greatest hope.

It's not enough that Liam survives, that he ekes out an existence. He needs to live a life, and already he is doing that. His interests ranged from Thomas the Tank Engine in preschool to dinosaurs and Ben Ten Today . . . girls tomorrow? Liam has a sense of humor and a sense of worth that are both larger than mine ever were at twenty-seven years, much less age seven. That is where my hopes lie. I can invest my hope in my son, because I have faith he will make the most of the life he's been given. I have faith in Liam.

Yes, I peered into Pandora's box situated inside my body and saw a future of pain and possible death, but Liam was the box itself. He was wrapped around all my fears but he also held all the hope and growing the cache of love that would maintain us. The hope is still in the box; the hope was always there in his broken heart. When he still was just Flipper the little Lima bean on that dark screen there flickered this shining light. That was the heart. Liam's broken heart is the source of all my worst fears and the host of my greatest hope.

I have to believe that I helped put that seed in him, that his hope-filled heart, no matter how broken it is, came from me and from

Jim. It came from the deep and bright love that we share, a love that yearned for a family and now rejoices in having these amazing children in our lives.

No matter how bad things have gotten, no matter how dark, I always find hope growing in the love of our home. It's in me and Jim and Moria, just as much as it is in Liam. Congenital Heart Disease did not give my life meaning, but my children and my relationship with Jim has. CHD just burned the hell out of everything else that could have made me lose focus of what *does* matter. It burned away many good things, too, and I've grieved those losses. Yes, Liam has a horrible disease, no doubt, but learning how to accept that changed me in beautiful ways. So, even for the fire, I am grateful.

40
And the Beat Goes On . . . For Now

I kneel and reach into the tub, squeezing baby oil in gleaming sheets over Liam's chest. Today, he is seven and a half, and this is the fourth time in eleven months that I've performed this baby oil ritual. Twenty-four hours and thirty minutes ago, I strategically pressed five thick adhesive foam pads to Liam's chest. I snapped leads to the metal nubs on those pads, and I turned on the Holter Monitor, a 24-hour EKG machine. For the past day, Liam asked every fifteen minutes, "Mommy, is it done yet?"

Each time he asks, we fish the Holter box out of his pocket and check the countdown on the display, call out the time together, and then slip the box back in the pocket of his over-sized orange hoodie. We go nowhere for a day, and then the Holter beeps, and the countdown is over. The unpleasantness is, however, just beginning.

Now that the box and leads are detached, I'm kicking myself. I forgot to ask the tech, who sent the Holter from the hospital, to include those orange scented pads that make tape removal slightly more tolerable. I kick myself again for forgetting that if I had snapped the leads to the metal spurs before I stuck the pads on my child, it wouldn't have hurt him yesterday when I had to shove them against his ribs. I expect to see bruises when the pads are off.

I kick myself once more for forgetting that the last time I strung the leads between the splits in the adhesive pads and under the excess foam making it easier for the oil to get underneath and loosen their grip. How did I get so stupid? Why did I forget the little things that would have made this easier for us both?

While I'm busy beating myself up, I work the sticky pads loose, slowly with more and more baby oil. Liam wants me to stop, "Why do you have to do that? Please, Mommy, don't pull yet. I'm not ready. Please, Mommy, don't."

I stop trying to wriggle my fingertips between my son and this foam and apply more and more baby oil. While I work the oil into the edge of the foam, Liam's scars glare at me accusingly. Thick and deep white stripes testify to six times his chest has been cut through to the bone, five times the bone sawed through and the ribs spread apart. Liam doesn't remember, but his skin hasn't forgotten. The twenty-one pucker marks are mementos of where chest tubes drained fluid off his heart and lungs over and over and over again at two different hospitals. The slow sucking of history is recalled in white dots that look like bullet holes.

I lean back and sit on my feet, still on my knees, I snap the oil shut and carefully place the slippery bottle on the bath mat and rub the excess oil from my hands on the dirty mat. I'll wash it later with the towels.

As I pull myself to my feet and feel the age in the backs of my knees, I tell Liam, "Lay on your tummy, sweetie. Pretend you're swimming, then the stickies will get all wet and come off easier."

"I like to lay on my back better so I can go under the water with my ears."

"OK," I say, as I run the washcloth through the water. "Then let's put this over your stickies so they get wet, OK? You can wear it like a blanket."

Liam nods, reclines, and I drape the sopping washcloth over the pads, hiding them for now. "Mommy, can you close the door so I can splash?"

I slide the glass shower door shut, I see myself in my bathroom mirror and I feel my age in my face. I can see guilt seeping from my eyes. I put these adhesive pads on my child with my own hands, and now I must remove them. Liam has been waiting more than a day to get these "stickies" off, and it's a slow dance to peel them back.

I cover my still-wet hands with copious amounts of soap, and as I turn on the sink to rinse, I hear Liam thrashing in the bath like a shark. He transitions so easily from annoyed to overjoyed. I hate that I'm going to come back, that I have to open the door and break into splash time to peel back the stickies.

I clean my room, put my dirty socks and pajamas in the laundry, pull out the baskets to make ready for the oily towels. I only clean when I'm upset. I always clean when I'm upset. I stall and listen to Liam singing in the tub, playing in the water.

It must be getting cold now. I go back in the bathroom, and I slide the door back. Liam is naked on his back, the washcloth still mostly covering him. His head is under the water, his eyes are closed, he is so peaceful, and I don't want him to hear me. I don't want to do what must come next.

"Liam, it's time."

He doesn't hear me, or maybe he pretends he doesn't hear me. I reach down. It's not far, I'm so short, and gently wiggle his big toe. His big blue eyes pop open.

"It's time."

"Oh, Mama," he says. He only calls me "Mama" when he wants to be dramatic. "Why do we have to do that?"

"We can't leave them on, they'll get all dirty. You'll feel better when they're off," I offer. I don't know if that's true, but Liam can't go to school tomorrow with five metal snaps poking through his shirt.

I kneel again, and I take the baby oil. I saturate the areas around each pad. Then, I start at the top, on the bony area on his right clavicle. I rub the oil with my index finger slowly and firmly into the pad, as soon as it starts to slip, I work my finger under and his skin tears a little. Liam winces. Eventually, the oil and the friction works the pad loose enough that it's hanging only by the corner, like a loose tooth ready to come out of a mouth with one last tug. I tug, Liam cries out, "Ouch, Mommy, don't do that!"

The first one is off, that was the easy one. For the next quarter of an hour, I peel them back. Slowly and methodically, but it doesn't matter. No matter how cautious I am I still take a layer of Liam's reluctant skin with each square of resistant foam. Liam and I both try not to cry. We both wince, but our tears stay balanced on the rims of our eyes.

These new marks that rise out of his allergic reaction will fade, but right now they sting. The old scars that I put into my son's flesh by signing a dozen forms will go on forever. These lines are the transactional record, the balance sheet recounting the price of this and every moment. The scars run like runes along Liam's flesh and predict company.

A new scar will come. A new scar is coming. Who am I kidding? A pacemaker is coming. That is the harbinger of the Holter. This insidious little box with its wires and pads that keeps coming back to our home like a bad penny.

Just like the last three times, Liam's cardiologist will call me again, like he always does. He'll call me in four or five weeks when I've all but forgotten this day and remind me of the knifepoint that promises to find Liam again. The next time, like the last time and the time before, we might change Liam's prescription. But, it's only a matter of time before the tinkering with drugs stops and I sign Liam over for his thirteenth heart surgery.

The twelve surgeries that came before have scarred the inside of his heart so deeply that it doesn't conduct electricity as it should. Liam's heart has never done anything as it should.

I stop myself from going into the future because I have this moment now standing over the tub, and I take it. I soothe Liam's blistered skin, I put more oil on each of the five rectangles of raised flesh and use a warm washcloth to gently, slowly rub away the tell-tale adhesive shadow that clings to orange fuzz from his sweat shirt.

When Liam is clean and we're both a little further from the edge of tears, I let him shower off and help him out of remnants of his slippery bath. In layers over each wound, I combine Benadryl to stop the allergic reaction, Bacetracin to prevent infection of these microscopic tears in Liam's skin, and Vanicream to sooth the sting. At least I could remember my concoction.

As I rub the last layer gently into the welts, I tell Liam, "I'm sorry, so sorry, but now we're done."

I pull out his new green sweater he picked out himself that I haven't let him wear yet. Now that it's on, he's moved on. "Don't I look sharp, Mommy?" he asks as he combs his hair.

"You're the most handsome boy in the world," I tell him with absolute honestly. Now Liam is ready to just be Liam and drop this twenty-four hour intrusion, and get on with his life. I get the laundry started and we head out to Fed Ex. It is a ritual, I always let him put the Holter package in the Fed Ex box. I give him the power to cast it away, but I know it will be back.

Liam doesn't know any different because this is his normal. It's taken me almost eight years to own it, but this is my normal, too. Only, unlike Liam, I know the difference between my old normal and our life as it is. Different—how perfect that *different* is a challenge word on this week's second-grade spelling test. This is our normal, but it is so different from what I expected and yet so much better than I ever dared hope.

41

The Last Word, an Epilogue for my Ladies, or
What to Expect when You're Expecting the Worst

I wasn't always like this. I wasn't always OK, and sometimes I'm still not. I still cry in the shower and veg out when I can't handle this load. I wasn't always well adjusted and capable of talking or writing through the hardest moments of my life without shedding tears. I've shed those tears, but they come from a deep well that never runs dry.

At the bookstore, I gaze at the titles I read when I was pregnant and have long since given away. With one ultrasound they ceased to apply to me. They weren't my books anymore. They were for women who were having normal happy pregnancies. Those books set expectations for bodies that created healthy babies. My body failed me, and worse, my body failed Liam.

Those thoughts are ugly, but they exist. They take shape in the dark corners of my mind and hiss at me like feral cats. I know they live in the minds of other moms like me—to the hissing voice in my head I say, "Shut the fuck up."

My body may not have grown Liam's heart properly, may have housed a negligent womb that allowed a strange extra lumbar to wrap itself around his tiny spine and undercooked his heart, but my body loves that child as much as the one it made correctly.

With one afternoon in December, my life changed forever. On the axis of a medical stool, the direction and trajectory of my existence swiveled and shot off into a completely different universe from where I was heading. Now, here you are, too.

I don't know what doctor's office or maternity ward you were in when your world shattered, but if you're one of my crew, it's happened to you. It happened and you have a pivot point, a time in your life where your identity fractured and you became a Heart Mom. I am so sorry you joined this club, but now that you're here, welcome.

What is my advice? How could I write this book without offering a scrap of advice to moms like me? I've told my story and you can learn what you choose from it, but I can't refuse you a little grain of advice. So, here it is.

What to expect when you're expecting a heart baby? Expect nothing, but don't expect the worst. Your unborn or newborn baby was not abducted by a pedophile; I am not the FBI. Do *not* expect the worst! Know the worst exists, but it hasn't found you yet, and it may never find you.

Know you are allowed, entitled, and encouraged to face the truth and that your fear of the truth is real, it's valid. The truth *is* out there, and it's a stroke, a heart attack, an infection. The truth is a nightmare and a tiny little casket. It may not happen to you, but it might. That is what people around you don't seem to understand.

Tragically, it will happen to someone. It happens all the time, and it will happen again and again to someone exactly like you and me. It might be you, it might be me. We never know who it's going to be, but when it happens it is never, ever fair.

It's true, it happens, and that fear is palpable and it's in your life until it's not. The fear only ends in death, yours or your child's. Everyday, you and I stick our hands in the jar and draw out a marble. Everyday that we get the white one is a blessing. Everyday in America, England, Australia, Uganda, Egypt, and China mothers just like us draw a black one, and every day children die from CHD. Don't let anyone who doesn't have to draw a marble minimize the effort it takes to reach in the jar or cast their judgment on how you get through your day. You have to live with your fear. This is your reality; this is my reality. I know my shit; welcome to the outhouse.

You don't have to let anyone but you (and a well-informed pediatric cardio thoracic surgeon or pediatric cardiologist) attempt to belay your fears. Someone who doesn't know what we face and is trying to minimize our fears is akin to approaching a rabid dog with a squeaky toy. They just don't get it. So don't allow them to make you feel worse than you do by their failed attempts to make you feel better.

It's OK to be angry that these people say the wrong thing, but only for now. They don't know any better, and eventually you do forgive them. It's OK to take your time so you can do it sincerely. It's not real forgiveness if given begrudgingly.

To forgive you need to understand where your anger comes from. Give yourself time to get wherever it is you need to be to gain the strength for forgiveness. That grace doesn't happen overnight. I forgive you for your anger because I understand it. But someday, you're going to have to let it go and forgive yourself.

You can't stay angry forever, so accept your anger, and let it run its course. If you fight it, you won't ever be able to let it go. Own your fear, face it, and then fight like hell to keep your hope. Don't latch on to the fear; it's poison. Latch on to your hope; it will sustain you. This is your fear, not your child's fear, so don't feed it to them. Deal with it so your child isn't burdened by it. Hiding from it doesn't help, and wallowing in it is worse. You've got to work through it or you go nowhere.

What to expect?

Expect that everything you thought you knew or would have is false. Expect that you alone need to compartmentalize your fear. Expect that bad things might and can happen, but nothing, not even the bad stuff, is certain. Be cautious, but be optimistic. Dream big and if you can't dream big, don't stop your child from dreaming for himself.

If that ugly fear comes to pass and your baby, your toddler, your grown child dies, at least you didn't waste what time you had with your child expecting the worst. Expecting the worst steals your joy, and haven't you lost enough already? It's better to have no expectations than only bad ones, believe me I know. I've been there.

Expect that your child's story and your story are going to be uniquely your own. Two separate stories. You may never experience many of the feelings or challenges that I have, but you probably will. I don't know for sure and neither do you. Expect that you're going to have to get through what comes, and befriend people like you who will understand and can help you. Expect that you are going to be angry again and again, and work through it day by day until you can start to feel more than fear and anger, and work through that until you can feel joy.

Expect that even if the worst thing happens, that it's going to be worse than you can even imagine, so try your best to not to imagine it. I know how hard that is. I practice what I preach and it takes more effort than I can put into words to keep the fear in check so I can ring in the joy, but it is possible. Keep practicing.

Know this, your worst fears may never find you, but what has found you is bad enough, so you need to address it.

So my last and best piece of advice is grieve. Grieve now, not just for what might happen, but for what has happened to you and what will never happen for you and your child. Grieve for all those things that your child cannot do or have—the sports, the roller coaster rides, the casual consent to ear piercing, the smooth skin and in tact bone—the whole heart.

Grieve for all those lost expectations. Grieve for the loss of your peace of mind because it's gone and you're never getting it back the way you once had. Grieve for the things you cannot do for you child. Grieve that you can't kiss it and make it better. Grieve for the truth that your child will find his own fear one day and when he does, all you can do is hold your baby as the threat of mortality hits all too soon. But take comfort in the fact that it's been a long time in coming for him and he's stronger than you are because you've given him your strength.

You will never ever get over it, but you won't move through it until you grieve. Fear and grief are the price of staying in the fight. Grieve for the anticipation so you can move through it and find stability until the next wave hits. If you avoid the anger and the fear, they will hunt you down and drown you from the inside out. Grief is how you metabolize the fear and anger. So, grieve, and forgive yourself for your anger. If you don't do this, if you don't work through it and let it out, you won't be able to separate your own fear from your child's life. You need to own your fear so that you don't let it spill over onto your child. You owe it to both of you to grieve properly so you can get on with living the life that you share.

Know that this grief is not a mountain we get over, but an ocean we swim through. We never surmount our grief, never overcome it, we just get through it, stoke by stroke, breath by breath until we reach the shallows where we can find our feet again, and slowly we reach the shore. And even when we're dry and warm again, we will always smell of the salt of our tears. We will always carry those grating grains of sand beneath our nails. We will never forget our swim through the ocean of grief, and that's why we will never "get over it." We simply get through it, and the tide always threatens to take us back out to sea. We have to find a way to live on the beach and see the beauty there, even as we fear being swallowed by the sea.

Grieve, my sweet broken-hearted sisters (and brothers, Heart Dads hurt, too). Cry for what you've lost, cry for what you fear. Just like I tell Liam, "Sometimes you have to cry, it's like going potty, if you don't let it out, you'll get sick."

When you can think about your child's broken heart only incidentally and abstractly and it is not the sole focus of your daily life, when it is just a peripheral shadow and not a pitch blackness that blinds you, then you'll breathe, you'll live, and you'll get through it. I can't promise you anything better than that.

(((Heart Hugs to the Heart Moms and Dads)))
Amanda
P.S. this is just advice. Like a Google Map. It's ink on a page, pixels on a screen. If you follow it verbatim, you might get lost. You're the one who has to find your own way through your fear. Don't let me or anyone else tell you differently. You'll know when you've arrived. I'm still on my journey too, but I'll meet you there.

Heart Warrior's Field Manual
Table of contents

History

The history of pediatric congenital heart surgery starts in the 1940s at Johns Hopkins University, the University of Minnesota, and Yale University and picks up speed in the 1950s with Johns Hopkins' Dr. Alfred Blalock, Vivien Thomas (a genius lab technician), Dr. Helen Taussig. Their Blalock-Taussig (BT) Shunt has saved tens of thousands of lives. In the 1980s at Boston Children's and later Children's of Philadelphia and Nemours, Dr. William Norwood invented and refined the eponymous procedure that would make Liam's life remotely possible. Damus, Kaye, and Stansel would adapt Norwood's work to children like Liam who were not actual Hypoplastic *Left* Heart patients, but not really BT Shunt only candidates. It's a rare subset, but part of a larger collective that sees about 6/1000 babies born missing major heart structures[1].

The early variations of the BT Shunt and Norwood surgeries were highly fatal, but the children who endured them and the parents who consented to them had no other choice but death. Those children were absolutely dying, and those doctors were their only hope. Over time, the courage and sacrifices of those Post-war American families and families in France, where the Fontan operation was being developed, made it possible for my son and thousands more to not only survive, but thrive and live amazing and full lives. Dr. Glenn added to the mix by staging the Fontan procedure into two separate surgeries to spare the patient the shock of a full diversion of blood flow all at once.

Talented surgeons since Blalock, Norwood, Fontan, Stansel, and Glenn have added to the success of the surgical intervention not only for hypoplasts but for children with atrial, ventricular, valvular, and other structural defects of the cardiovascular system. Doctors

---

[1] Hoffman and Kaplan, Journal of the American College of Cardiology, 2002; 39:1890-1900

like Starnes, Lacour-Gayet, Fraser, Mee, Hanley, Burke and a handful of others of their caliber in places like Boston, Philadelphia, Ann Arbor, and San Francisco have inverted a 90% mortality rate year over year for kids like Liam.

I recommend visiting the Johns Hopkins Medical History and the Yale University web sites site (Google it for most current versions) to learn about the earliest days of CHD treatments and the visionaries who gave Liam and so many other the gift of hope.

Glossary of Native Terms
(or words Microsoft refuses to acknowledge)

Note: This glossary is directly relevant to the text in this book. I do not go into great detail about heart defects Liam does not have, treatments he would not receive, or experiences common to many CHD patients, but not to us. For instance, Liam's never crashed or stroked (that I know of), so nothing about that is included. He never had a J or Gtube and had an NG tube only briefly, so nothing about feeding issues is in here either. That said stroke and feeding issues are huge complications faced by many but not most CHD families. Watch my website, www.amandaroseadams.com, for more detailed information about congenital heart disease, collaborative care, stories from other families, and additional resources for the Heartland.

Disclaimer: While the information in this glossary may prove a helpful starting point, it IS NOT and is not meant to be comprehensive. No matter what you read in any book or on the Internet ALWAYS consult your pediatric cardiologist with your questions (or your adult congenital heart specialist if you're a teen or adult). If they don't answer you (and I'm not saying if they don't give you the answer you *want* to hear, but if they ignore you outright) find a new doctor and ask that one. It is your right and your responsibility to own your healthcare information, participate as a team member in decisions about your care, and be respected in that role by your healthcare providers. Sometimes you have to work harder and reach further. I'm sorry, but that's just how it is.

Atria: The average healthy human heart has two atrial chambers. The left atrium receives oxygenated blood from the lungs through the pulmonary vein. The right atrium receives deoxygenated blood the body has already used from the superior vena cava and inferior vena cava.

After his first open-heart surgery, Liam was left with one large atrium that receives blood from the pulmonary vein and both the inferior and superior vena cava. During his second open-heart surgery the superior vena cava was removed and attached to his pulmonary branch artery. This was redone during his third open-heart surgery During his fourth open-heart surgery Liam's inferior vena cava was removed and a Fontan conduit sewn to the side of his atria to allow blood overflow back into the heart. The conduit was then routed to flow into his pulmonary branch arteries as well. Now there is no systemic venous blood flow to Liam's heart at all.

Atrial fibrillation (A-Fib): Liam may or may not have been born with A-Fib. Because the area of the heart that causes this issue is close to parts of Liam's heart that were missing or malformed, A-Fib may be endemic to his other birth defects, but surgery probably made it worse. After Liam's second major surgery, the Glenn shunt, he had a prolonged episode of A-Fib as his heart's swelling decreased. This repeated itself for every surgery and cath since. Now Liam is in a persistent state of entering and leaving A-Fib wherein his sinus node fails and his atrium or upper chamber (he only has one –see the previous and subsequent entries) wiggles instead of squeezes. As long as Liam's ventricle squeezed in response, Liam avoided a pacemaker. Now, the A-fib is persistent enough that medication can't stop it, and Liam needs a pacemaker in the near future.

Atrial Septal Defect: A hole between the two upper chambers of the heart. Liam had a couple of small ones that became non-issues when his entire atrial septum was surgically removed by Dr. Starnes during the DKS procedure. For some children with CHD, this is the only heart defect they have and it is highly treatable if diagnosed early.

Aorta: In a healthy heart, the aorta ascends from the dominate left ventricle to feed the body oxygen-rich blood. Liam's aorta not only ascended from the wrong side of his heart, but because the pulmonary valve it was attached too was feeding it a mere trickle of blood, it developed to be about 10% of the size it should have been to sustain his life.

Additionally, this hyoplastic aorta failed to provide significant volume to feed his aortic arch, so he had a severe coarctation as well. During his first surgery, Liam's aorta was dissected from his pulmonary valve and grafted to his pulmonary artery to allow the blood volume from the left side of his heart to feed his body.

Aortic Arch: is fed by the aorta and diverts oxygen rich blood to the brain and arms. Liam had a severe kink (coArctation) in his aortic arch, which could lead to massive stroke if untreated. Dr. Starnes surgically corrected Liam's coarctaion. Like an ASD, a CoArc is sometimes the only heart defect a child might have and while a dangerous defect if untreated, is frequently treated in a cath lab now. Liam's condition was too complex and required surgical intervention.

Aortic Valve: is the valve that, in a healthy heart, is found on the left ventricle of the heart and passes oxygen rich blood to the aorta. Liam's aortic valve was attached to his pulmonary artery, so the left side of his heart was pumping blood to his lungs. However, due to his fetal heart structures, this blood was diverted to his aortic arch and allowed him to develop in utero.

Had those structures failed at birth, Liam would have flooded his lungs with blood and died rapidly of oxygen deficiency to the brain or a pulmonary embolism. This is why in utero heart screening mid term is so vital.

Cardiac MRI: Also called MRA, this is a magnetic resonance imaging screen of the heart itself. Liam had one before his Fon-tempt. If Liam gets a pacemaker in coming years, MRA will no longer be an option for him. Though it does not measure venous or lung pressure like a cardiac cath, it is less risky and a nice option for patients and cardiologists.

Cardiac Anesthesiologist, Pediatric Variety: This M.D. is usually a pediatrician who does fellowships in both cardiology and anesthesiology in order to administer anesthesia to babies and children with heart defects. Anesthesiology is complicated even in completely healthy patients, for children with deformed hearts it is both an art and a science. Without these folks, surgeries and caths for kids like Liam would be too dangerous to attempt. Kudos to these amazing doctors!

Cardiac Catheterization. Pediatric Variety: During a cardiac cath, the patient (Liam) is taken to a sterile cath lab where he is put under general anesthesia and a catheter is inserted into the femoral artery in his groin to access his heart. Sometimes, due to the DKS reconstruction of his aorta and pulmonary arteries, the doctors also accessed Liam's carotid artery in his neck.

Anyway, once the catheter is in the arteries it's threaded into the heart to measure pressures and do all kinds of fancy things like add a stent, test closing the hole left open in Liam's Fontan conduit, and coil off all kinds of peripheral or collateral veins that keep growing even though we don't want them. Sigh. . . infection risk exists as does the risk of bleeding, stroke, and cardiac arrest. Also, Liam's sinus node always gets extra persnickety when poked in a cath.

Cardiac Intensive Care Unit, Pediatric Varity: This is just a personal opinion, not backed by any medical certification of any sort, but I would never allow Liam to be treated surgically for any reason by a hospital that did not invest in a dedicated cardiac intensive care unit. Some hospitals have NICUs (Neonatal Intensive Care Unit) and PICUs (Pediatric Intensive Care Units) but no CICUs, and that's not cutting it for my kid. Now that I know better, only the centers that do high enough volume of surgeries to hire the best staff and maintain a CICU would even be under consideration for my child.

A CICU has nurses and attending critical care professionals fully devoted to the care of cardiac patients. Whereas, a hospital with only a PICU might have a trauma patient treated by the same nurse as a cardic surgery patient – not good enough says this author. At least, not good enough for my child. Any nurse or attending touching Liam must know as much or more about cardiology than I do, and that's not always the case in every PICU where the nurses must be jacks or jills-of-all-trades to their patients. Noble, yes, honorable, absolutely! Wonderful people work in a PICU and help cancer patients and brain injury patients. I'm not disparaging them in the least. But when given the choice, as we are in America, I'll take the CICU every time for my child with half a heart. Note that some hospitals have a "functional" CICU within their PICU where specialized nurses are assigned to cardiac patients. Ask about this if they don't have a dedicated CICU space.

Cardiologist, General variety: If you are a sixty year old with no previous history of heart problems, this is your guy. If you are a heart warrior – stay away, far away! Seriously, regular cardiologists are amazing folks worthy of our respect, but they have NO BUSINESS treating children or adults with CHD unless they've done a fellowship in pediatric cardiology OR the emerging field of Adult Congenital Heart Disease. No fellowship or experience with CHD – no touching my kid, not even when he's fifty.

Cardiologist, Pediatric variety: Here's your man (or woman). This doctor is first and foremost a PEDIATRICIAN who treats the developing bodies of children and then a cardiologist versed in all the possible known permeations of malformed hearts and their associated venous and arterial structures. This guy/gal knows the hemodynamics of an altered heart and the impact on the liver, digestive, and respiratory systems.

Your PedCard MUST answer your questions. He/she is not remotely obligated to tell you what you want to hear, but this person should be honest with you and help you understand the situation so you can make informed decisions. If he/she doesn't, even if you have to go a thousand miles to find one who does, get thyself to a better communicator.

Note: There is an emerging field of ADULT CHD doctors. These are not necessarily pediatricians. They may be internists or general cardiologist who go on to purposefully study heart defects and their treatments and how they affect the adult body. We need these people because the pediatric cardiologist is primarily a pediatrician – which is exactly what you need for the first sixteen to eighteen years – then you need the new guy. And with more and more children surviving CHD into adulthood, we need a lot more of these experts.

Cardiothoracic Surgeon, Pediatric/CHD variety: (see also God – just kidding God, please don't smote me!). This person, when he (I've met two she's – so there are some, but typically it's still a 'he') is at his best saves several lives per week. When he's at his worst, he should retire. This is a dangerous and difficult job, saving babies many wouldn't ever touch.

When choosing a cardiothoracic surgeon (and yes in MOST cases you really do get to choose and if you don't feel like you're getting options – stamp your feet until someone pays attention) always, always, always expect them to explain the surgery in detail and if they don't offer, you ask:

1) How many of this particular type of procedure have they done in their career?
2) How many at THIS hospital?
3) What's the morbidity rate for patients with this procedure?
4) Is that rate higher or lower than the national average?
5) Do you perform heart surgery on adults who don't have CHDs, and how often? (RED FLAG – if this doctor doesn't

have enough business just doing CHD surgeries you should find one who does).

A very esteemed surgeon told me that if hospital's have mortality rates of higher than 3-5% on Norwoods, BT Shunts, Glenns and Fontans, they're not doing enough of them and they're not doing them well enough. These are 2010 numbers, not 2003 when Liam was still on the forefront of surgical successes. So if they tell you 10% or 20% in 2012 and it's not a new procedure for the rarest of the rare defects that I've never even heard of – get thyself on the phone with thy insurance company for a second opinion. (If you have to be airlifted to save your child's life – just think about that for a second – do you really have to think about it?)

Central Line (See Also Central Venus Catheter in more scholarly texts): A central line is like an IV but the catheter for the fluid is threaded from the entry point (in Liam's case always the neck or groin, but can be placed in the chest) all the way to the heart and can administer medication as well as venous pressures. They also withdraw blood from the line to measure blood gasses, which gives the most accurate oxygenation reading.

During postoperative recovery, this is one of the first things to go because it is pretty risky to have this plastic thing hanging around inside your swollen heart – infection and what-not. PICC lines are the same but they're threaded from the arm instead of neck/groin/chest. Liam had a PICC line for over six weeks and we had to take him home with it to administer his Vancomyacin in 2006.

Chest tubes: Liam has had twenty-one in his life. They are thin plastic tubes that stretch for stripping of fluid which is collected and measured, and sometimes sent to pathology. During surgery small x-shaped incisions are made in the torso, and the tubes are inserted to release fluid or air from around the lungs and prevent wet or collapsed lungs. They are very painful to have pulled, and the removal should always include a sedative and a pain medication (Versed of Chloral Hydrate + Morphine or Fentanyl) beforehand. The holes need to be stitched and leave pucker-shaped scars. According to Leslie McCall, chest tubes were the most painful part of open-heart surgery.

Chloral hydrate: Medicine that makes babies and children very sleepy before surgery or other procedures. Administered in liquid form, Liam hates it. So, I didn't let them give it to him before his caths in the summer of 2008, which made him traumatized by being gassed. I will regret it for the rest of my life. Wish I had my own Chloral hydrate right now . . . sniff. Don't skip the chloral, better to fight to get it down than fight to get them unconscious.

Coarctation: a kink or constriction of tissue in the aortic arch.

Damus, Kaye, Stansel Procedure (DKS) or Modified Norwood: In Liam's case, Dr. Starnes grafted/patched Liam's aorta and pulmonary artery together. He also removed his atrial septum, creating only one upper chamber in the heart.

Before surgery, Liam's pulmonary blood flow from his heart to lungs came from his pulmonary artery which came off the left side of his heart. His blood flow crossed his ventricular spetal defect and drained, rather than was pumped out of an opening where his pulmonary valve would be if his heart formed properly into his aorta which was also on the wrong side of the heart. This would have been purely depleted oxygen if not for it mixing together in his heart. He could not live like this and his organs were suffering from oxygen depletion including his kidneys, liver, and the heart muscle itself.

During the surgery, Dr. Starnes added a Gore-Tex® tube to replace pulmonary blood flow. As the aorta was grafted to the pulmonary artery to supply blood to the body, the tube was grafted to another artery (I honestly don't know which one and it stymies cardiologists to this day who see his heart on an echo) to supply blood to the lungs. This artificial tube was a modified Blalock-Taussig Shunt and was replaced during Liam's Glenn procedure three months and one week later.

Finally, during this surgery, Dr. Starnes removed a section of Liam's aortic arch (coarctation) and reconnected the ascending aorta. In all, you could say, Liam had four different open-heart surgeries in one, and all in under an hour on an organ the size of a small egg or golf ball. At the time the mortality rate for this procedure was 20%.

Digoxin: In Liam's case this is used to stop his atrial flutter. His atrial flutter is caused because Liam's heart's all scarred up and doesn't contract properly. This can cause clotting issues because the heart is not pumping regularly. It's possible, without treatment (Digoxin) he'll need a pacemaker to control his atrial flutter. Digoxin has not prevented his atrial fibulation though.

Ductus arteriosus: is a connection between an unborn baby's pulmonary artery and his aortic arch. Because an unborn baby doesn't use his lungs, the ductus arteriosus diverts the blood that would normally go to the lungs back to the body for use. Since the mother's body oxygenates her unborn baby's blood, this flow is sustained until birth. See also: Foramen ovale and Ductus venosus.

After Liam was born, this connection was kept open by prostaglandin for two weeks until his DKS surgery.

Ductus venosus: is a connection between an unborn baby's inferior vena cava and his umbilical cord. This allows his mother's oxygen to enter his body, travel to his heart, and be pumped to his aorta through the pulmonary artery's ductus arterious connection with the aortic arch.

Echocardiogram (Echo): This is a sonogram or ultrasound of the heart. Liam's first echo was with Dr. Doom, and he has had at least seventy of these procedures including transesophageal echos through his throat and esophagus during surgery to make sure he had no internal bleeding before they closed his chest. I can now tell what structures we're looking at during an echo and have explained them to Liam at his last echo so he understood. As a baby/toddler Liam had to be sedated with hydrochloral or Versed to be subdued for an echo, now he asks questions. This is one of the least invasive and most useful diagnostic tools.

Enalapril (Captopril): This is a blood pressure medicine that Liam takes and has taken since he was two weeks old to ease the pressure of altered blood flow on his narrowed and constricted vascular system.

Fentanyl: A very strong drug that works fast to stop intense pain. Liam had double the recommended dose before his sternal reset in 2006, and he was still in extreme pain. Wikipedia says it's 100 times more powerful than morphine, and yet he screamed.

Flat as a Pancake: After a cath, patients must lay absolutely still to prevent their femoral arteries from "popping a clot," and bleeding out. This was particularly difficult when Liam threw up bile and then dry heaved after his last two heart caths. . . sigh. Popping a clot when Liam was on blood thinners to get that cath into his heart led to sandbags being placed on his groin, even as he continued to dry heave . . . sigh . . . so much blood – not a nice memory. "Flat as a pancake, sweetheart, flat as a pancake," says I.

Foley Catheter: If you've ever had surgery you know what this is. If not – it's a tube that goes into the urethra to collect urine, which is then weighed and compared to the amount of saline administered to determine if a patient is retaining too much fluid or is too dehydrated. It's one of the last things to go during the postoperative phase and is a sure sign that recovery is imminent.

Fontan Procedure: This is the surgery where the inferior vena cava is dissected from the heart and attached to the artificial conduit that then connects to the pulmonary branch arteries. In Liam's case, the conduit was sewn to his atria and a hole placed in his atria between the conduit and his heart so that if too much blood backed up in his lungs, it could be pushed back through the hole in his heart.

That hole is called a fenstration, and because the pressure in Liam's hypoplastic arteries was so high in 2006, it was larger than average, as was the conduit (they run 16-23 mm and Liam's is 22 mm). Smaller conduits are used on children who can tolerate higher pressures.

Note: There is an older type of Fontan procedure called the lateral tunnel or LT Fontan, where a baffle is run through the atria instead of outside of it (extra cardiac or EC Fontan is the type Liam had). In my observation of hundreds of families, LT Fontans are increasingly less common, but are still done. I'm certain any surgeon who still does LT Fontans has a very good reason based on the patient's anatomy to do it that way. If that approach or a human or animal homograft instead of a Gortex conduit is used in an EC Fontan you should talk to your surgeon about why those differences are necessary for your child. I'm not remotely suggesting that you question their wisdom, but having it explained to you will teach you more about your own child, and that is always a good thing. You're simply asking for education not justification.

Fon-tempt/Glenn-Again: Liam's left and right pulmonary arteries had grown hypoplastic from the diminished blood flow of both the BT shunt and the Glenn flow over time. His arteries were only two millimeters and needed to be eight to support the increased blood flow of the Fontan. This was untenable, so while Liam's heart was stopped his arteries were splayed and Gortex patches were applied to make the arteries bigger. The junction of the superior vena cava to the pulmonary branch artery was also moved to a new position and the artery repaired where it was removed.

Foramen ovale: this is a natural, not defective, hole between the right and left atria in an unborn baby's heart. This hole allows more oxygenated blood passed by the ductus venosus to the right atria through the inferior vena cava to make its way to the baby's brain by pumping out the left side to the aorta.

This hole was kept open with prostaglandin in Liam's body to allow continued mixing. His other atrial septal defects and the Foramen ovale were cut away during the DKS surgery when the entire septum was removed. In some babies the hole won't close naturally and is then considered a birth defect and may be surgically corrected like an ASD later in life.

Glenn Shunt Procedure, Bidirectional: Liam's superior vena cava was dissected from his heart and attached to his pulmonary branch arteries to drain blood returning from his arms, head, and upper torso directly to his lungs. This is a common procedure and done in most children with single ventricle hearts, even if a Fontan is avoided in some cases.

At one point postoperatively, his oxygen saturation was 44% and he was the color of blueberries. He improved, but his sinus rhythm was never fully restored and the Glenn had to be redone seventeen months later.

Hypoplastic: means, essentially, too small to function properly. Liam's right ventricle was hypoplastic, meaning it was too small to function. His aorta was hypoplastic, meaning too small to function as an aorta. His pulmonary branch arteries were also hypoplastic.

Mitral Valve: the valve between the left atria and the left ventricle. Because Liam only has one atria and one functioning ventricle, this is his only internal heart valve. It currently regurgitates (throws blood back up into the atria when the left ventricle squeezes instead of passing all of the blood through from the atria to the ventricle and keeping it there). This regurgitation is worrisome and may lead to future procedures for Liam.

PICC Line: See Central Line

Prostaglandin (PGE): are human messenger molecules that control smooth muscle tissue and prevent the fetal heart structures from closing on themselves until the diminished amount of PGE in the neonate's body after birth signals those structures to close. Since Liam needed his fetal heart structures to remain open for him to survive until his first surgery, he was on a continuous PGE drip for his first fourteen days of life.

Pulmonary Artery: is the artery that, in a healthy heart, ascends from the right ventricle to feed the two pulmonary branch arteries that provide deoxygenated blood to the lungs for oxygenation. That blood is then passed back to the left atria by the pulmonary veins.

Liam's pulmonary artery ascended from his aortic valve on the left side of his heart. It was feeding his aortic arch through the ductus arteriosus. If this connection had been closed before surgery, Liam would have lost blood to his brain and either stroked or simply died.

Because the right side of his heart was malformed due to the missing tricuspid valve, his pulmonary valve was not functional, and his pulmonary artery could not be moved to the pulmonary valve. Therefore, the aorta was removed from the pulmonary valve and grafted to his pulmonary artery. Now his pulmonary artery serves as his aorta.

Pulmonary Valve: is the valve that, in a health heart, feeds the deoxygenated blood from the right ventricle to the pulmonary artery for delivery to the lungs.

Second Opinions: I've never sought one, but I would in a second if I questioned decisions or the options presented to me. We've been very blessed with good cardiologists and a strong team approach at both hospitals where Liam received heart surgery. That said, if he needed another one tomorrow, it would not be a planned experience and it would not be typical, so in that case I would be likely to seek a second opinion.

No parent or patient should feel awkward or outside of their rights to seek a second opinion. If the other doctor/institution confirms what you're being told at the first, it just elevates your confidence. If you're given better options, then it was entirely worth doing.

Stent: A stent is a wire mesh tube that is inserted into a vein or artery to open in wider to allow adequate blood flow either toward or away from the heart. Liam has a stent placed in his left pulmonary branch artery (LPA) because that stretch of artery, despite being augmented twice surgically, was still too constricted to allow adequate blood flow to his lungs.

Liam's stent covered part of his lung tissue and had to be pried open in two or three places to keep blood flow moving to his lungs. The stent helped, but the placement during a cath procedure is somewhat risky.

Tricuspid Atresia: is the absence of a tricuspid valve which results in the absence of a functional right ventricle.

Tricuspid Valve: is, in a healthy heart, the valve that allows blood from the right atria to pass to the right ventricle on its way to the lungs. Liam had absolutely no right ventricle. Rather, he has what might best be described as a knot, like in a piece of wood, but no opening at all on the wall of what was his right atria.

Oxygen-rich blood that entered the right side of his heart through the inferior vena cava (fed by the ductus venosus and his umbilical cord) sloshed across his foramen ovale and other holes between his two atrium, ending up in the left atrium and feeding his left ventricle, where it sloshed back to the right ventricle and fed his aorta. Because the blood volume to the right ventricle was so limited the muscle structure never grew large enough to be a functioning chamber of his heart, and Liam only survived gestation because of the foramen ovale, ductus venosus, and ductus arteriosus feeding his oxygenated blood to his body.

Vancomycin: In 2006 this was the strongest antibiotic on the market and used (I know it was at least six and it may have been eight) to treat Liam's near-fatal staph and strep infection. We had to administer it ourselves three times a day once Liam was home.

Ventricular Septal Defect (VSD): This is a hole between the left and right ventricles. In some children it's a serious heart defect that can be treated either in a cath lab with a patch that cells grow over and close or in open-heart surgery where it is sewn shut. It's highly treatable when it is detected early and the only CHD present.
However, in Liam's case it was the one defect that kept him alive the first two weeks so any blood at all could get to his body from his malformed (practically nonexistent) right ventricle that was mis-attached to his aorta.

A few months ago during an Echo, I could see Liam's right ventricle as a little spatter of blood crossed his VSD. It looked like a tiny little closet or alcove under the stairs against a larger room – his left ventricle. Liam saw it too and it was his first inkling about what his heart looks like and why it's "special."

Versed: Happy juice that made Liam fail to remember having chest tubes pulled, PICC lines placed and a number of other indignities over the years.

Viagra: Invented for heart disease – its side effect was a marketing gold mine. Several of our very young friends have been on this drug following the Fontan to reduce pulmonary artery pressure that might have caused Fontan failure. It was suggested for Liam if the arterial stent were to fail to bring his oxygen saturation up, but we've avoided it to date.

Second Opinions and Changes of Venue

First let me say in full disclosure that I've never sought a
change of venue for Liam. I've never asked for a second opinion,
but I would if I thought it necessary. I have changed doctors and
hospitals by switching from PSL's program to The Children's
Hospital when we returned from LA. I also have the benefit of
having my child treated by three different practices, meeting
doctors at dozens of practices throughout the US from my
advocacy work, and talking to parents who use even more
hospitals and doctors through the same efforts. If I didn't know
what I know, I would likely have sought a second opinion on
many occasions, and I've not ruled it out for the future by any
stretch.

What I learned about the differences in programs came from
the beginning. Jim and I learned and discussed how the Denver
program was a fledgling hope in 2003, compared to the intense
training and experience of the cracker-jack CTICU staff at CHLA.

Yes, Dr. Lacour-Gayet performed many successful DKS and
traditional Norwoods in his time in Europe, but the nurses in
Denver had not attended to such precarious patients. They were all
still ramping up when Liam was at CHLA. Before Lacour-Gayet,
the most complicated babies either got wait-listed for transplant
(Dr. Dooms M.O.), or they got sent to Los Angeles or Children's of
Philadelphia. HLHS babies frequently went to Dr. Starnes from
Denver if transplant matches would run too long. So the novelty of
Denver's program was one valid reason, of which I was completely
oblivious at the time, for me to be glad that we went to CHLA.

The second benefit of being at CHLA was that it gave me a
glimpse of what Denver could become, what to expect and
demand from the CICU (Cardiac Intensive Care Unit) staff there.
It taught me things that made me a better Heart Mom for Liam
and in time a better leader for other Heart Moms.

I do worry that our family still feels guilty they weren't there when they imagine Jim and me in that honeycomb bleak maze of a waiting room during Liam's first major dance with death. They shouldn't feel any guilt, at least not for me. I'm glad it was only me and Jim. I'm glad I didn't have to baby-sit anyone else, answer their questions, smile to alleviate their pain, or feel the weight of their worry. Instead, I was alone in LA with Jim, the person I feel the most at home with. I only held my fear in a little ball until I could hold my child again.

In LA, I didn't sing or dance for anyone else. I imagine Jim feels the same way, but we don't talk too much about that day, though I'm sure we both remember it vividly. It was the first time we offered our child back to God and waited for the verdict.

The lessons here are that if you take your child a few blocks or a thousand miles for the best possible care, you're doing what is necessary. It's not an inconvenience if it saves your child's life. And while you're on this pilgrimage of survival, you are not beholden to take care of anyone else. If you need the emotional support and distraction of an entourage, then have one. If you're a solitary creature, then be one. Do what you need to do to get through what will be the hardest days of your life.

I don't want YOU, fellow Heart Moms and Dads, to learn what I learned through domestic air travel a thousand miles from home. That said, if you interview your closest surgeon and determine that your child's odds are 5% better a thousand miles away, then by all means make that flight.

Dozens of Internet services and the Better Business Bureau exist so you can interview three contractors before you accept a bid for repairs on your home. We're talking about your child's life. I'm going to give you the short list of questions to ask if your baby is diagnosed that I didn't know to ask when Liam was first diagnosed.

While Question 1-3 are very specific to hypoplastic right, 4-7 are appropriate for any heart defect.

1. Is there any transposition of the great vessels or narrowing of the aorta, aortic arch or pulmonary artery? This is very important because this complication changes your first surgical stage dramatically. If they tell you no, then YAY! Odds are in your favor for lower risk during the first surgery. If they say yes, this means you want one of the BEST hospitals in the nation for your baby.

2. Which valve is affected and is it stenotic or is it full blown atresia? Stenosis of the pulmonary artery may indicate more options than any other diagnosis. Atresia of the pulmonary artery may also leave some doors open. Stenosis of the tricuspid valve may limit your options, and tricuspid atresia (unless other weird things are going on) pretty much means you're on a Fontan path as of 2011. Let's just say that we've come a LONG way in the years since I was diagnosed at 23 weeks, and if it's Pulmonary Stenosis or Pulmonary Atresia, get thy records to another hospital for a consultation about biventricular repair BEFORE you head down the Fontan path. It may be that the Fontan is unavoidable for you, but for the first time in history it might not be, so don't waste the opportunity to find out because you're shy about getting a second opinion.

3. Once you get answers to one and two, ask about the hospital, the surgery they're recommending (depending on dx expect one of these:

   A) Norwood/DKS

   B) BT Shunt

   C) Pulmonary Artery Banding

   D) Cath procedure valvoplasty or septostomy or both depending. D. is not open heart surgery, but it is not without significant risks on a newborn - but less risky than A, B, or C in most good facilities.

   E) Very rarely, in utero procedures may be an option. This is very rare and has mixed results, and if you want to know more you should ask your pediatric cardiologist about it.

4. After the doctors tells you what type of surgery to expect, ask how many of those they do each year, what their statistics are, how that compares to other leading hospitals, and if there is another hospital in your state that has a better success rate. Don't be shy or embarrassed to ask. These are totally appropriate questions and I tell you this - if you're asking this out of the gate they'll know you mean business.

5. Ask what makes your baby similar or different from other case, any concerns that set your baby apart from other cases. You want to know your child's details as best as they can determine them.

6. Ask when they will want to see you again and what they'll be looking for at that time.

7. Ask about delivery nearby and transportation to the facility after you give birth. More and more hospitals are letting the moms deliver on site, but not all. It doesn't hurt to ask and ask if they have fetal diagnosis navigator or coordinator - this is a newer thing but it's a growing trend and good for you. You might meet this person first if they have one.

Supplies for the Battlefield

Special Note: I understand that if you're airlifted without notice, these aren't options, BUT your friends should be able to help you. Hint for friends and family – you can provide supplies and actually deliver on the, "if there is anything I can do" offer.

Camera: Your child deserves to have baby pictures, even if they're scary pictures. And God-forbid, if your baby doesn't make it, you deserve those pictures too. If anyone says anything to you about this, you go to my blog at **www.amandaroseadams.com** and find the "Photo Rant" post and send it to them. Let NO ONE make you feel bad about photographing your child; it's photojournalism mixed with primal love.

CarePages: **www.carepages.com** - it's free, it's easy, and it prevents you from having to update everyone on the phone. Also, it's slightly more private than Facebook, and you're less likely to get flamed by some unfeeling jerk for expressing what you're really feeling. If that happens you can delete them!

Change: For the soda and snack machines when the cafeteria is closed. I recommend a roll of quarters.

Clothes: Sure, you want to pack light, but when and where are you going to do laundry? Bring more underwear than you think you'll need and some extra t-shirts. Just because you're trapped doesn't mean you should be uncomfortable.

Contact List: Anyone you might possibly need to call about a pet, a sprinkler system, or if the worst thing happens, so you can hand it to someone else and you won't have to give bad news to anyone yourself.

Entertainment: Be it trashy magazines, Sodoku, or crossword puzzles, or just an iPad (wish we'd had that in 2006), get yourself something to play with that isn't *War and Peace*.

Eye mask/Ear Plugs: I once spent eighteen hours in a window bed listening to the two most annoying human beings on the planet, and when they finally fell asleep the snoring, if you can call it that, it was beyond description. Sleep deprivation is inevitable on the battlefront, so give yourselves whatever comfort you can find.

Face cloths: Get yourself some nice disposable facial washcloths you can put in a baggie. You will feel so much better if you can just go wash your face with something soft that smells good.

Friend/Family Right Hand: Someone you trust to update your Carepage for you when you can't do it yourself for whatever reason. Someone who will rally the troops for support when you need it or tell people to stay away because of infection risks, etc. Your bodyguard who will also feed your husband when he refuses to eat.

Fruit: Not only is it good for you, but it will remind you that there is life beyond Snickers bars and light beyond the florescent glare of your time in the hospital.

Gum: Lest you be tempted to make too many trips to the candy machine.

Insurance details: Some of the larger insurers have a special program for CHD. Call yours right away to find out if they do and get in touch with a nurse coordinator as soon as possible. Some of these programs will provide reimbursement for shelter and food when you are displaced for optimal care. They can also, typically, give you statistics from the hospitals you're considering regarding volume of patients treated and morbidity rates.

Lotion (good stuff): There will be blood—on your knuckles—from all the hand-washing. You will wash your hands because you do not want your baby to die from a senseless infection, and your hands will crack and bleed and hurt, but you will keep washing them. Get some Crabtree & Evelyn or Burt's Bees, or some such gardener quality salve for your hands. Share with your nurses too!

Music: A mobile or other musical toy will be worth its weight in gold to soothe your baby and your own soul.

Notebook: Get yourself a nice one with lots of pockets to keep things you're given. Take notes and log your questions for follow up. Put pretty stickers on it to make you smile. You can also vent your frustrations or write out things before you post them for the world to see or say something you might regret later.

Pen: See Notebook.

Slippers: I remember my sensible tennis shoes digging into my feet and me loosening the laces. I wished, every time I went, that I had slippers, and then never remembered to bring some. You really can't go barefoot, so get yourselves some nice slippers.

Snacks: There is only so much candy machine you should and can consume. Bring some of your own favorite comfort foods.

Sweater/Sweatshirt: You will get cold.

Tissues: GOOD ones. You're going to miss home and miss comfort, so get yourself a big box of Puffs or Kleenex, because the sandpaper available to you in the hospital might cut your skin, but it's not going to 'cut it' for your face. Take your comforts where you can.

Toys: For surgeries after the age of two months distractions are needed.

Watch: Just in case a clock isn't readily viewable. And it helps with your notebook.

Safe Harbors

Note: Review all information with your pediatric cardiologist before making medical decisions. With complex Congenital Heart Defects, there are absolutely no guarantees. Children still die every day around the world even at the very best hospitals, but fewer of them die and more and more of them thrive each year. To increase your child's odds you want to get the best possible care with the lowest risk by going to the best possible facility.

If you are fortunate enough that your child is diagnosed while you're still pregnant (I know you don't feel fortunate because it happened to me, but we are), you have time to find the absolute best hospital. The best hospitals will typically:

- Be affiliated with an outstanding medical school. Harvard/Boston, USC/CHLA, Baylor/Texas Children's, CU/Denver, etc.
- Invest the money to train and operate a Pediatric CARDIAC Intensive Care Unit. Why?
  - Because they invest in their staff's education and professional development focused on a specialty for all who will treat your child.
  - They aren't doing cardiology "on the side" and keeping the kids with heart surgery in the same space as kids with cancer or brain injuries – different needs, different expertise. If I was the mother of a child with brain injury, I wouldn't want my nurse trying to figure out the next kid's over heart problems either. Alignment of skills is CRITICAL in critical care.
  - They are more likely to have support staff (child life and social workers) who can help you with your specific needs.
- Explain the surgery options to you patiently and in detail and make resources available to you for follow up questions.
- Have many families that come from other towns, states, and even foreign countries seeking their expertise. I can't stress this

enough, unless you live in a major metropolitan area, you will likely need to travel to find a hospital that can treat your child.

- Do a high volume of the procedure your child requires. So, a hospital that does five Norwoods per year is far less likely to produce the results of a hospital that does 20 Norwoods per year. Why?
  - o Because the nurses have been there and done that and will know what to watch for and be the most responsive.
  - o The surgeon and his team will typically get your baby off of bypass faster and be better prepared to deal with the equipment and complexity of the surgery.
  - o They know what good and bad recovery looks like and how to respond to your child's needs.

Disclaimer: Am I saying all cardiac programs with low volume and no CICU are bad choices? No, I'm simply saying that you may have better choices. I will concede there are some old, established, and excellent programs that lack a dedicated CICU, but they are rare. I don't judge any parent's decisions, I just pray that they make informed choices.

For more information and a stronger education, please see Dr. Redmond Burke's website for surgical outcomes: www.pediatricheartsurgery.com

USA Friends of the Mission

Organization	Primary Focus	Link and Notes
Adult Congenital Heart Association (ACHA)	Patient education and advocacy, research	**http://www.achaheart.org/** Excellent resource for teens and their parents as well as adults with CHD.
The Children's Heart Foundation	Research	**http://www.childrensheartfoundation.org/** Funds research *only* for congenital heart disease! Best investment of your friends' good will and donations.
Facebook Groups	Mostly support	**www.facebook.com** (search on CHD) Recommendation: Find a few good friends on Facebook and chat about sensitive things privately. Offer support to those who need it, it's good for your karma! See the Internet Warnings for more information.
Hypoplastic Right Hearts	Emotional support and parent education.	**www.hypoplasticrighthearts.org** I made this! This was my first nonprofit that I founded. We do only allow families with Hypoplastic Right Diagnoses to keep the discussions focused and the education relevant to all. But we're just like a gated community in the heartland, where we all come out and make friends with the other folks.

Mended Little Hearts	Local Emotional Support	**http://mendedlittlehearts.org/**
		The greatest way to meet people in the Heartland who live near you. They're also progressively partnering with the ACHA and the CHF and pulling the Heartland together. Great people who are in it for the right reasons.
		If you don't have a chapter- start one and I'll put you on my web site as a heart hero!
Ronald McDonald House Charities	Housing and Food and Emotional Support	**http://rmhc.org/**
		The most amazing place that you never want to have to visit. So, if you're in a good place in your life, visit because you want to and help these families by bringing food, donations, or your services. It's called the house love built for a very good reason – it's true.
Saving Little Hearts	Emotional Support	I've known the founder Karin for years and years. She sends gift bags to patients and families in the hospital and has an amazing conference every year! Great organization and if you live in the South, try to get to their conference.
Donor Alliance	Organ Transplant Coordinatio n and Support Services	Regional outlet for Colorado and Wyoming, their web site **www.donoralliance.org** has great information and resources. Search on "organ donation" and the name of your state for similar resources near you.

How to Find Local Resources:

1. Call your hospital and ask for the cardiac social worker or child-life experts (sometimes it's the volunteer office).
2. Talk to your social worker/child-life specialist/volunteer coordinator about services and support groups.
3. If you don't have a support group associated with your local children's hospital, contact Mended Little Hearts (**http://mendedlittlehearts.org/**)about their chapters or starting your own.
4. Remember, 1/100 babies is born with CHD and there are two million North Americans with CHD, so there are people near you. It might take some effort to find them at first, but it will be worth it when you can stand in a room with people who've been where you are.
5. If you need financial assistance, call your city, county, and state government offices and ask about services for disabled children. You can also call the special needs social worker at your local hospital that delivers babies, even if yours was born elsewhere, to ask about county or city services. I can't promise you you'll find what you need, not all entities offer services to all income levels, but this is the best place to start.

Words of Warning about the Internet

I love the Internet. I love Wikipedia, Google, Carepages, and **www.hypoplasticrighthearts.org**. I even have begrudgingly come to love Facebook and Twitter. But be warned and be safe, take note of the following things:

- Not everyone on Facebook is there to comfort you. Some will just want to play the "my child is the sickest child" game. Flee these people, do not befriend them. They are either too steeped in their grief to give comfort to others, or they're just crazy. Either way, if they're going to derail you on your journey through your own grief, avoid them.

- Beware of spammers and liars (people have actually made up imaginary children), and Münchausen by Proxy people on Facebook. They are all initially strangers, and it's ok to avoid them.

- Question EVERYTHING you read online, and ask your pediatric cardiologist about what you've read. Much of it is old, misinformed, or inappropriate to the nuances of your child's condition. Some of it is highly medical and hard to understand. Ask your doctor, you're on the same team. Liam's cardiologist and I are on Team Liam.

- Do not compare apples to oranges. If a child's heart is identical to your child's heart and their treatment path is different it's TOTALLY appropriate to ask your doctor for insights, and learn from that experience. But if a child's condition is remotely or even marginally different from yours, don't compare your child to theirs. It's perfectly good and right for you to learn about other children to help you understand your own child better. But you only have your own child to raise. What you share with other parents is information, not competition, and no one's opinion online matters one tenth as much as your medical care team.

- Don't let other people judge you, and choose your friends wisely. I've seen mothers torn to shreds over circumcision, parenting style, termination, and even photographing their sick child. Sigh . . . judge not lest ye be judged, and if someone is judging you, unfriend them, delete them, whatever. Heart family or not, no one has the right to tell you you're doing things wrong. You're doing your best, and only your child's medical care teams' opinions should matter as much as yours. Everyone else is secondary. That said, be careful what you share in mixed company and seek those folks who will offer you the best support.

Tactical Guide for Civilians on the Home front

So, your daughter/sister/best friend just found out her baby, this child she was over the moon to be expecting, will be born dying. Yep, that's heavy. You hurt. You hurt to see your loved one in such pain, and you hurt for this child who was going to be part of your life. You hurt in all kinds of ways but you cannot hurt as much as she does.

I know you're close friends, but for the next few years you'll be on the "outside" with a lot of this because your friend truly is in a state of grief. It's not personal. She has to go inside herself to survive something this harsh. You *have* to give her time to process and figure it out, but stay on standby - many a friend has been lost to parents in this situation because it was too much for everyone to endure.

First: Just listen to her about whatever she wants to say, and don't tell her it's all going to be OK. Telling us that it's going to all be fine really makes us mad because it's not fine, and it's never going to be fine, it's essentially either your baby has his chest ripped open 2-3 times or he dies, or both - it's a lose/lose/lose situation, and playing it down really doesn't help. Downplay is about the worse thing people can do to us.

Second: Acknowledge that you don't know what she's going through - own that. A lot of people try to compare what they've been through to that, and short of your child having a near or full death experience there is no comparison. I once blew up at a lady comparing her college aged daughter getting her wisdom teeth out to what it's like for a child to have a debilitating chronic condition - it's not the same.

So, tell her that while you can't understand how hard it is, you know it's amazingly overwhelming and that you're here for her no matter how hard it gets or what happens. Don't try to understand how much it hurts, just know that it does and try to help her by responding to her cues.

Another similar thing is for people to say, "People die every day," "Any of us could be hit by a bus, you can't live in fear all of the time," kind of crap—the randomness of lightening is not an accurate comparison to the 5-20% mortality rate for newborn babies having certain neonatal open heart surgeries. To marginalize her experience or her fear as something unfounded is insulting. I'm sure you wouldn't do that, but some people don't know what to say, so they say stupid things. When in doubt, just shut up and give her a hug!

Third: Don't leave it up to her to tell you how to help, think of your own ideas and see if that would help. So many people tell us, "If you need anything don't hesitate to ask," but I never knew what to ask for until after. Asking your friend to figure out what she needs is simply giving her a chore and that doesn't help anyone. Here are some things you can do for her:

- Ask her if she still wants to have a baby shower and if she does have one that is positive and beautiful - make her know this baby is welcome and wanted by everyone and has his/her own cheering section from day t-10 and into infinity. Let her know that all of her family and friends are behind her hope will bolster her fighting spirit. If she doesn't want to have the shower (some people don't) offer to do it when the baby is home and better no matter how long that take. Remind her that her baby will be a cause for extra celebration because he/she is a champion.
- Buy her a nice journal to keep notes and information in during the baby's treatment - something with pockets and dividers where she can keep notes and keep track of what's happening.
- Get her a hospital care kit with a disposable camera, nursing pads, a good book or magazines, some nice lotion, just to let her know you know she's going somewhere difficult and while you can't be

with her for the entire lonely and difficult journey, you're behind her all the way. Also, SNAP-FRONT baby clothes that don't have to go over the head are great gifts because heart babies are hard to dress, and those little gifts make long hospital stays a little nicer because you can actually put some real clothes on your baby. A boppy pillow is good for under your arm when you hold the baby in the hospital for a long time. Sometimes we don't get to hold our babies for whole weeks and when we can it's a battle with cords and tubes, so we hold them for a very very long time. See if you can find a plastic cover to keep it sterile. Thinking of her comfort is a great kindness.

- Don't send flowers when the baby is born, they can't be in the NICU and they are often thrown out in the chaos of treating a heart baby, but DO send flowers and balloons to celebrate coming home from the hospital. Get your other friends to participate. Ehen we FINALLY brought our son home from CA after one month (we live in CO and he had been airlifted) there were no flowers, no cards, nothing to celebrate a new baby. We only had get-well wishes and prayers that reminded us Liam nearly died, not the tokens most new parents receive to celebrate life. Whatever special things you got for your own healthy baby, make sure your friend doesn't miss out because she's already missing out on so much.

Fourth: Give her space, call and check on her, don't forget her, but don't push. If she doesn't want to talk about it, don't make her. If she does, do NOT change the subject; just let her know you're open. The conversations will be hard because she's working through "why me." Some people never get past that question and it really ruins their lives, let her work through it. Being stilted will limit her enjoyment of her child and make it harder for her to fight any postpartum depression.

Stand up for her, if someone else says something inappropriate, call her on it. Share this advice with other friends, help her enforce hand washing and no smoking and any other limits necessary for the baby's health. You really will have to walk on eggshells for a while because your friend will be wounded and in pain, and slights or comments made right now will stick with her a lot longer than they would under normal conditions. We don't mean to by hypersensitive or thin skinned, but the minute you hear your child will be born fighting for his life, you go into survival mode, and having a friend like you who is sensitive and wants to do the right thing will really help her get through it.

Things to Do

You say things like, "Anything you need, just ask," but she won't ask. She is catatonic, and she is broken. You want to help her but you don't know how. So, here is my advice to you, the good friend who isn't running to the hills when the shit goes down. You are good people, and you deserve good advice:

1. Check the Supply List in the field guide and make her a basket.
2. Find someone to befriend her husband. He needs support just as much as she does, and he needs someone to listen without judgment. Help her help him.
3. Refer to the end of the Never Better, or It's Complicated chapter for the right things to say.
4. Let the couple decide if they still want a baby shower or not. I wanted mine because I needed it. To me it was a testament of faith in Liam's life by all the people in our lives. Don't assume they won't want to do it, but make sure they still do before anything proceeds.
5. Don't disappear, even if she's unbearable, know that she's grieving and not in her right mind. Know that what seems like her being selfish is merely her self-preservation.
6. Pick up the slack, if she needs help with older kids, help with errands, or if you're a coworker and she just needs a little help getting ready to go on leave, step up and step in to help. And

don't expect glory or credit for it; just do it because it's the right thing to do and you'd want someone to do the same for you.

7. Don't tell her everything is going to be all right – you don't know that. Tell her you pray for her child, her strength, her future, but don't make bold or blind assurances. The odds may be in her favor, but eight thousand CHD babies die in the USA each year, there's no way for you to know who will make it and who won't.

8. Don't tell her how strong she is, because she doesn't want to have to be this strong.

9. Support her decisions and listen to her closely so you can give her support when she questions herself later.

10. Rally the troops. Get your friends together to pamper her, spoil her, or just do some little nice thing. Organize meals, or organize silence. Organize a group to walk at a CHD walk in their honor or bring meals to the Ronald McDonald House for them and their new friends.

11. Be a bully, not to her, but to her one ridiculous relative, or annoying former friends. Keep people away if she wants you to, but take your lead from her. Run interference so she doesn't have to, and feel free to call the entourage on whatever rude comment they've made.

Things To Say

When I started writing this book, all my Heart Mom friends said, "Make sure you put a list of all the stupid shit people say in it." I did in the first draft and then my good friend, who is not a Heart Mom read that draft and asked, "But, what *can* we say?"

It's a fair question. People outside of this do-or-die, submit your kid to butchery and torment or watch them whither to death situation don't know what to say. Sometimes they're trying to be supportive but it doesn't translate. So here are some things you can say and do that shouldn't hurt.

Disclaimer: There are some people who are so sensitive that you can't possibly ever do anything right, so just give them a hug and be quiet. For the rest of us, here's your list:

- I'm sorry this happened to your family, but I'm glad you have medical options to help you.
- Can we bring you some fresh fruit in the hospital?
- Do you need your sidewalks shoveled/lawn mowed when you're in the hospital? (or don't even ask, just do it)
- Can I take your other kids to the zoo/museum/park/etc. so they can have some fun?
- Can I come sit with your heart kid and read him a story so you can take a nap or a shower? (or go cry in private . . . this is really important, don't go expecting to visit the sleep-deprived parents and think you're going to get conversation, if they want to stay and visit, give them that option without expectation).
- Hey, I was going to get a rotisserie chicken on the way home, want me to bring you one too? (You can only eat so much hospital cafeteria food before you feel like you should to be admitted yourself)
- I know you're really afraid and that you have really good reasons for your fear. I'm not trying to take that away from you, I just want you to know I'm here and I will listen.
- Do you need a hug?
- Do you like soduku? Crosswords? What kind of junk magazines would you like to have with you in the hospital?
- Wow, people sent you a lot of stuff for your kid! Would you like me to take some of it to your house for you so you don't have to worry about all of it? I'll even write thank you cards for you!
- I was at the store and saw these cute blank notes, so I got them for you and some stamps in case you need to be able to send anything out while you're stuck here.
- Guess what, I picked up your mail and here are all of your bills, and I grabbed your checkbook too! (Seriously, this is helpful

because these folks are sitting in the hospital worrying about what they can't get done at home).

- I know it's a private thing, but just so you know, if you need help with all this time off work and the medical bills, let me know and I'll see if I can get my church, HOA, school, fraternal org, etc. to do a bakesale/garagesale/silent aucton/ etc. to help you guys out. No pressure, just know we're here if you need us and people want to help.
- Would you like me to stop by your house and get you some more clothes so you don't have to worry about doing so much laundry while you're here?
- What's your favorite kind of gum?
- Did you forget anything (dental floss, etc.) that I could run out and get for you? Or better yet, let me run you over to the store real quick so you can get a break.
- Want to take a walk?
- Wow, your baby has been through so much, but he still has such a great attitude, smile, laugh – whatever, (just don't focus on how he looks – we all know he doesn't look good so don't say that).
- When you get home and settled back in, let me bring you a Starbucks. (or just keep on bringing the lattes)
- We all really care about you and we know this is harder than we can ever really know.
- Do you need a hug? (repetition on purpose).
- Wow, I can totally understand why you can't let people smoke around your baby and are so sensitive to viruses with his compromised lungs and all. I didn't realize before that these heart problems also affected the lungs so much.
- Of course I will wash my hands, in fact I brought you this great smelling new soap and lotion set! Let's share!
- I realize that this is a life-long problem and you're going to have ups and downs. Please know that we like to know your ups as well as support you in your downs because we're with you for the whole ride.

Notice: I never once thought to ask, "What can I do for you?" because that's like a pop quiz. They don't know, so don't make your suffering friend work to make you feel better. You do the heavy mental lifting and figure it out.

The only big no-no that cannot be excused as foot in mouth, or misplaced concern is this:

Unless she is the mother of your child or your own mother, never, ever, ever tell the mother of a child who is near to death how hard this is emotionally on *you*. You don't get to do that, I forbid it. No matter how hard it is for you to see a child like that, unless it's your child, zip it, lock it, and put it in your pocket. We'll forgive you for just about anything else

A Heartland Amandafesto

It is important that all members and supporters of the Heartland know the top issues affecting us today. I have outlined them below with remediation tactics you can do from your own computers and mailboxes.

Problem One: Issues with Continuous Care.
1. Across the nation, teens and young adults with CHD are dropping out of care.
2. When they finally get sick enough to seek out care, they are often misdirected to adult onset cardiologists with no expertise in congenital heart disease.
3. There are not enough adult congenital heart specialists practicing and they're often isolated to the largest population centers, making them difficult for patients to see.
4. Many teens and adults with CHD are lacking medical coverage and have trouble navigating the system to get adequate care in a timely manner.
5. Many medical records, especially for adults with CHD have been lost over the years.
6. There is no national tracking of these records or an active or comprehensive national registry for children who have had open-heart surgery.
7. Often when a patient seeks acute care several years after surgery, specialists are starting from square one just getting a sense of their anatomy and how to treat them.

Reasons: Many patients/parents either were expressly told or bought into the idea that they were "cured" by surgery and are uneducated about long term complications and the need for follow up care, or they are in denial about the same issues. Before the 1980s we never saw large numbers of children surviving into adulthood with CHD, and for the first time in history there are more adults than children with CHD and that number is growing each year.

Solutions: Parents need to have the expectation that, even after successful surgery, a heart defect is a chronic and life-long condition that needs routine follow-up care to prevent critical complications later in life. Society needs to recognize how prevalent CHD is and support electronic medical records and best practices to keep and share information across time and geographies in the interest of the patient and the patient's quality of life. Medical schools need to establish more Adult CHD career paths for physicians to increase the number of practitioners to help the growing number of adults with CHD. Patients and parents need to be more effective advocates and partners to bring these needs to light in the public and take responsibility for them at home.

Problem Two: Research and information is lacking
1. Much of what is available about CHDs and available to parents is dated and inadequate to enable intelligent questions, facilitate meaningful dialogs, or solicit informed consent.
2. CHD is the single most common defect, kills more babies globally than any other disease, and yet it is underfunded compared to other ailments. Specifically, according the Children's Heart Foundation:
    o   In the private sector, (the American Heart Association) only 1% of every dollar received at the major private funder of cardiovascular research goes to any Pediatric cardiac research.
    o   Likewise in 2007, the National Institutes of Health's NHLBI (National Heart, Lung and Blood Institute) allocated less than 3% of every dollar invested in research to any Pediatric cardiovascular research.
3. The research done has been very successful but hasn't gone far enough. It's truly a mixed blessing because without the progress

made in the twentieth century so many children would not be alive as adults today. Yet, now those lives are compromised. Tens of thousands who would have died ten or twenty years ago are now saved every year, but what does their future hold? Imagine how the absence of an answer to that question rocks the world of an adolescent who is envisioning his future. Yes, as a mother I'm grateful you saved Liam's life, but doctors, researchers, society, and myself included, owe Liam and the millions like him a more stable future with more information.

4. Transplant is not an option. There are simply not enough hearts for transplant need with all the kids who are currently living with half a heart or other severe forms of CHD. Transplant is only another form of palliation, and for kids with hypoplastic hearts, their bodies don't want a full heart at age twenty-five because their bodies are used to a different system. They want to keep working with a half heart, as compromised as that is. We need artificial hearts for the newborns and artificial half-hearts or assist devices for the half-hearted who are here before the artificial heart arrives. We need stem cell research to prevent organ rejection today and to prevent artificial heart rejection in the future. There are a million good ideas and possibilities out there, and we need to make them happen because what's here today won't save Liam or the thousands upon thousands like him tomorrow. This is urgent. This is not negotiable.

Reasons: Every disease needs money. That's just the way it is. I believe that there are four specific elements that have limited funding for CHD (as compared to diseases like autism or breast cancer) and they are lack of awareness in the public, lack of knowledge in the general medical community and nonprofit sector, excessive denial on the part of parents of and patients with CHD, and missed opportunities on the part of CHD researchers.

Solutions:

1. Awareness: The public has no idea that CHD is as common as autism or that at least half of children diagnosed with CHD will have at least one open-heart surgery to survive it. Yet, when you talk to individuals they can always come up with at least one person they know who has congenital heart disease, but they know it as a hole or some other descriptor. We need to re-brand the collection of defects to improve awareness.

2. Knowledge: When I've spoken with employees of the American Heart Association, they often do not know that Congenital Heart Disease is different from the adult onset cardiovascular disease they routinely encounter in their volunteers and constituents. If they don't understand, we're already in trouble. Likewise I've encountered OB-GYNs and pediatricians in my own experiences who don't know a quarter of what I know about CHD, yet it is the most common birth defect. More shockingly, many mothers are urged and even goaded into terminating babies like Liam by general practitioners or obstetricians who attended medical school fifteen or twenty years ago and have learned nothing about CHD since. The world has changed, and other medical professionals need to get with the program so that CHD research becomes the priority it needs to be.

3. Denial: Denial is so dangerous. Aside from the acute danger on an individual level, this endemic denial that anything is wrong or that it's someone else's problem has an enormous impact on mobilizing public support for CHD research. Historically, some cardiologists have been collaborators in this lie, telling parents their kids were "fixed," and free from follow-up care or failing to provide sufficient detail about the child's surgeries for future reference. Maybe they believed that the kids were fixed and wouldn't need long term care, but that hasn't borne out across the one million adults living with CHD. It's a bit too easy a few years out from major surgery to want to buy into this idea that it's in the

past, but CHD will come back in some form for many patients. Maybe a fraction of the families will be the lucky ones with no complications down the line, but that's big gamble to take with the futures of so many on the promise of a fantasy. The Heartland needs to wake up and get out there, especially those families who aren't in the hospitals, who have gotten through the really hard times. We owe it to the ones who are struggling, the ones who haven't made it and our own kids' whose future's we've bought on credit, hoping the research will be there. It's our responsibility to make sure it gets delivered.

4. Doctors, doctors, doctors: PhDs and MDs alike. Guess what? You have an untapped goldmine of interested supporters who are itching to help you get your research funded. Look at the autism and breast cancer movements – we're just as passionate as them. It's time you harness our horsepower. What we need is leadership and direction. Our cause is true, let's work together.

Problem Three: Bad or no screening at all. When it comes to CHD kids, the following areas have been historically lacking:

1. Insufficient screening for infants and children with CHD at birth. Recently the Department Health and Human Services finally advised pulse ox screenings for all newborns. Ideally, this will prevent thousands of CHD deaths in the coming years because low oxygen is a huge indicator of congenital heart defects. A low score prompts follow up screening not just for acute cases like Liam's but for kids whose defects might not cause damage for years, but by the time they're detected might be irreversible. This is a good thing, but not every state has agreed to do so. Maybe in the coming years this problem will be solved.

2. Insufficient screening for CHD before birth. I've heard time and time again from mothers who had a twenty-week ultrasound and their children's hypoplastic ventricle was still missed. This is partially because with certain version of this type of defect it gets proportionally smaller as the pregnancy progresses, but in some

cases it's just inadequate screening. I'm more concerned with the women, who like me, are denied a mid-pregnancy ultrasound because of an initial screening earlier in the pregnancy. It should not be an either/or thing; every pregnant woman should be given a full screening of her fetus' vital organs prior to birth. To withhold this screening is to increase the risk of death for kids who are missed.

3. Inadequate sports physicals and pediatric screening. Every time I hear about a kid who dies on an athletic field or roller coaster, I think CHD, and I've yet to be proven wrong. Autopsies bear it out time and again. Often this is cardiomyopathy or some other birth defect with conduction that causes irregular beat. Sometimes it enlargement of the heart from a structural defect that then causes conduction issues, but I've yet to follow a news story like this and find some other cause for premature death.

4. Strong-arming parents into late term terminations. No parent should be made to feel guilty for not having a termination, especially by someone who doesn't know anything about the status and possibilities of modern pediatric cardiology. This is wrong, and while I respect all parents' rights to choose what is best for them and their families, they should never make such a huge decision without all of the most current and relevant information.

Reasons: Money. It costs money to screen kids for oxygen levels (about $10 whole dollars) and screen fetus (about $500, thought that's typically covered it's the repeat that's the problem) and EKGs and training (about $100) for sports screenings at general practitioners and pediatricians. As a parent whose child has nearly died and whose friends include many who've lost children, this cost per screening seems low compared to the eight thousand infant lives lost each year to CHD or the routine news stories about that basketball player, track star, football hero, or gymnast who dropped dead after a game.

Solutions: Screening and education. Simple screening. It may not catch every case, but we give mammograms, prostate exams, and colonoscopies as a matter of routine to our older citizens to preserve their golden years. Do our youngest citizens deserve less when they have so much more living ahead of them? Education is as simple as requiring a couple of hours of pediatric cardiology training every few years for those doctors and midwives treating pregnant women and newborn babies as well as pediatricians and general practitioners giving children sports physicals.

Problem Four: Poor Communication Across Disciplines

1. What do pediatric gastroenterologists, neurologists, pulmnolists, nephrologists, orthopedists, and cardiologists have in common? Kids with CHD, and yet many parents of these kids with CHD have to juggle these specialties and moderate communication across disciplines. That is not in the mommy job description in any parenting handbook I've read. How do we know when these defects and complications are related when they're always treated in isolation?

2. We have poor and limited resources and counseling options to deal with the challenges we face. A great deal can be leveraged from grief counseling, but we need more specific health care for both caregivers raising children with chronic life-threatening disease and adolescents and adults living with these birth defects long past childhood.

3. We need better communications between cardiology and OB/GYNs, midwives, and general practitioners. What happened to me should never, ever happen again. Any midwife or any person treating pregnant women should know exactly who to contact for the best congenital heart care.

4. We need better communication in cardiology departments for long-term care. They've got the crises covered, but we need to

have more comparative statistics over the long term, not just at one institution, but across institutions for maximum information sharing.

Reasons: Everyone is busy, and each discipline has plenty of its own kind to treat. Yet, we routinely see kids with CHD afflicted by multiple defects.

Solutions: As a society we need to recognize that CHD is common and it's not going away. We need to make this big disease a priority in training and communications across disciplines. It's not fair for parents or adolescents or adults with CHD to be the go-betweens in such complex and difficult information exchanges. It's not fair to save so many lives and leave them lost for support in establishing their quality of life.

All children's hospitals treating CHD need to have outreach programs in place with to maintain contact with those who are delivering the babies whose lives they will save. Information should be readily at hand for referrals and assistance. No mother should ever have to find her own pediatric cardiologist the way I did. Almost every one of these problems could be solved with better communication at a relatively low price. It's as much about doing more, it's about doing it better.

Problem Five: CHD REALLY is a disability – sorry folks it just is!
1. Many parents don't file an IEP or a 504 form for their kids when they start school. Then if there is a stroke, infection, long hospitalization or other issue their kids are not protected and families have to fight school districts after fighting for their kids' lives.
2. Until 2011, kids with single ventricles had to fight for social security coverage. This problem has thankfully been resolved, but sadly, there were a select few very healthy hypoplasts who resented that legislation because they didn't want to be

considered disabled.

Reasons: If you spent thirty minutes with Liam without knowing about him, without reading this book, you would not believe me when I tell you he is disabled. But he is disabled. He only has half a heart and his respiratory system and liver function are compromised if not yet impaired. They are both at risk along with his heart for long term failure. He doesn't have the stamina of other kids and he has orthopedic defects on top of that. If he can get an office job as an adult, then he'll probably be fine to work 30-40 hours a week, maybe. Manual labor is highly unlikely for someone with Liam's anatomy. Still, many parents of and patients with CHD would like to ignore this fact. It's one thing to be in denial for yourself, but when you withhold or fight remediation for your less fortunate peers, that's just narcissism.

Solutions: Documentation is crucial. The disabilities of children with severe or moderate but unmonitored CHD escalate with age. Liam is getting a pacemaker sooner rather than later. If it happens during the school year, I have his 504 in place to protect him so he will get his homework and adequate time to recover from surgery and do his work. I'm also protected because Liam is usually covered with deep black bruises on any bony part of his body that might bump anything at all. This is from aspirin therapy, and that is noted in his 504 plan. The school and the school district is protected because Liam's condition is a point of record and the institutions can plan accordingly. Doctors can help by providing details and helping with preformatted descriptions of the impacts of the disease and limitations for each patient.

The goal is not to limit Liam or kids like him, but to protect them from being limited or victimized because of their preexisting medical conditions. We don't want to focus on what they can't do, but we need to be realistic that there are limitations. We can't wish away CHD and hiding from the disability leaves the disabled more open to being excluded from social protections put in place to protect everyone.

For more information about 504 plans and special needs trusts see my web site at www.amandaroseadams.com.

The Last Resort (Heart Transplant)

As I mentioned in the narrative, many people believe that a transplant is a simple fix for severe congenital heart disease, but it's not. A heart transplant is many things, but quick and easy don't make the list.

According to Donor Alliance, "There are currently more than 100,000 people in the U.S. waiting for organ transplants. Each year, approximately 6,000 people die waiting for an organ transplant that would have given them a second chance at life with their families. In addition, each year hundreds of thousands of people benefit from donated tissue that is used for life-saving and reconstructive purposes."

Liam could have easily been one of those 6000 in 2003 and I have a friend whose son just had his transplant this spring after a thirteen-month wait. Transplant is not quick, and to top it off, you are waiting for another person to die. Sometimes that person is a small child or newborn baby. Organ transplant is not easy.

It's also not easy to get "on" the list. A person has to be just sick enough to be dying but not so sick that he can't survive the transplant itself. It is a strange limbo that has strict rules about behavior and proximately to the hospital, which takes many families far from home and their support systems to wait for something that many never happen.

Dr. Shelley Miyamoto at The Children's Hospital Colorado told me, "A transplant is just exchanging one disease for another." Transplant is not easy. The following risks follow transplant recipients through their lives:

- Incredibly expensive anti-reject medication and other medications to keep the body's compromised immune system in check.

- Frequent hospitalization for infection and complications.
- Increased risk of cancer from the anti-rejection medication.
- Organ rejection itself.
- Social isolation due to health concerns.
- The emotional trauma of coming so close to death and owing one's life to another's passing.
- Guilt for requiring so much emotional and financial support from family and loved ones.

Transplant is not easy. It is an altered state and a last resort. It also requires more people to join the donor pool by registering to be organ donors. Even if a recipient is fortunate enough to find a good match, the risks that follow the person through life are daunting. There is a better way, but it is found in technology and the future.

Cardiac assist devices and mechanical hearts are not where they need to be to replace organ donation. Even if they were, kidney, lung, liver and other tissue donation is still necessary. But there is hope through stem cell research where the patient's own stem cells can be grafted to valves, pumps, and other artificial devices to one day eliminate rejection and dependence on death to save life.

The Children's Heart Foundation and the National Institute of Health fund this kind of research that may one day save Liam and countless other children and adults with not only CHD but adult onset cardiovascular disease. Please support NIH funding by supporting politicians who support science and research. Please support the Children's Heart Foundation and make an investment in research that saves lives and preserves hope. And until we get to the point where we have viable mechanical alternatives, please make sure you've signed your organ donor card.

The Final Word About Raising a Heart Warrior

Always, always, _ALWAYS_, consult your doctor with your questions, fears, etc. If your doctor is not supportive of your need to understand what is happening, find one who is.

I use a triage mechanism with both of my kids – is he/she peeing, pooping, sleeping, able to wake up, able to cry, able to stop crying, responding to my voice, and not running a fever? If the answer to all of these things is yes, then I calm myself down and call the regular nurse line either at the pediatrician or cardiologist's office for advice. I the answer is no, I'd go to the ER, and I have gone to the ER for both of my kids at least once. Each time I was right to go, and if if I was wrong, better safe than tragically distraught. If you need more than my guidelines, you do what's right for you.

This book is my gift to every mom who faced down the threat of death to her child and wished she didn't have to be as strong as she is. This book is my gift to every scared parent who thinks he or she is crazy; you are not crazy. This book is the book I wish I had had when Liam was still inside me to teach me what I learned the hard way. So here are my final lessons, Heart Moms and Dads, the rest is up to you.

- It's not going to be easy, but will be beautiful.
- This is not your fault and you are not being punished.
- Grieve for what you've lost; it's ok and it's healthy. You have lost so much and it will take time to see what you've gained.
- You have every right to be afraid, this is scary, but you don't get to decide, so let go of trying to control the situation and the fear won't be as bad.
- It's OK to cry and it doesn't mean you're weak.
- You will find the strength to get through this.
- Your friends and family will surprise you.

- You will laugh again, you will be happy again, you will smile again, but no I'm sorry, you can never be the same as you were before this happened.
- No matter what happens, it is all worth it.

For General Book Club Readers:

Thank you for reading Heart Warriors and welcoming it to your book club! Book Clubs are special places that celebrate friendship and personal growth, and as a writer I'm deeply touched by anyone who would consider Heart Warriors for their club selection.

Please remember, this is just a guide and all of your questions and comments about the book are valid because they come from your heart, half or whole.

Question One: Adams touches on themes of entitlement in her expectations of pregnancy and motherhood. What do you think her experience says about the American sense of entitlement?

Question Two: Knowing that it is nonfiction, how does Heart Warriors impact you differently than it would have if it were fiction? If it were fiction, what do you wish had happened differently to the characters and how do you think that would have changed their lives?

Question Three: Adams primary goal in telling her family's story was to elicit empathy, not pity or apathy. Do you think she succeeded?

Question Four: Congenital Heart Disease is the single most common and lethal birth defect in the world both in the most advanced and the most underdeveloped nations. Did you know anything about CHD before you read Heart Warriors? How has this book impacted your view of this disease?

Question Five: Adams is ambivalent about abortion in general, but adamant that it was not the right choice for her. What are your thoughts on her decision? What are your thoughts on the consequences for Liam?

Question Six: As Amanda recovers from her grief in waves and rebuilds her own ability to be empathetic, she must recognize that the needs of the CHD Heartland are not greater or lesser than any other constituency fighting a disease. How would you face a conflict where "your cause" must compete with other causes for limited resources?

Question Seven: What are your thoughts on Jim and Amanda's marriage?

Question Eight: How did the experiences in Heart Warriors change Adams? What did she lose and what did she gain?

Question Nine: How would you parent Liam and Moira? How do you view Adams' challenges in parenting?

Question Ten: What did you think about Click Clack and the woman who told Amanda Liam was lucky to have Congenital Heart Disease?

Question Eleven: Did you find the Adams family likable? Why or why not?

Question Twelve: Would you recommend Heart Warriors, and if so to what kind of reader?

For Heartlanders:

This is a guide for Heartlanders to host a book club around Heart Warriors. Heart Moms or Adult Survivors can get together, or a Heart Mom and Dad can bring their extended family and friends together to talk about their own experiences.

Please remember, this is just a guide and all of your questions and comments about the book are valid because they come from your heart, half or whole.

Question One: Adams found out about Liam's heart before he was born. Was that your experience too, or was it different? How was your diagnosis experience similar to or different from Amanda and Jim's?

Question Two: Amanda talks about her stages of grief and being stuck on the anger. What has your grief journey been like?

Question Three: If you are a family member/friend of a Heart Mom or Adult Survivor, how did reading Heart Warriors affect your understanding of what your loved one's experience has been like?

Question Four: What do you think Liam's book would be like when he's an adult? What do you think he would say about his parents and his CHD? How about Moira's memoir of her own life?

Question Five: What was the hardest part about reading Heart Warriors for you?

Question Six: Did Heart Warriors motivate you to be a stronger advocate or do more to further CHD research or support programs?

Question Seven: What are your thoughts on Jim and Amanda's marriage?

Question Eight: How did the experiences in Heart Warriors change Adams? What did she lose and what did she gain? How does this parallel your own experience?

Question Nine: How would you parent Liam and Moira? How do you view Adams' challenges in parenting?

Question Ten: What did you think about Click Clack and the woman who told Amanda Liam was lucky to have Congenital Heart Disease?

Question Eleven: Did you find the Adams family and their story relative to your own lives?

Question Twelve: Would you recommend Heart Warriors to readers who have not been impacted by CHD?

Acknowledgements

First, most, and forever I thank Jim, my beloved, my childhood sweetheart, and my best friend for twenty years. I thank you for never complaining about "the book," for loving it even as it gobbled up so much family time, for always having faith in it and me, for reading it in less than a day, and for giving me the alphabetical advantage on the bookshelf. I thank Liam and Moira, my heart and soul for enduring a mother who is at times more absent minded and nutty professor than nurturing mommy no matter how much she tries to bend her nature. I thank them and for feeling my love and believing in it. There is nothing more real my love for you.

I thank Dr. Remond Burke for his beautiful foreword and for saving my friends' children's lives and the lives of thousands of children like them.

I can never thank the following people enough, for without them this book would have been far too short and far too tragic: Dr. Vaughn Starnes, Dr. Francois Lacour-Gayett, Dr. Henry Sondheimer, Dr. Paul Wexler and all the people at Genassist, Dr. Richard Porreco, Dr. Sarah Badran, Dr. Masato Takahashi, Dr. Gerald Bushman, Dr. David Moromisato (who called from his home to check on Liam and I will *never* forget that), Dr. Laura Hastings, Dr. Mark David Twite, Dr. Robert Friesen, Dr. Melvin C. Almodovar, Dr. Deb Kosic, Dr. Chen Chan, Dr. Dennis Chang, Dr. Michael Schaeffer, Dr. Dunbar Ivy, Dr. Sean O'Leary, and Dr. Kristen Sampera, and every other doctor that ordered blood work, put in PICC lines and chest tubes, ordered and read x-rays and cardiac MRIs, tracked Holter results and otherwise kept Liam alive. I also thank Children's Hospital Los Angeles, The Children's Hospital in Denver, Presbyterian St. Luke and Obstetrix, and the University of Colorado and USC medical schools and anyone who supports these institutions for making the amazing possible.

For every doctor in that long list there are a dozen nurses, techs, and important people whose names it is my greatest shame and regret that I cannot remember especially given all the hours and passion they've given us. So I thank the best of the best on behalf of the greatest profession on the planet. Esther Carpenter is an angel on earth, and Mark Legault should take a bow, but they're too busy saving lives. Nurses Judi, Kescia, and Darcy in LA and nurses Darcy, Maggie, Jillayne, Julie, the Jen-Squared on 3N, and James Brown (there is such a nurse-person and he's awesome) and dozens more in L.A. and Denver. Thank you to every other amazing nurse no matter where you work whose feet have ached as much as their hearts for all that they gave, thank you on our own behalf and on behalf of all the hearts you've saved. You deserve your own book; you are beautiful souls.

I am so grateful to my mom Debbie, Jim's mom Karen, his dad Bill and my step-dad Doyle, to Great-Grandma Jane & Great-Grandpa Jim, Aunt Jenny & Uncle Matt, Aunt Sara & Uncle Jeff, and my niece Avery & my sister Megan for all the help with garage sales and heart walks and their faith in the mission and our fight. I thank my baby sister Rhonda and Mike and the girls for always being there to take Moira and give her safe harbor when we needed her most. Thank you, Ruth Kron, and all the Chosa girls who support us with quilts and love. I thank every soul that prayed for Liam. The all-star supporters like Great Aunt Shirley, Cousins Charlotte, Cindy Hoskinson and Janice Mount – we are so blessed by your concern and your prayers. Gary Reed, there are no words for the comfort and support you offered when we needed it most, thank you.

Thank you to Lex, Lisa, Twyla, Dian, Sue, Deb, Jen, K.C., Maggi & Kim, Micki & Peg for always being there for me at HP. Thanks to Vu, Todd, James, Andy, Kevin, Steve, CBart, Robert S.

Paddy, Kevin Heapes and David Markey and all my guy friends at HP too. I was very blessed to have so many people in our corner during my years in the cubicle. Thanks to Ruby, Brandy, Dawn & Heather, and Catie and Sherrie my forever and new friends and August puzzle pals for crying when I told my story and convincing me it should be written down. Thank you Brie & Thea for the baby showers and the love.

Thank you, Lynn & Fred at Behler Publications, for your faith in this project and your honesty in life. Laura Resau (and Jen Luy for introducing us) thank you for all your support during my neurotic events, and if you are reading this acknowledgement section, dear reader, go forth and buy Laura's amazing books! Thank you to Kristin Henderson for your inspiration and encouragement. Thanks, Claire Gerus, for never actually rejecting me and for being the most single most good and honest agent that ever lived. Thank you to Victoria Strauss for looking out for writers everywhere – good karma is going to get you!

I thank Dian Hansen (again), Corey Radman, Chuck Jaffee, Sheryl Kippen, and Beth Delaney for reading the book when it was still rough and "scabby," and offering me the gift of complete honestly and to help me "bleed" my way back to the readers who are the only real reason to write a book in the first place. I thank Pam Wolf, Kay Theodoris, Patricia Stolty, Diana Holgvin-Balogh, and Josey Bierma for helping me with our shared craft. Thank you Northern Colorado Writers (Kerrie, Jen & Pat) for creating an environment for growth and creativity, and Heather Janssen for fostering creativity and sisterhood in our community. You all inspired me to keep at it.

I thank my cousin Lori Casper for the great proof read. I also thank Micki Yonkaits and Danica Tutush, two sisters who along with their mom, I wish I could adopt! I am grateful to so many people for their support and encouragement. I thank Amy Black and the Beta Sigma Phi Ladies – I think I may have raised

more for charity than you got off of selling our house - everyone
needs a realtor like Amy!

And, the Bees, the glorious beautiful Bees who proved
unequivocally that there IS a market for this book. Thank you,
thank you, thank you, and Cheers! (I love my hand-painted
glass) to: Deb Riggen, Sue Hilligrass (and her daughter,
husband, and in-laws!), Adria Lopour, Susan O'Neill, Vara
Saunders, Audrey Matheny, Janette Haver, Jeanne Wilbur, Robin
Hadley, Lisa Edwards, Denise Coffey, Janet Mesce, Dorothy
Nelson, Cathy Emery, Patty Baer-Henson, and Millicent Runyon.
You gave me the faith I needed to keep trying.

Finally, to my ladies…Dorothy Morrison, Kristen Sherman,
Melissa French, Rachel Stutesman, Sally Martell, and to Heart
Dad Rabbi Eli Kagen – thank you for reliving what you lived
yourselves with me and Liam by reading and contributing to the
editing of this book. It means all the more to have your input.

From the Heartland, thanks to Julie, Susan, Lucy and Traci
for talking me through the last months of my pregnancy and Jen
H., Ginny C., and Melissa L. for helping me through the first
years of Liam's life. Kim & Tommy, Angela & Tim, Barbara,
Stephanie T., Stephanie M., Debra, Sharon & Toby, Cathy, Bruce,
Lori & Bill, Kim McCall, Jen Dooley, Valerie B., Des, and Jackie &
Dawn Down Under, and Kristien in the EU. Thank you
advocates Debbie DeGrace, Betsy, Bill, Ellen, and the rest of the
CHF champions. Thank you living warriors Jan, Dr. George
Warren, Alissa T., Nick Z., Jessica, Ana, Joel Down Under and a
shout out to heart-sis Lisa too, Tessa, Nels and Jeni B. To my lost
heart heroes Steve, Joanie & Leslie – thank you. Thank you to
our oldest and newest comrades in the CHD cause Jen & Kevin
Bohn and Lynn & Wyatt from post op day one in CHLA to new
friends Alison, Kimberly, & Lauren on Facebook. Thank you Dr.
Kay, Dr. Fraser, Dr. Breitbart & Dr. Justino who have never
treated Liam but saved countless lives and joined the
bandwagon with the Children's Heart Foundation and/or

Hypoplastic Right Hearts. Thank you to every heart mom and dad and adult survivor and heart warrior, physician and nurse, echo tech and radiology tech and respiratory therapist everywhere who stands up to make a difference. What a family we are!

If you don't know me and you got all the way to this page, thank you for reading this book! You, dear reader, rock – yeah I'm talking to you! Thanks!

I'm sure I forgot someone, and I'm really sorry, but my boundless gratitude grows every night that I put two children to bed and every morning that I wake up with their father and find we're so blessed to still have a complete family. I am the luckiest woman in the world, and every day reminds me to take nothing for granted and accept all blessings with gratitude. Wishing the same for you.

(((((Heart Hugs)))))

Amanda